D0065157

Criminal Justice?
The Legal System Versus
Individual Responsibility

Criminal Justice?
The Legal System Versus
Individual Responsibility

Robert James Bidinotto, Editor

The Foundation for Economic Education, Inc.
Irvington-on-Hudson, New York

Criminal Justice? The Legal System Versus Individual Responsibility
Second Edition

The Foundation for Economic Education, Inc.
30 South Broadway
Irvington-on-Hudson, NY 10533
(914) 591-7230

Publisher's Cataloging in Publication
(*Prepared by Quality Books Inc.*)

Criminal justice?: the legal system versus individual responsbility
  / Robert James Bidinotto, editor ; foreword by John Walsh. — 2nd
  ed.
    p. cm.
    Includes index.
    ISBN: 1-57246-016-4 (hc.)

  1. Criminal justice, Administration of. 2. Crime. 3. Criminal
behavior. 4. Criminal psychology. I. Bidinotto, Robert James.
HV7405.C75   1995   345
                                QBI95-20231

Library of Congress Catalog Card Number: 95-61017

First edition, November 1994
Second printing, February 1995
Second edition, October 1995

Cover design by Doug Hesseltine
Manufactured in the United States of America

To Margaret and Katrina, for believing—
and to the individual victims of crime.

Foreword

by John Walsh
Host, "America's Most Wanted"

For my wife and myself, the sunny Monday morning of July 27, 1981, started like any other. It didn't end that way.

On that day, a nameless, faceless stranger kidnapped and murdered our six-year-old son, Adam.

The loss of a child is every parent's worst nightmare. It's terrible enough when the loss is due to some accident or disease. But to lose your child to the depravity of a vicious predator—that's the kind of unspeakable nightmare no parent should ever have to experience.

Yet in modern America, such nightmares have become all too common.

It seems incredible that in the greatest nation on earth, horrors such as these can even occur, let alone become routine newspaper items. I made it my business to learn why such things are happening, and what we might do to stop them from happening.

Ever since that black day 14 years ago—and in the eight years I have been with "America's Most Wanted"—I have met thousands of victims, and helped to catch more than 350 criminals. I've learned firsthand how brutal the system is to victims, and how lightly it treats the criminals.

It's a system where expediency rules; where punishments bear little relationship to crimes; where, too often, vicious crooks are treated with sympathetic leniency, while their victims are dismissed with cold indifference. It's a system that everyone—cops, citizens, and criminals alike—has come to regard as a joke.

Obviously, this isn't what the framers of our Constitution designed or intended. They created institutions of law "to establish justice" and "to insure domestic tranquility."

But in today's legal system, those goals seem like afterthoughts. Can anyone truly believe that justice or public safety is being sought when probative evidence and voluntary confessions are routinely excluded from trials? When criminal defendants are allowed to bargain for reduced charges and punishments? When child molesters

vii

get probation instead of jail, and chronic sex criminals are freed to rape again and again? When violent criminals, even killers, are granted weekend passes from prison? When inmates serve, on average, just a third of their court-imposed sentences? When our response to prison overcrowding is to give early releases to convicted predators?

Ordinary Americans are outraged about this erosion of our justice system. But they aren't specialists in the law, and don't know how to reform it. I've tried to educate myself on these issues, and do whatever I can to return some measure of safety to our communities. But the job has been difficult, and often demoralizing. Allies always seem to be in short supply. So are good ideas—the ammunition we desperately need to fight back against injustice.

That's why I'm so pleased about the publication of *Criminal Justice?* In these pages, crime victims, law enforcement officials, and ordinary citizens will find the allies and ammunition they need to fight back against criminals—and against those who make excuses for them.

I first met Bob Bidinotto several years ago. At the time, Bob was investigating the legal system's kid-gloves treatment of sexual predators and child molesters. Even before we met, I had read several of his eye-opening *Reader's Digest* exposés of our justice system.

Bob's commitment to crime victims was obvious even then—and you'll find it on every page of this book. He has never lost sight of the fact that victims are people, too.

Bob Bidinotto has been right on target about the criminal "injustice" system. He has been a loud voice for victims like myself. Now, in *Criminal Justice?*, he has brought together some of the finest thinkers on the subjects of crime, criminals, and our legal system.

They shed new light on the dark recesses of the criminal mind. They expose the shortcomings of our laws and institutions. Most importantly, they offer common-sense reforms that will put considerations of justice and public safety back on the front burner of our legal system.

I believe that *Criminal Justice?* will become the bible for an ever-growing, silent segment of American society—its crime victims. Loaded with indispensable facts and sound reasoning, this book is a must read for anyone who knows the system is broken, and wants to change it.

Acknowledgments

"Criminal Responsibility," "Subverting Justice," and "Restoring Responsibility," by Robert James Bidinotto, originally appeared in the July, August, and September 1989 issues of *The Freeman*. Copyright © 1989 by Robert James Bidinotto.

"Crime: The Unsolved Problem," by Melvin D. Barger, originally appeared in *The Freeman*, February 1980.

"Stalking the Criminal Mind," by David Kelley. Copyright © 1985 by *Harper's Magazine*. All rights reserved. Reprinted from the August 1985 issue by special permission.

"The Basic Myths About Criminals," from *Inside the Criminal Mind* by Stanton E. Samenow. Copyright © 1984 by Stanton E. Samenow. Reprinted by permission of Times Books, a division of Random House, Inc.

"Crime in the Welfare State," by David Walter, originally appeared under the title "Crime in America," in *The Freeman*, September 1971.

"Plea Bargaining: An *Un*necessary Evil," by Ralph Adam Fine, originally appeared in the *Marquette Law Review*, vol. 70, no. 4, Summer 1987. Copyright © 1987 by Ralph Adam Fine. Reprinted by permission.

"The Paradox of the Exclusionary Rule," by Caleb Nelson, condensed from *The Public Interest*, no. 96, Summer 1989. Copyright © 1989 by National Affairs, Inc. Reprinted by special permission of publisher and author.

"The Urge to Confess," from *Escape of the Guilty* (Dodd, Mead & Co.), by Ralph Adam Fine. Copyright © 1986 by Ralph Adam Fine. Reprinted by permission of the author.

"The Insanity Defense," condensed from *The Reign of Error* (Beacon Press), by Lee Coleman. Copyright © 1984 by Lee Coleman. Reprinted by permission of the author.

"Ten Deadly Myths About Crime and Punishment in the U. S.," by Charles H. Logan and John J. DiIulio, Jr., originally appeared in *Wisconsin Interest*, vol. I, no. 1, Winter/Spring 1992. Reprinted by permission of the authors and the Wisconsin Policy Research Institute, Inc.

"How to Reduce Crime," by Morgan O. Reynolds, originally appeared in *The Freeman*, March 1984.

"The Case for More Incarceration" was originally published in 1992 by the Office of Policy Development, U. S. Department of Justice.

"Truth In Sentencing: Why States Should Make Violent Criminals Do Their Time," by James Wootton, from a *State Backgrounder* published by the Heritage Foundation, December 1993. Reprinted by permission of the author and the Heritage Foundation.

"How States Can Fight Violent Crime," by Mary Kate Cary, condensed from a *State Backgrounder* published by the Heritage Foundation, June 1993. Reprinted by permission of the author and the Heritage Foundation.

"Community Supervision That Works," by Edward F. Leddy, and "Crime and Moral Retribution," by Robert James Bidinotto, appear originally in this volume.

About the Contributors

Melvin D. Barger is a retired corporate public relations executive and freelance writer who resides in Toledo, Ohio.

Robert James Bidinotto, a Staff Writer for *Reader's Digest,* is author of investigative articles on parole, probation, prison furloughs, sex offenders, and criminal records. One of them, "Getting Away With Murder," sparked a national controversy on crime during the 1988 Presidential campaign, and was selected by the American Society of Magazine Editors as a finalist that year for Best Magazine Article in the "public interest" category. He has published widely, and appeared in broadcast forums such as CNN's "Sonya Live," CNBC's "Rivera Live," and the Canadian Broadcasting Corporation radio network.

Mary Kate Cary has served as a congressional aide, a speech writer for President George Bush, and Deputy Director of the Office of Policy and Communications at the U. S. Department of Justice. She is currently a Deputy Director of Communications, the Republican National Committee.

Lee Coleman, M.D., practices psychiatry in Berkeley, California. For over two decades, he has written for both popular and professional journals, and has regularly explained to juries why psychiatry's impact on legal cases brings confusion rather than clarity. He is author of *The Reign of Error* (Beacon Press, 1984), and is currently writing a book on how psychiatry created the current epidemic of false accusations of sexual abuse.

John J. DiIulio, Jr., Ph.D., is a senior fellow at the Brookings Institution in Washington, D.C., and Professor of Politics and Public Affairs at Princeton University, where he is Director of the Center of Domestic and Comparative Policy Studies. A recognized authority on criminal justice issues, he has appeared on national television discussions, such as the PBS's "Think Tank," and has written for scholarly journals as well as popular publications, such as *The Wall Street Journal.* Professor DiIulio is the author of several books, including *Governing Prisons* (Free Press, 1987), *No Escape: The Future of American Corrections* (Basic Books, 1991), and *Courts, Corrections and the Constitution* (Oxford, 1990).

Ralph Adam Fine has been a circuit court judge on the Wisconsin Court of Appeals in Milwaukee since 1988. Before that he was a trial judge for nine years. He is author of *Escape of the Guilty* (Dodd, Mead & Co., 1986), *Fine's Wisconsin Evidence* (Butterworth), and *The Great Drug Deception* (Stein & Day). Judge Fine is senior contributing editor for the four-volume treatise *Evidence in America* (Michie), and a frequent contributor to professional journals. He also has analyzed criminal justice issues on such national television programs as "60 Minutes," "Nightline," "Reader's Digest: On Television," "The MacNeil-Lehrer News Hour," "Crossfire," "Larry King Live," and "Both Sides, With Jesse Jackson." Judge Fine teaches trial advocacy, evidence, and appellate advocacy in programs around the country, including the National Law Center in Washington, D. C.

David Kelley, Ph.D., received his doctorate in philosophy from Princeton University, and has taught philosophy and cognitive science at Vassar College and Brandeis University. He has written and lectured extensively on issues in philosophy, politics, and public policy. His articles have appeared in journals ranging from *Barron's* and *Harper's*, to *The Sciences* and *Cognition and Brain Theory*. In addition, he is author of *The Evidence of the Senses* (Louisiana State University Press, 1986) and *The Art of Reasoning* (W. W. Norton, 1988), a widely used college textbook. Dr. Kelley is founder and president of the Institute for Objectivist Studies in Poughkeepsie, N. Y.

Edward F. Leddy, Ph.D., is a professor of criminology, and Director of the Criminology Program at St. Leo College in Norfolk, Virginia. For nearly two decades, Professor Leddy was an adult Parole Officer in New York. He worked extensively with felons, drug addicts, and other criminals "in a law-enforcement-oriented department."

Charles H. Logan, Ph.D., is a criminologist, and Associate Head of Sociology at the University of Connecticut. Dr. Logan has been a Visiting Fellow at several agencies of the U.S. Department of Justice, and an editor for *Criminology* and the *Journal of Research in Crime and*

Delinquency. A noted expert on prison privatization, he has served as a staff member on the President's Commission on Privatization and written many journal articles on the subject. He is the author of *Private Prisons: Cons and Pros* (Oxford, 1990).

Caleb Nelson, former Managing Editor of *The Public Interest,* has written for *The Atlantic Monthly, Commentary, The American Journal of Legal History, The American Spectator,* and other publications.

Morgan O. Reynolds, Ph.D., is a professor of economics at Texas A & M University. A prolific writer, researcher, and lecturer, Dr. Reynolds is author of *Crime By Choice: An Economic Analysis* (Fisher Institute, 1985), and numerous studies of punitivity and the economics of criminality. He was recently on the research staff of the Joint Economic Committee of the U. S. Congress in Washington, D. C.

Stanton E. Samenow, Ph.D., a clinical psychologist in Alexandria, Virginia, is a pioneer in the study of criminal psychology. For eight years, he was a research psychologist at St. Elizabeths Hospital in Washington, D.C. There he co-authored, with the late Dr. Samuel Yochelson, a pathbreaking, three-volume study, *The Criminal Personality.* Dr. Samenow was a member of three Presidential task forces on crime and drugs, including President Reagan's Task Force on Victims of Crime. In addition to his clinical work with criminals, he is a consultant and lecturer on criminal psychology and behavior to law enforcement organizations internationally. His books also include the acclaimed *Inside the Criminal Mind* (Times Books, 1984) and *Before It's Too Late* (Times Books, 1989).

David Walter is chief financial officer of a manufacturing company in Pennsylvania. He is co-founder of the Society for Individual Liberty and the International Society for Individual Liberty.

James Wootton is founder and president of the Safe Streets Alliance in Washington, D.C. From 1983–1986, he was Deputy Administrator of the Office of Juvenile Justice and Delinquency Prevention at the U. S. Justice Department. There he helped to establish the National Center for Missing and Exploited Children in Arlington, Virginia, and the FBI's National Center for the Analysis of Violent Crime in Quantico, Virginia. The author of the Chapman "truth in sentencing" amendment to the 1994 federal crime bill, Mr. Wootton has appeared in forums such as the "Today Show," "Good Morning America," the C-SPAN cable network, "NBC Nightly News," *Newsweek,* and hundreds of radio talk shows. His columns also have been syndicated nationally.

Contents

Introduction to the Second Edition by Robert James Bidinotto   xvii

Introduction   1

I. CRIME: WHO'S RESPONSIBLE?

Criminal Responsibility   5
     Robert James Bidinotto

Crime: The Unsolved Problem   26
     Melvin D. Barger

Stalking the Criminal Mind   34
     David Kelley

The Basic Myths About Criminals   47
     Stanton E. Samenow

Crime in the Welfare State   59
     David Walter

II. THE FLIGHT FROM RESPONSIBILITY

Subverting Justice   65
     Robert James Bidinotto

Plea Bargaining: An Unnecessary Evil   84
     Ralph Adam Fine

The Paradox of the Exclusionary Rule   102
     Caleb Nelson

The Urge to Confess   112
     Ralph Adam Fine

The Insanity Defense   138
     Lee Coleman

Ten Deadly Myths About Crime and Punishment in
     the U.S.   156
       Charles H. Logan and John J. DiIulio, Jr.

III. RESTORING RESPONSIBILITY

Crime and Moral Retribution   181
Robert James Bidinotto

How to Reduce Crime   201
Morgan O. Reynolds

The Case for More Incarceration   209
Office of Policy Development,
U.S. Department of Justice

Truth in Sentencing: Why States Should Make Violent
Criminals Do Their Time   233
James Wootton

How States Can Fight Violent Crime   250
Mary Kate Cary

Community Supervision That Works   270
Edward F. Leddy

Restoring Responsibility   276
Robert James Bidinotto

Index   297

Introduction to the Second Edition

When the first edition of *Criminal Justice?* appeared, some readers may have doubted that our justice system was quite as bad as the book suggested. Of course, at that time Americans had not yet been fully exposed to such excruciating spectacles as the trials of Colin Ferguson and O. J. Simpson.

In December 1993, in full sight of dozens of witnesses, Ferguson shot 25 people on a Long Island commuter train, killing six. Though he had a history of mental instability, he nonetheless was judged sane by court-appointed psychiatrists. Ferguson promptly insisted on acting as his own lawyer. For weeks, he was permitted to grill his own victims, incoherently and insultingly, as they took the witness stand to accuse him.

The reason for this sickening farce? Had Ferguson been ruled insane by the court, he might have spent just a short spell in a mental hospital, then been freed whenever psychiatrists ruled him "restored to sanity." So, to keep this killer locked up for good, Ferguson had to be ruled competent to stand trial—and allowed to abuse his victims in a grotesque charade of a judicial proceeding.

The endless Simpson trial further jaded an already cynical public. From the weeks and weeks of pretrial skirmishes to suppress vital evidence—to the high-profile squabbles among the jet-set defense attorneys, their efforts to exonerate Simpson by smearing the police and DNA experts, and the transformation of the judge, prosecutors, lawyers, and witnesses into public buffoons and pop celebrities—Americans saw, naked and exposed, a legal system gone utterly mad.

More specifically, what we saw was proceduralism gone mad—proceduralism elevated to an end in itself. Such trials have made it painfully obvious (even to many hesitant to accept the arguments in *Criminal Justice?*) that the original, substantive ends of our system—the quest for truth and justice—have all but disappeared. Arrests, trials, prisons, and their attendant personnel, policies, and procedures, have largely degenerated into governmental full-employment programs for law school graduates.

xvii

However, worse than the outrages perpetrated in the courtroom are those the system continues to inflict upon ordinary citizens on our streets. High-profile horror stories—such as the arrest of repeatedly convicted violent offender Richard Allen Davis for the kidnap-murder of young Polly Klaas in California—usually provoke new bursts of public indignation, and sometimes even the change of a few laws. Yet those who man the legal system invariably try to ignore the public's demand for reforms, or undermine any that are enacted.

Consider Pennsylvania's parole system. In 1994, convicted killer Reginald McFadden, supposedly serving a "life" sentence, was freed after the state Pardons Board recommended a commutation. McFadden promptly went to New York state, where he was arrested after a string of rapes and murders. There was great public outcry—reminiscent of the 1988 Willie Horton episode—which impacted the outcome of the 1994 Pennsylvania governor's race.

However, the only subsequent change in the system itself was a game of musical chairs among board members. The release of chronic, violent offenders, under a variety of pretexts and procedures, continued unabated. Some 68 percent of Pennsylvania inmates applying for early parole that year were granted their wish. This amounted to the release of some 7,000 serious felons.

Robert "Mudman" Simon was one of them.

Simon had been serving an indeterminate 10-to-20 year term for the 1974 murder of a woman. He won release despite a history of prison disciplinary problems—and the fact that, in 1992, his sentencing judge had written the parole board, warning that Simon "has no respect for human life and I believe it would be only a matter of time before he would kill again."

But in November 1994—at the same time state voters were delivering a clear message about such policies—he was quietly freed by the state Board of Probation and Parole. The prison infractions and the judge's warning were ignored. So was the victim's family: they were never notified of his release, as they had requested, and as is required by state law.

Simon was paroled on condition he avoid both alcohol and the "Warlocks" motorcycle gang of which he had been a member. But though he soon relocated to Williamstown, New Jersey, a town frequented by the gang, his parole was not revoked. On April 29, 1995, just months after his release, Simon and fellow Warlocks member

Charles "Shovel" Staples were arrested for gunning down police Sgt. Ippolito Gonzalez during a routine traffic stop.

Again, a great outcry. Yet again, the only new reforms considered were minimalist ones. Now, before paroling violent criminals, the board is first supposed to notify the governor. Also, the parole board may be expanded from three to five members—apparently on the grounds that the way to prevent future abuse of taxpayers is to force them to pay for more bureaucrats. The obvious solution—an end to indeterminate sentencing and the parole system—is still stubbornly resisted.

By whom? and why? You'll have to read on.

The reception of the first edition of *Criminal Justice?* was unexpectedly gratifying. Though the book was then available solely through mail order, sales seemed propelled by word-of-mouth. Law enforcement and crime victims groups made substantial bulk purchases; one organization distributed the book to every member of the U.S. House of Representatives, and to key senators.

As editor, I was invited to appear at a number of forums and on talk shows, while some of the book's contributors—notably, Judge Ralph Adam Fine and Professor John DiIulio—were asked to testify before a new and more receptive Congress. For the first time, elected officials at the federal and state level seemed willing to question some of the reigning dogmas about exclusionary rules, plea bargaining, and the plethora of "revolving door" policies that infuriate ordinary Americans. Still, I was frustrated by the book's unavailability in bookstores and libraries, which blunted its potential impact on the national crime debate.

That is why I am so pleased by the publication of this new trade edition of *Criminal Justice?*, which at last makes it accessible to the general reading public. And those who made this possible deserve my special thanks.

This book exists only because of the boundless efforts and unflagging patience of Beth Hoffman, indefatigable Managing Editor at the Foundation for Economic Education. Without Beth, neither edition would ever have seen the light of day.

To detail the many special contributions of the rest of the FEE staff would require another chapter. From proofreading to typing, correspondence, taking phone orders, arranging publicity, getting and channeling information—they did everything. I consider the following people, then, as unlisted contributors to this volume: Mary Ann Murphy, Greg Pavlik, Bill Watkins, Bill Fox, Bettina Greaves, Tom Schrader, Kathy Walsh, Janette Brown, Mary Sennholz, Felix Livingston, Kyle Swan, Royce Janszen, Harriet Bender, and Barbara Dodsworth. My thanks to one and all.

Two other special thank-you's are in order. First, to FEE President Dr. Hans Sennholz—renowned economist, author, teacher, and champion of human liberty. His belief in me, and in this book—and his willingness to commit the resources necessary to its success—are things writers are seldom lucky enough to obtain from their publishers. They are things I shall never forget.

Finally, my deepest gratitude to John Walsh. Few have been forced to confront the reality of crime, and the failures of our legal system, so directly or brutally as he. Few of those who have, have managed to transcend such cruelties so courageously or constructively.

John Walsh is a living inspiration to everyone who cares about justice. His willingness to lend his good name and kind words to this volume moves me beyond measure.

—ROBERT JAMES BIDINOTTO
May 26, 1995

Introduction

The polls indicate that crime is now the number one concern of the American people. Moreover, Americans are disenchanted with the criminal justice system, which they see as increasingly unfair and ineffectual.

One reason for their worry and dissatisfaction is the wide chasm between their views, and those of social scientists and public officials, concerning the causes of crime, and the role of the criminal justice system in addressing it.

The ordinary citizen believes individuals are responsible for what they do, and thus should be held accountable for harm they do to others. Accordingly, the criminal justice system's role is—as our Constitution promises—"to establish justice" and "to insure domestic tranquility." The ordinary citizen's views are thus premised in *morality*. But, of course, he has no voice in academic debates on such matters, and little influence upon the legal institutions which academics have sculpted and staffed.

The academic and legal establishments start with contrary premises, and as a result, have a different view of what the police, courts, and prisons ought to be doing. Whatever their many disagreements, today's social scientists seem all but unanimous in the view that the individual criminal bears little, if any, personal responsibility for his deeds. Wedded to the philosophical premises of determinism, they contend that the individual offender is shaped by a wide variety of forces—biological, psychological, or social—over which he has little volitional control. As a result, public institutions should abandon "just deserts" and moral considerations for *utilitarian* measures intended to address the "root causes" of criminality.

Years of researching crime have led me to the counter-intuitive conclusion that, on this issue, the general public is right, and the "experts" dead wrong. Not surprisingly, however, I have found scant scholarly literature supporting that view.

To begin to fill that void, in 1989 I published an extended essay, in the form of a series of three articles for *The Freeman*, the monthly magazine of The Foundation for Economic Education (FEE). Titled "Crime and Consequences," the series attempted to provide a summary of what I had learned about our modern crime explosion, and of my views concerning criminal responsibility. FEE then issued the essay in booklet form, and the public response was heartening.

I have long been aware of the need for a more comprehensive treatment of the themes raised in that essay. That is why I was delighted when Dr. Hans Sennholz, President of FEE, invited me to compile and edit a book of criminal justice readings, to be built around my *Freeman* series.

This collection is the result of his invitation. In it, distinguished scholars, journalists, and criminal justice professionals address the problem of crime *consistently* from the premise that individuals bear primary moral responsibility for criminal actions. Though the contributors cannot be expected to agree with each other in every detail or recommendation, they stand united on the important principle of individual autonomy and accountability. To my knowledge, this volume is unique in that perspective, and unparalleled in the theoretical and empirical arguments marshaled in its support.

I have followed Dr. Sennholz's structural prescription, organizing the other contributions around my own series of articles. While a few of the crime statistics I reported in Part I, "Criminal Responsibility," are somewhat dated, I have decided to let them stand, since the points they make remain valid.

I had hoped to limit my offerings to those three pieces. However, I was unable to find in the literature a satisfactory essay addressing the topic of retributive justice. Dr. Sennholz agreed with me that such a discussion was essential to this volume; I therefore beg the reader's indulgence for offering additional thoughts of my own on that crucial issue.

My deepest appreciation to all of the contributors and publishers who graciously allowed me to reprint their outstanding works, or who provided me original material for this book.

My further gratitude to Dr. Sennholz for proposing and encouraging this project; to FEE editor Beth Hoffman for her wise counsel and tireless efforts in shepherding it through the production process; and, of course, to the hard-working FEE production staff, Christopher Dunn, Mary Ann Murphy, and Gregory Pavlik, who somehow transformed the very raw material I provided into a work of quality.

—ROBERT JAMES BIDINOTTO
May 30, 1994

I. CRIME: WHO'S RESPONSIBLE?

Criminal Responsibility

by Robert James Bidinotto

During the 1988 Presidential campaign, the issue of crime loomed large—due, in part, to this writer's *Reader's Digest* article on the now-infamous Willie Horton case.[1] That story offers a fitting introduction to the subject of America's seemingly intractable crime problem, and what's wrong with our criminal justice and correctional systems.

Horton was a habitual criminal, sentenced in Massachusetts to "life with no possibility of parole" for the savage, unprovoked knife slaying of a teenage boy. However, like many other alleged "lifers" in that state, after only ten years in prison he was transferred to an unwalled, minimum-security facility. There, he became eligible for daily work release, as well as unescorted weekend furloughs, from prison.

Following the example of ten other "life-without-parole" killers over the years, Horton decided not to return from one of his furloughs. Instead, months later, he invaded the home of a young Maryland couple, where for nearly 12 hours he viciously tortured the man and raped the woman.

Not even a "life without parole" sentence for a gruesome murder had been enough to keep a killer off the streets—a fact which incensed enough Americans to become a major election issue. It also reopened the public debate about the criminal justice system in America. For as the campaign rhetoric grew heated, many citizens began to discover that the Horton episode was not an isolated exception. Instead, they learned that, in today's criminal justice system, justice is the exception.

Now that public awareness of, and concern about, such matters is intense, it seems an opportune time to reconsider the way in which we approach the problem of crime.

Permit me to begin on a personal note. My work on the Horton story put me in touch with police, parole, and probation workers; with politicians, prosecutors, and prison reformers; with judges and jurists, therapists and theorists, corrections officials, and—most important—crime victims. The faces of victims have haunted me ever since. So at the outset, let me declare my bias without apology: it is for them. Today, they are too often the forgotten people in our legal system; and their cries for justice must be heard and answered.

The more I have learned, the more I have realized that what happened in the Horton episode is symptomatic of a whole approach to crime which has gained sway during the past three decades.

In this volume that approach will be explored in its many facets:

- the reasons for the surge in criminality during the past three decades;
- the various theories which purport to "explain" crime;
- the nature of criminals;
- the criminal justice system which confronts them;
- the correctional system which tries to reform them; and
- the ways in which our approach to crime might be changed.

The Crime Explosion

Across the nation, our system of dealing with crime has utterly broken down.

To put things in perspective, we must first grapple with some numbers. Crime itself continues to increase, with no end in sight. The number of crimes reported in 1987 was 12 percent higher than in 1983 and 21 percent higher than in 1978.[2]

Not only is the number of crimes increasing; so is the crime rate—the number of reported crimes per 100,000 people. From 1964 to 1980, the property crime rate increased nearly 2.5 times, while the rate of violent crime tripled.[3]

Though these rates declined somewhat during the first half of this decade, they have been rising steadily since.[4]

Such statistics tend to depersonalize the issue. It's quite another matter when you are personally assaulted or robbed; when your wife or daughter is raped; when your neighbor's home is burglarized; when an employee embezzles funds from your business. Such things happen to us more frequently than we realize. In 1986 alone, about one household in four was touched by some kind of crime—meaning that at least someone in each of those homes fell prey to a criminal.[5]

Another gauge of the crime explosion is the rapid growth of

prison populations. In 1960, there were some 200,000 inmates in federal and state prisons; by 1987, there were 581,609.[6] This might seem proof of a growing "get-tough" attitude toward crime. Yet the percentage of serious crimes committed which resulted in imprisonment actually fell sharply throughout the 1960s and 1970s. In 1986, the ratio of prison commitments to total crimes was 32 percent lower than in 1960.[7] This means that a third fewer of total crimes were being punished with imprisonment. It also means that, despite rapidly increasing prison populations, the crime rate is growing even faster than we've built cells to hold all the new criminals.

And in fact, even these statistics paint too rosy a picture.

The Federal Bureau of Investigation (FBI) announced that, in 1986, 13.2 million serious crimes, from murder to auto theft, were reported to local authorities.[8] However, the FBI's statistics cover only eight specific "index crimes." Moreover, its numbers reflect only those incidents reported to police. In fact, the FBI's annual Uniform Crime Reports grossly understate the total number of crimes which actually occur.

In an effort to get more reliable numbers, the American Bar Association (ABA) recently compiled information from various sources, including crime-victim surveys. The ABA estimated that, in reality, about *34 million serious crimes* had been perpetrated nationally during 1986—some 2.5 times what the official numbers indicate.[9]

This means that other official data—such as computations of arrest and imprisonment rates—do not begin to convey how serious the crime problem is. For example, FBI statistics show that only one of every five serious crimes reported to police are "cleared" by an arrest.[10] But if the ABA is correct, we must multiply by 2.5 to account for *unreported* serious crimes. This reveals that there is actually *only one arrest for every 12.5 serious crimes committed.* Put another way: only eight serious crimes in 100 result in so much as an arrest.

What are the chances that even this small percentage of arrested criminals will ever see the inside of prison? Consider now what happens within the criminal justice system.

"Criminal Justice": An Overview

Of the eight felons arrested per 100 serious crimes, one or two are teenagers who are routed to the juvenile justice system (which is far more lenient than the adult system). This leaves only six or seven adults apprehended for every 100 serious crimes committed. Of these, many are released for lack of sufficient evidence or on technicalities; a few are acquitted after standing trial. Of the tiny number remaining who plead guilty or are convicted, most receive dramatically reduced sentences, or are allowed simply to "walk" on probation, thanks to "plea-bargain" arrangements.

The results? According to the federal government, for every 100 serious crimes *reported* in 1986, only 4.3 criminals went to prison.[11] But adjusting once again to account for *unreported* crimes, we find that in 1986, only 1.7 percent of the most serious crimes were punished by imprisonment. In other words, only 17 perpetrators were put behind bars for every 1,000 major felonies.

In calculating his chances of being punished, then, any would-be criminal would logically conclude that the odds are definitely on his side—that today in America, crime *does* pay.

Hence the phenomenon of the career criminal. Most crimes are committed by repeat offenders, often arrested but rarely imprisoned. For example, in 1986, Massachusetts state prison inmates each had an average of 12.6 prior court appearances. Since, as we have seen, the typical criminal gets away with 12.5 felonies for his every arrest, simple multiplication (12.6 × 12.5) suggests that, on average, many of the Massachusetts inmates had committed well over 100 crimes. Few of these inmates were teenagers: their average age was 31. Yet despite their status as career criminals, 47 percent of them had never before been incarcerated as adults.[12]

The career criminal knows, too, that even in the unlikely event he's ever sent to prison, all is not lost. If he's been convicted of multiple felonies, he stands a good chance of getting "concurrent sentences," to be served simultaneously instead of consecutively. This greatly reduces the time he'll spend behind bars. And he also knows that prison sentences almost never mean what they say.

In most jurisdictions, parole eligibility comes after serving only a fraction of the nominal term handed down by a judge. In addition, from the time he enters prison, the inmate is offered a *de facto* bribe of *automatic deductions from his sentence* for each day of good behavior (called "good time"), as well as additional deductions for blood donations or participation in various rehabilitation programs. These may count either against his prison term itself, or his post-release parole supervision time.

Furthermore, virtually every state offers the inmate a wide array of outside release programs. After serving only part of his sentence, the inmate can become eligible to leave prison walls and work at a job (work release), attend classes (education release), or simply visit his family and friends for several days at a time (home furloughs). The public's image of the hardened criminal leaving prison handcuffed to an armed guard is many years out of date. In many current release programs, even dangerous killers (such as Willie Horton) are simply turned loose without any prison escort—presumably in the "custody" of a family member or friend.

In summary: even among that small percentage of hardened, repeat offenders who are apprehended, convicted, and imprisoned, few will spend very long under lock and key. And within a short time after release on parole, most resume their criminal careers. Proof of this lies in many studies showing that paroled inmates have high rates of "recidivism" (or relapse into crime). Depending on how recidivism is measured, fully a third to half of all paroled inmates are returned to prison within a year or two—and this despite the very low chance of being arrested for any of their subsequent crimes.

As every criminal knows, the "criminal justice system" is a sham. As we shall later see, the consequences are undermining the motivation and integrity of those who man the institutions of the law. Worst of all, millions of victims, who hope for justice, find that some of the worst crimes against them are perpetrated *after* they go to court.

Irrationality of this magnitude doesn't "just happen." Nor would it long be tolerated, without a complicated framework of abstract rationalizations to soothe, confuse, and dismiss critics. Like most compromised institutions, today's criminal justice system is the handiwork of what I call the "Excuse-Making Industry."

The Excuse-Making Industry

This industry consists primarily of intellectuals in the social science establishment: the philosophers, psychological theorists, political scientists, legal scholars, sociologists, criminologists, economists, and historians whose theories have shaped our modern legal system.

It also consists of an activist wing of fellow-travelers: social workers, counselors, therapists, legal-aid and civil-liberties lawyers, "inmate rights" advocates, "progressive" politicians and activists, and so on.

It was this industry which, in the 1960s and 1970s, initiated a quiet revolution in the criminal justice system. Its proponents managed to rout the last of those who believed that the system's purpose was to apprehend and punish criminals. Instead, the Excuse-Making Industry was able finally to institutionalize its long-cherished dream: not the punishment, but the *rehabilitation* of criminals.

Prisons were renamed "correctional facilities," and state bureaus of prisons became "departments of correction." Many aspects of the legal and prison systems, outlined above, were implemented about this time. These reforms dovetailed with other products of the industry: massive government-spending programs to eradicate what it called "the causes of crime." Welfare programs mushroomed; academic standards declined so as not to "discriminate" against the "disadvantaged"; "elitist" moral standards were scorned by various "liberation" movements.

Summing up the unintended consequences of these efforts, Charles Murray has written: "The changes in welfare *and* changes in the risks attached to crime *and* changes in the educational environment reinforced each other. Together, they radically altered the [social] incentive structure." This became especially evident in the area of crime: crime rates began to take off while penalties for crime lessened. Soon, "a thoughtful person watching the world around him . . . was accurately perceiving a considerably reduced risk of getting caught. . . . It was not just that we had more people to put in jails than we had jails to hold them . . . ; we also deliberately stopped putting people in jail as often. From 1961 through 1969, the number of prisoners in federal and state facilities—the absolute number, not just a proportion of arrestees—dropped every year, despite a doubling of crime during the same period."[13]

Clearly, it wasn't the intention of the social-science establishment that crime rates soar. The Excuse-Making Industry is no diabolical, centrally directed conspiracy, harboring some warped, unfathomable desire to foster criminality. Rather, it's a sprawling intellectual consensus, consisting of many diverse, competing, and often conflicting elements—but united in a single premise: that the criminal isn't responsible for his behavior.

There are many variations on the theme that binds the Excuse-Making Industry.

There are sociologists, who hold that environmental, racial, social, and economic factors have "driven" the criminal to his anti-social behavior—a view echoed by economists, usually of a Marxist inclination, who argue that criminals are formed by their membership in an "exploited" economic class.

There are Freudian psychologists, who contend that criminals are helpless pawns of emotional drives rooted in childhood; and behavioral psychologists, who believe criminals are clay, shaped by "negative reinforcers" in their families and neighborhoods.

There are biologists, who cite the alleged correlation between criminal behavior and possession of a so-called "mesomorphic body type"; other biologists and geneticists, who think criminality is caused by genetic, physiological, or biochemical deficiencies; and still others, who believe there may be a racial or ethnic "propensity" to criminality.

There are eclectics, who think a combination of such "causes" can "explain" crime.

But whatever the variation, the theme is a constant. The criminal is not responsible for his actions, because man is not a causal agent in any primary sense. Forces and circumstances outside his control "cause" him to behave as he does. He should be forgiven, or treated therapeutically, or placed in a better environment, or counseled to "cope" with his uncontrollable inner demons. But he must not be held accountable for his actions—and, under *no* circumstances, punished for what he "couldn't help."

For all its internal bickering, the Excuse-Making Industry's common theme may be summed up in a single cry: "He couldn't help it, because. . . . " Arguments arise only in answer to the question: " . . . because *why?*"

Consider some of the commonly advanced "explanations" for criminal behavior.

The Sociological Excuse

In the musical *West Side Story*, one juvenile delinquent incisively satirizes the sociological theory of crime, telling the local cop, Officer Krupke: "We're depraved on accounta we're deprived."

In his book, *Crime in America,* former U.S. Attorney General Ramsey Clark offered a more formal summary of the view that crime is "caused" by external social and economic factors.[14]

This is probably the most widely held view of criminal causation—and probably the easiest to refute. Whatever might be said of the prevalence of unsavory social conditions today, surely they were even more prevalent in decades and centuries past, and are more prevalent today in Third World nations. Yet despite the fact that conditions and circumstances have been constantly improving for the vast majority of people, crime today is *increasing;* and it is increasing faster in America and other developed countries than in most poorer parts of the world.[15]

The sociological excuse (of which Marxist "class warfare" theory is a subset) flies in the face of common sense and empirical evidence. Even within the same poor, inner-city families, some youngsters become criminals, while the majority do not. Sociology (including Marxism), based on the collectivist premise that men are interchangeable members of undifferentiated groups, cannot account for such obvious diversity in individual behavior under identical circumstances.

Or consider the following example: "During the 1960s, one neighborhood in San Francisco had the lowest income, the highest unemployment rate, the highest proportion of families with incomes under $4,000 per year, the least educational attainment, the highest tuberculosis rate, and the highest proportion of substandard housing of any area of the city. That neighborhood was called Chinatown. Yet in 1965, there were only five persons of Chinese ancestry committed to prison in the entire state of California."[16] Clearly, factors other than economics and ethnic status affect the propensity toward criminality.

How, then, do we explain the disproportionate numbers of poor and black inmates in prisons?

For one thing, those who are better-off financially can afford better lawyers, and manage to "beat their raps" more consistently than those forced to rely upon court-appointed attorneys or legal-aid lawyers.

We might also consider a heretical thought: not that "poverty causes crime," but that *criminality causes poverty.*

While most poor people behave responsibly and work hard to

better themselves, some do not. The majority's responsible behavior has a much greater likelihood of leading many of them out of poverty; but the minority's irresponsibility is an almost sure path both to continued poverty, and to criminality. Irresponsible youths tend to be self-indulgent and short-range in their thinking. They disrupt their classes, drop out of school, develop criminal associations, drink, gamble, get involved with drugs, malinger on the job, or simply refuse to work at all. These are hardly habits that lead to upward mobility or which keep one out of trouble. Also, the ranks of the poor are infused daily with new members: people who were once better-off, but whose irresponsible attitudes and actions have caused them to lose their jobs or families, to become addicted to drugs, or to associate with people of bad character.

If good people have a much greater likelihood of ascending from poverty, and if bad people have a much greater likelihood of sinking into or remaining in poverty, is it any wonder that the ranks of the poor contain a disproportionate number of criminals? Character, it has been said, is destiny. It should come as no surprise that prisons are filled disproportionately with people who are both criminal *and* poor. But it was their criminality which caused their poverty, not the other way around.

There is empirical evidence to support this hypothesis. In a classic study of male criminality, Sheldon and Eleanor Glueck conducted in-depth surveys of 500 young delinquents, matching them with 500 non-delinquent boys of similar ages, ethnic backgrounds, I.Q.'s, and housing in comparable slum neighborhoods. Even so, the delinquent boys' homes were more crowded and less tidy, and had lower average family earnings, fewer breadwinners, lower educational levels for parents and grandparents, greater histories of family discord, higher incidence of public welfare support . . . and crime.[17]

These facts may be characterized as symptoms of *irresponsibility*. Since the boys' impoverished environments were virtually identical, the chief differentiating factor between the two groups seemed to be exposure to differing sets of attitudes, values, and *morals*. Even though all the boys came from the slums, the "bad boys" more frequently came from homes in which irresponsibility and criminality were prevalent; and those factors were correlated with even lower income and living standards. This bears out the "crime causes poverty" hypothesis.

Moreover, these influences by no means had a uniform impact on the boys: plenty of the "good boys" were exposed to bad moral influences, too; and many of the "bad boys" came from better moral environments. This is a telling argument against the collectivist premises of the sociologists. "Influences" are not the same as "causes": one's response to his environment (these facts seem to say) is *individual.*

As for the reasons why members of racial minorities constitute a disproportionate share of the inmate population, the facts lead to interpretations other than "racism."

As mentioned earlier, Charles Murray has presented overwhelming evidence that welfare-state programs increase incentives for irresponsible behavior among their presumed beneficiaries.[18] Historically, such programs have been directed toward the poor, particularly blacks and other minorities. Murray shows that during the 1960s and 1970s, when government programs for these social groups expanded enormously, a host of symptoms of irresponsible behavior among these same groups followed, including a virtual explosion of criminality.[19]

Based upon such evidence, we can safely conclude that the disproportionate incarceration rate of minorities is caused, not by their having some "racial predisposition" to criminality, nor by a "racist" legal system singling them out for arrest and imprisonment. It stems, rather, from the pernicious, unintended consequences of welfare-statism, which has increased incentives for irresponsibility among targeted minorities—most notably, urban blacks.

The sociological "deprivation" theory of crime also cannot explain the fact that "white-collar" crimes are increasing as fast as street crimes. From 1978 to 1987, forgery and counterfeiting went up 23.5 percent, fraud soared 41.8 percent, and embezzlement skyrocketed 56.3 percent.[20] Such crimes are not typically perpetrated by those languishing in the social environment lamented by Mr. Clark. The bookstores are currently loaded with similarly sordid tales of "high society" crimes, crimes by doctors and Wall Street con artists, and crimes by high-living drug lords. One wonders how sociologists would have accounted for the crimes and perversions in the courts of Nero and Caligula; clearly, these folks weren't "depraved on accounta they're deprived."

As Robert M. Byrn put it: "Not all criminal offenders come from a deprived background, and only a small portion of our disadvantaged citizens become criminals. Organized crime was not reformed when it moved into legitimate business. White-collar offenders frequently hold good jobs and live in respectable neighborhoods. Could it be, after all, that the problem is moral as well as social?"[21]

The point is simple. In various places at various times, there may arise a statistical correlation between crime and any number of socioeconomic factors. But criminality cannot be *causally* attributed to external social and economic factors alone. To excuse criminals because of poor social environments leaves unexplained the crimes of those from good social environments. And the sociological excuse is an insult to millions of others from the poor backgrounds, who have *not* turned to crime.

The Psychological Excuse

Where the sociological excuse for criminality blames forces *outside* the criminal, the psychological excuse blames forces *inside* the criminal. Both, however, share the view that whatever these forces are, the individual has no power to resist or control them.

Whether we treat criminals punitively or therapeutically depends upon the issue of "criminal responsibility": whether the individual has control of his actions. This issue is at the core of the debate over punishment vs. rehabilitation. For if the individual is not responsible, then we should not engage in what famous psychiatrist Karl Menninger denounced as "the crime of punishment." Such psychological determinists believe "the idea of punishment must be completely eliminated."[22]

Freudian Psychoanalysis. Most of us would agree that some people are so mentally impaired they shouldn't be held accountable for acts normally regarded as criminal. But the notion, promoted by many psychological theories, that virtually *all* people are driven to act by inner forces beyond their control, undermines the very premise of criminal responsibility.

This notion is the legacy of Sigmund Freud, the father of psychoanalysis. Freud authored the view that the individual "can't help himself" because he is driven by dark inner forces beyond his control, that frustration of these basic inner "drives" is the source of mental illness.

"I feel," he wrote, "that the irrational forces in man's nature are so strong, that the rational forces have little chance of success against them." To Freud, *human nature* was, at root, virtually criminal. "Every individual is virtually an enemy of civilization. . . . Men are not gentle creatures who want to be loved, and who at the most can defend themselves if they are attacked; they are, on the contrary, creatures among whose instinctual endowments is to be reckoned a powerful share of aggressiveness. As a result, their neighbor is for them not only a potential helper or sexual object, but also someone who tempts them to satisfy their aggressiveness on him, to exploit his capacity for work without compensation, to use him sexually without his consent, to seize his possessions, to humiliate him, to cause him pain, to torture and kill him."[23]

Freud's influence on American psychiatry, and on the culture in general, has been nothing short of enormous. In a society groping for meaning and direction, his explanation of human behavior became dominant. By the late 1960s, a national survey found that "Sigmund Freud's is the only doctrine that has had any wide acceptance in psychiatry today. . . . " Another psychiatrist wrote in the *International Journal of Psychiatry* that "as far as the large segment of educated opinion in the United States is concerned, the attitude of acceptance of Freud's theory has won out." Likewise, Richard LaPiere, a Stanford sociologist, wrote in 1959 that the Freudian ethic is "the ethic that is most commonly advocated by the intellectual leaders of the United States," and described it as "the idea that man cannot and should not be expected to be provident, self-reliant, or venturesome, and that he must and should be supported, protected, socially maintained."[24]

This ethic remains a cornerstone of the Excuse-Making Industry's efforts to rehabilitate criminals (and, incidentally, to replace American capitalism with a paternalistic socialism). Yet how effective has the theory of psychological causation been in actually rehabilitating psychiatric patients?

In 1959, psychologist Hans J. Eysenck analyzed 19 reports covering 7,000 psychiatric patients from 1927 to 1951. He found that the rate of improvement or cure was only 64 percent. The spontaneous recovery rate for patients receiving no psychotherapy was 66 percent. In another study, Canadian psychiatrist Raymond Prince spent 17 months with Nigerian witch doctors and concluded that their rates of therapeutic success rivaled those of North American clinics and hospitals.[25]

More pertinent is the effectiveness of psychotherapy in rehabilitating criminals. In the most ambitious effort ever made to evaluate criminal rehabilitation efforts, Robert Martinson, Douglas Lipton, and Judith Wilks surveyed 31 different programs between 1945 and 1967. These employed individual or group psychotherapy (Freudian psychoanalysis as well as other techniques) to reduce criminal recidivism rates—the percentage of inmates who, once released, return to crime.

Their conclusion: "With few and isolated exceptions, the rehabilitative efforts that have been reported so far have had no appreciable effect on recidivism." For group therapies in particular, there were "few reliable and valid findings concerning their effectiveness." Individual psychotherapy seemed only to improve certain criminals who had been judged "amenable" to treatment; but in other cases, criminality actually *increased* after treatment. These findings have been confirmed in a number of other studies.[26]

Theories are only as good as their demonstrable relationship to the facts of reality. Most psychological theories are based upon sweeping inferences drawn from dubious causal assumptions. The main problem is that these can't be demonstrated. At root, the psychological excuse simply boils down to the truism that all actions are motivated. But this doesn't tell us much. It doesn't tell us whether those motives are causal primaries, or simply the results of something else, over which we have a measure of volitional control. And it doesn't tell us whether those motives, once they arise, can be overridden or channeled by the individual.

We're often tugged by competing emotions. To say that somebody had an impulse or inclination to commit some crime tells us no more than the fact that "he felt like it." Well, we already know that. The existence of civilization, however, is evidence that we do have some power, at some level, to choose which emotions will prove decisive.

But the psychological excuse assumes that emotions are causally irreducible and irresistible. In effect, it equates all desires with *compulsions*.

Another problem with the psychological explanation is that it isn't one explanation. There are many psychological theories, each contradicting all the others. In practice, this means that no two psychologists or psychiatrists seem to agree on the specific "causes" of any given person's actions.

In a review of the relevant literature on the reliability of psychiatric diagnoses, Wisconsin Circuit Court Judge Ralph Adam Fine reported the following:[27]

In one study, pairs of psychiatrists diagnosed 427 psychiatric patients, and were able to agree only 50 percent of the time; in another study, 54 percent of the time.

Case histories of 34 patients at the UCLA Neuropsychiatric Institute were given to ten staff psychiatrists, ten psychiatric residents, and ten untrained college students with diverse backgrounds. There was no statistical difference in the rates at which any of the groups selected the right diagnosis.

Two University of Oklahoma researchers filmed an actor playing a happy, problem-free scientist. They showed the film to 156 undergraduate students, 40 law students, 45 graduate students in clinical psychology, 25 practicing clinical psychologists, and 25 psychiatrists. Each group was told that the man looked normal, but had been previously diagnosed as "quite psychotic." Result: the actor was diagnosed as mentally ill by 84 percent of the undergraduate students, 90 percent of the law students, 88 percent of the graduate psychology students and clinical psychologists, and 100 percent of the psychiatrists. Later five identically composed groups were shown the same film of the same actor, but were told that he "looked like a healthy man." *All of them* diagnosed the actor as free of mental illness.

A final example. Eight normal volunteers, led by a Stanford psychology professor, presented themselves to twelve psychiatric hospitals in five states, complaining of hearing voices that said "empty," "hollow," and "thud." Except for their identities, they answered all other questions truthfully. All were admitted, at which point they behaved normally. Their hospitalizations lasted from seven to 52 days, upon which time they were released with diagnoses of "schizophrenia in remission." However, 35 of 118 actual mental patients in the same hospitals voiced suspicions that the eight were utterly sane people sent to "check up on the hospital."

These anecdotes make some serious points. If even supposed "experts" in the psychiatric field cannot tell whether a person is basically sane or insane, how can they tell what subtle "forces" cause him to act as he does? If they cannot reliably or objectively "explain" the causal antecedents of any given individual's actions, on what grounds do they justify their general theories purporting to "explain" so complex a thing as criminal behavior? On what grounds do they presume to offer "expert testimony" in courtrooms concerning the motives of defendants, or to design "rehabilitation" programs for criminals?

At present, psychological theories of causation have more in common with demonology than science: they excuse outrageous behavior, but explain little.

Behaviorism. Thanks to the failure of Freudian and neo-Freudian therapies, there has been a flourishing of competing theories of causation, the most notable being behaviorism. In its most pure form (as in the theories of B. F. Skinner), behaviorism proposes an almost mechanical model of human action: that man is little more than a stimulus-response machine, like a rat or pigeon, instead of a conscious, thinking entity with some power of choice. This billiard-ball approach to human causality, say behaviorists, is "objective" and "scientific," unlike the "subjective" approach of psychoanalysis.

Behaviorism thus ignores the "inner state" of an individual or his past history, concentrating on altering his present behavior strictly by "conditioning" him with rewards and punishments (called "reinforcers"). It is not going too far to say that the behavioral approach to human change is essentially the same as that used by dog trainers.

Whereas Freudian psychology is the foundation for the "therapeutic" approach to crime, behaviorism "reinforces" the sociological approach. It lends weight to such environmental excuses for criminality as poverty, "peer pressure," racism, and the like. Behaviorists believe that people will change their "responses" if we change the "reinforcing stimuli" in the external environment. (Some have taken this to mean the eradication of the profit motive and capitalism.)

But proceeding on the premise that individuals are no more complex than pigeons apparently has its limitations. For one thing, so-called "behavior modification" programs don't seem to have much more lasting impact on criminals than do those based on conventional psychology.

One study examined 24 such programs between 1965 and 1975, all aimed at altering the behavior of institutionalized delinquent youths by use of rewards and punishments. Almost all succeeded—

while the youths remained in the institutions. But when four of the programs followed up on their subjects after they were returned to the community, three reported no significant, lasting reduction in the young criminals' recidivism rates. The fourth program reported such a reduction, but it wasn't a carefully controlled sample. Other similar studies have been unable to demonstrate any lasting impact of behavior modification.[28]

It seems, then, that even criminals are more complex than dogs. Behaviorism, in refusing to consider that an individual's thinking and values might play a role in his motivation, joins conventional psychology as another failed theory of human action. While both provide a wealth of excuses for criminal behavior, neither helps us understand, alter, or prevent it.

The Biological Excuses

This last group of excuses for criminality consists of variations on the "bad seed" theory: the view that one is genetically or constitutionally predisposed toward criminality. In fact, these theories have more empirical support than do sociological and psychological theories.

There are certain physical attributes which repeatedly have been shown to correlate statistically with increased criminality: being male, having lower-than-average intelligence, having certain temperamental traits (such as hyperactivity), having a certain body type (heavy-boned and muscular). In addition, evidence from the studies of twins tends to show that the likelihood of finding a criminal twin, if the other twin was criminal, was statistically significant and even greater for identical twins than for fraternal twins. This held true even in studies which accounted for environmental factors. A systematic Danish study of over 14,000 adopted children also showed that adopted children whose biological parents had been criminals had a measurably greater likelihood of becoming criminals themselves—even more than if their adoptive parents were criminals. This held true even for adopted siblings raised apart.

The best summary of such evidence appears in James Q. Wilson and Richard J. Herrnstein's comprehensive examination of criminal causation, *Crime and Human Nature*. They conclude that while "the average offender tends to be constitutionally distinctive," he is "not extremely or abnormally so." But as moderate behaviorists, they believe such "predispositions toward crime are expressed as psychological traits and activated by circumstances."[29]

In fact, these interesting correlations are far from being causally decisive. Even in the studies cited by Wilson and Herrnstein, the correlations occurred in only a small minority of cases. Whatever effect such traits have on personality, the link to criminal behavior is statistically weak. Inherited factors, for example, may predispose someone toward aggressiveness, a high degree of physical energy, and a short temper. But why do some individuals with such traits become professional football players, while others become street criminals? A family argument might "cause" one short-fused man with a heavy, muscular body to storm out of the house, cursing, and "let off steam" by chopping wood—while a similar man will begin to batter his children.

Personality traits only define general capacities. There's no evidence that what one *does* with those capacities is predetermined. Hence, even the "biological explanations" do not pose convincing excuses for criminal behavior.

Determinism, Free Will, and Criminal Responsibility

Like the characters in the fable of "The Blind Men and the Elephant," each member of the Excuse-Making Industry grabs onto one part of human nature, then assumes it constitutes or explains the whole. Psychologists focus on a person's emotional life; biologists focus on his brain, genes, or anatomy; and sociologists and behaviorists focus on his family and neighborhood. Each of these does so in the name of "science," rejecting free will—the premise that the individual can make some primary, irreducible choices about his thoughts, feelings, or actions—as "unscientific" or mystical.

The Excuse-Making Industry is premised on the philosophical doctrine of *determinism*. Determinists hold that, in any given moment, there's only one action that an individual can take, an action determined by the sum total of all the causes operating on him up to that point. To a determinist, human thoughts, feelings, and actions are all necessitated by antecedent factors; the individual has no choice about them. By contrast, a free will theory posits that some action—or choice, or thought—is *not* necessitated by antecedent factors, but is under the direct, volitional control of the individual.[30]

This is no digression. The issue of free will versus determinism is *the* key to resolving any argument about the causes and cures of crime. If determinism is true, then man truly "can't help" what he is or does; he is not the sculptor of circumstances, but the clay. Then, the entire idea of criminal responsibility—and of a criminal justice system to punish wrongdoers—is absurd. If, on the other hand, man has some measure of irreducibly free control over his thinking, feeling, or behavior, then he *does* ultimately bear responsibility for what he does—and the quest for justice makes sense.

Determinism certainly *sounds* scientific; it seems firmly rooted in cause-and-effect thinking. Everything requires a cause; thus human thoughts, feelings, and actions require antecedent causes. By contrast, at first blush, free will (or volition) sounds "causeless," hence unscientific. How can any human decision be "causeless"?

As many philosophers have noted, however, the apparent conflict between "causality" and "free will" rests upon a dubious view of causality—what has been called the "billiard-ball" theory. By this view, certain *events* are caused by preceding *events*. The action of one billiard ball hitting another causes the second to move. Likewise, the action of a man stabbing someone is caused by preceding events—in his childhood (the psychological excuse), in his neighborhood (the sociological excuse), or in his biochemistry (the biological excuse). In the first case, the struck billiard ball had no choice but to move; in the second case, the "affected" man had no choice but to stab.

There is, however, an alternative view of causality. By this view, it isn't actions which cause subsequent actions; rather, *entities* cause actions. This leads to a much more complex interpretation of causality, in which "external forces" acting on an entity are only one element "causing" subsequent events. The most important cause, however, is *the nature of the entity itself*: its matter, form, properties, and potentialities, in conjunction with outside forces.

This theory of causality, then, would hold that there are a number of forms of causality in nature. Inanimate objects respond passively; organisms are goal-directed from within; animals act on the basis of perceptual-level consciousness, showing psychological causation, while man has the additional abilities to think, introspect, and direct his awareness.

By this theory, man has final self-control in certain areas. This doesn't violate the law of cause-and-effect, for we act completely in accord with our nature as conscious, reasoning entities. Human volition, then, isn't an affront to the law of causality: it's an instance of it.[31]

There are various doctrines and theories of free will, of course. Some posit total control over thoughts, feelings, and actions; some suggest that only thoughts might be under direct control; still others argue for a more narrow control, over the level and focus of consciousness. For our purposes here, resolution of this question doesn't matter. What does matter is whether determinism is a respectable intellectual alternative. It is not.

No, free will cannot be "proved." That's because *proof presupposes free will.* It's impossible to prove or to know anything if one's thinking processes aren't free—if the outcome of our thinking is predetermined by forces beyond our control. Volition lies at the starting point of all knowledge and proof, not at the conclusion of some logical chain. It doesn't need to be "proved," for it's a building block of proof itself.

This poses a fatal dilemma for determinism, and for the whole Excuse-Making Industry which stands upon it. Knowledge presupposes the freedom to validate or refute a belief by a self-directed thinking process. However, those who claim to know that determinism is true must logically concede that they, too, "can't help" what they think, feel, or do. Yet if that is the case, then they can't claim to "know" that determinism is true—*for they were forced to believe in its validity.*

The dilemma is inescapable: the excuse-makers are slaves to their own theory. To claim knowledge of the validity of determinism, or to try to persuade others, presupposes a freedom which their own theory denies them. Determinists want to have their free will, while eating it.

It's therefore no wonder that the Excuse-Making Industry has failed dismally in its efforts to reform criminals. By not taking into account the free will of the criminal, it's ignoring the very factor which is *decisive* to his criminality: his responsibility for his actions.

Instead, it has shaped the institutions of the law to excuse him from justice.

1. Robert James Bidinotto, "Getting Away With Murder," *Reader's Digest,* July 1988.

2. Federal Bureau of Investigation, *Crime in the United States* (Uniform Crime Reports, 1987), p. 41. (For updated crime statistics, see "The Case for More Incarceration" and "How States Can Fight Violent Crime" in Part III of this volume.)

3. Charles Murray, *Losing Ground* (New York: Basic Books, 1984); from data on p. 256, Table 18.

4. *Crime in the United States,* p. 41, Table 1.

5. Bureau of the Census, *Statistical Abstract of the United States,* 1988 edition, p. 163.

6. *Ibid.,* p. 154, Fig. 5.2.

7. Bureau of Justice Statistics, *Bulletin,* "Prisoners in 1987," April 1988, pp. 1, 5.

8. *Crime in the United States,* p. 41.

9. American Bar Association, *Criminal Justice in Crisis,* November 1988, p. 4.

10. *Crime in the United States,* p. 155.

11. Bureau of Justice Statistics, *Bulletin,* p. 5; shown as 43 imprisonments per 1,000 of the following reported crimes: murder, non-negligent manslaughter, rape, robbery, aggravated assault, and burglary.

12. Massachusetts Department of Correction 1986 Annual Report, Appendix E, p. 20.

13. Murray, pp. 167, 170.

14. Ramsey Clark, *Crime in America* (New York: Simon & Schuster, 1970), prefatory remarks.

15. James Q. Wilson and Richard J. Herrnstein, *Crime and Human Nature* (New York: Simon & Schuster, 1985), ch. 17.

16. *Ibid.,* p. 473.

17. *Ibid.,* pp. 175–179. The Glueck study had many other far-reaching conclusions, and has been savaged by sociologists for decades.

18. See also Robert James Bidinotto, "Paying People Not to Grow," *The Freeman,* October 1986.

19. Murray, especially chapters 8, 12, 13, and 14.

20. *Crime in the United States,* p. 168, Table 27.

21. Robert M. Byrn, "The Morality of Punishment," *America,* Jan. 15, 1972. Quoted in J. Weston Walch, *Debate Handbook On Criminal Justice* (Portland, Me.: self-published, 1976), p. 89.

22. Richard X. Clark, quoted in Walch, p. 52. Also Wilson and Herrnstein, pp. 489–490.

23. Quoted in Frank Goble, *Beyond Failure: How to Cure a Neurotic Society* (Ottawa, Ill.: Green Hill Publishers, 1977), pp. 37–38.

24. *Ibid.,* pp. 39–40.

25. *Ibid.,* pp. 41, 43. Also Wilson and Herrnstein, pp. 378–379.

26. Stanton E. Samenow, *Inside the Criminal Mind* (New York: Times Books, 1984), p. 193. Also Wilson and Hernnstein, pp. 377–379.

27. Ralph Adam Fine, *Escape of the Guilty* (New York: Dodd, Mead & Co., 1986), pp. 203–208.

28. Wilson and Herrnstein, pp. 381–384.

29. *Ibid.*, pp. 102–103. See especially chapters 3–7.

30. David Kelley, "The Nature of Free Will," recorded lecture given in Toronto, Canada, in October 1986.

31. The author is indebted to David Kelley for the general argument presented in this section.

Crime: The Unsolved Problem

by Melvin D. Barger

What causes crime? Why do some individuals possess tendencies which lead them to commit acts of violence and predation: robberies, assaults, rapes, and other felonies? What sets the habitual or occasional criminal apart from the mainstream of society? More important, what can be done to "change" criminals into productive, law-abiding citizens?

The theory that has partly governed public policy for many years is that crime is caused by an unjust society. A most eloquent spokesman for this point of view was Ramsey Clark, who served as assistant attorney general in the Kennedy Administration and attorney general in the Johnson Administration. Here's how Clark described the crime problem in his well-known 1970 book, *Crime in America*:

> If we are to deal meaningfully with crime, what must be seen is the dehumanizing effect on the individual of slums, racism, ignorance, and violence, of corruption and impotence to fulfill rights, of poverty, unemployment, and idleness, of generations of malnutrition, of congenital brain damage and prenatal neglect, of sickness and disease, of pollution, of decrepit, dirty, ugly, unsafe, overcrowded housing, of alcoholism and narcotics addiction, of avarice, anxiety, fear, hatred, hopelessness, and injustice. These are the fountainheads of crime. They can be controlled. As imprecise, distorted and prejudiced as our learning is, these sources of crime and their controllability clearly emerge to any who would see.[1]

And how would such conditions be changed? In that same volume, Clark explains that it's a "matter of will." If society becomes willing, the conditions that cause crime can be changed, and then crime will be greatly reduced.

Clark's theory has a plausible sound and anybody who visits a large state prison will find scores of inmates from deprived backgrounds. Some of them are not really criminals in the true sense of the word; they are simply badly adjusted and disturbed people who need to be institutionalized. There are others with personal problems that got them into trouble.

But if a visitor searches out the professional criminals—both in prison and out—he may find that the theory doesn't hold up at all. There are men, and some women, who have numerous advantages in their lives and yet they seem to become criminals by deliberate choice.

For example, neither John Dillinger nor the notorious Alvin Karpis really were deprived as youngsters, nor were they getting revenge on an unjust society. The fact is, the criminal life simply gave them power, excitement, and recognition that they couldn't have found in most straight professions. Far from being driven to crime by necessity and despair, both men had fierce appetites for the danger and rewards of their lawlessness. It is even possible that John Dillinger would have considered his short life well spent, for his crimes brought him a dubious fame that he couldn't have achieved in any other way. Even Karpis, who spent more than 32 years in federal prisons for his crimes, did not seem to regret his choice of a criminal career. Indeed, his personal story, published after his release in 1969, carried few regrets and tended to glorify and defend his criminal career.[2]

In the introduction to that same book, a quotation from Ben Hecht sheds some light on the nature of the criminal mind. Hecht had been working on a biography of Mickey Cohen, and this portion was later published:

(Wrote Hecht): I have been talking to Mickey Cohen for a number of years and mingling with his underworld entourage. Out of my contacts has come what I think may be a major piece of anthropological lore. The criminal has no hates or fears—except very personal ones. He is possibly the only human left in the world who looks lovingly on society. He does not hanker to fight it, reform it or even rationalize it. He wants only to rob it. He admires it as a hungry man might admire a roast pig with an apple in its mouth.

I was pleased to find this out, for I have read much to the contrary. Society does not, as sociologists and other tony intellectuals maintain, create the criminal. Bad housing, bad companions, bad government, etc., have little to do with why there are killers, robbers and outlaws. The criminal has no relation to society to speak of. He is part of man's soul, not his institutions. He is an old one. A thousand preachers, summer boy's camps, plus a congress of psychiatrists can barely dent even a minor criminal. As for the major criminal, he cannot be touched at all by society because he operates on a different time level. He is the presocial part of us—the ape that spurned the collar. . . .

The criminal at the time of his lawlessness is one of the few happy or contented men to be found among us. . . .

Alvin Karpis certainly was that kind of criminal. In his biography, he discussed the few times he had accepted regular employment in the straight world. To Karpis, such a life was boring and pointless, and he quickly abandoned it for the lure of crime. He considered himself a professional thief, and he took considerable pride in his competence and in his standing among other gangsters. If he suffered any remorse for his crimes or saw anything evil in the robberies or kidnappings he carried out, it was not evident in his autobiography. In reading it, one almost has the feeling that Karpis would have selected such a life again if he could have returned to his youth and had choices to make.

Not all criminals have been as open as Karpis about the attractions of a criminal career. In any prison, it is always possible to find convicts who seem to have changed and who have shown appropriate responses to counseling and other supposedly rehabilitative programs. Some of them, of course, are sincere people who really have changed. Other convicts, however, are usually cynical about the motives of their fellow inmates. Quite often, the "rehabilitated" inmate is really only a perceptive and cunning person who produces the responses that counselors and prison authorities are seeking.

This is not to say that brutal prisons are good institutions for society or that one should abandon hope in possible methods of rehabilitation. We should admit, however, that crime is a lot like cancer. We may know more about it than we did in former days and we may have some criminals who have dramatically changed for the better. Still, both crime and cancer are unsolved problems and nobody has answers that promise wholesale improvements in crime statistics.

Self-Responsibility

One recent development is that some thoughtful people are beginning to question the belief that the criminal is simply the victim of bad social conditions. They are taking another look at the problem and are concluding that the criminal is, after all, responsible for his behavior. This was the conclusion of a psychiatrist, the late Dr. Samuel Yochelson, who with a clinical psychologist named Stanton Samenow studied 252 male hard-core criminals. They also interviewed people connected with the criminals, including prison and probation officials, families, girlfriends, employers, and associates.

Yochelson and Samenow eventually made a basic assumption that flew in the face of popular theory about the roots of crime. This assumption was: *The criminal can and does choose his way of life freely in his quest for power, control, and excitement. Moreover, he can choose to change if he musters courage or will to endure the consequences of responsible choices.*[3]

This assumption was surprisingly close to Ben Hecht's thoughts after spending time with Mickey Cohen and his underworld friends. The criminal, like the rest of us, possesses a human will and is capable of making choices. Every human being is controlled by the fact that choices may lead to unpleasant or unwanted consequences. For many of us, it is often necessary to make hard or difficult choices because we want to avoid certain consequences. For example, many people choose to plod away at boring, unsatisfying jobs simply because they need to make a living and do not want to live in destitution or dependency. Most people, in fact, do not manage to find a great deal of power, control, or excitement.

It's true that most criminals may not completely understand their own motivations. However, this too is changing. Yochelson and Samenow started a therapeutic program aimed at helping criminals understand themselves and voluntarily change their thought patterns and actions. The program was unapologetically moralistic and was aimed at helping criminals change into responsible citizens. They had promising success with a small group of persons who were willing to change. In the process, they also discovered that a criminal who comes to the program has "to wean himself from the high-voltage jolts he got out of crime to a steady current of satisfaction from self-respect and responsible living." This process may even produce withdrawal pains similar to those experienced by a recovering drug addict!

Helping the Individual to Help Himself

While the work of Yochelson and Samenow is still controversial among professionals in the mental health and psychiatric fields, it is likely to attract other disciples who have become disillusioned with the conventional, deterministic theories about criminal behavior. Their findings also are consistent with the results obtained by self-help and religious groups which have worked with criminals. Prison inmates have been helped by voluntary efforts such as Alcoholics Anonymous and the Dale Carnegie speech training program. The significant element in these programs is that of personal responsibility. The individual is guided to understand himself and to take voluntary steps to change his own thoughts and behavior.

At this point, none of these programs has helped more than a small percentage of the criminal population. Crime is still an unsolved problem, and nobody has found ways of changing the majority of criminals. From time to time, the nation's prisons come under attack for their failure to rehabilitate criminals; some of these institutions also are rightly criticized for their brutality and bestial living conditions. However, there is nothing about the prison system that should logically lead to recovery or rehabilitation of criminals. Prisons are state- or federally-run institutions with bureaucratic managements which are forced to respond to political pressures. The primary purpose of a prison is *custody,* and in any conflict between that purpose and rehabilitation, custody always wins.

And until rehabilitation measures can produce a better record of results, custody will continue to be society's principal way of dealing with criminals. Maintaining a prison is expensive and difficult, but there is a grim logic in the concept of custody. John Dillinger held up no banks while he was in prison at Michigan City, Indiana, and Alvin Karpis neither robbed nor kidnapped anybody after he landed in Alcatraz. There is also a strong feeling in society that violators should be punished. Even Jonathan Kwitny, a knowledgeable and seasoned reporter who writes on crime subjects for *The Wall Street*

Journal, has stated that the main problem with criminal justice now is that the system doesn't punish violators—organized or unorganized—after they are convicted.[4]

Punishment as Deterrent

Perhaps another argument in favor of strong custodial measures and swift punishments is to deter others who may be weighing the possible advantages of a criminal life. Whether it works this way or not, the public apparently believes that it does and supports the maintenance of prison systems.

But there is no reason why self-help programs cannot be offered even in maximum security prisons. And while no self-help program has produced spectacular results in helping criminals change their lives, some of the *individual* changes have been dramatic. The present author knows several persons whose lives were completely transformed in prison by accepting certain new ideas about themselves and society. One man made such a complete change that he was later named to *head* a prison camp in another state. Another person who once had been associated with the Detroit underworld became so completely rehabilitated that he was named deputy sheriff of the county where he lived (legally possible for felons if they receive a complete pardon). Still another person had been considered institutionalized; that is, he was believed to be incapable of functioning in society. However, he eventually met all the conditions of a parole and has lived an exemplary life for more than ten years.

Three greatly changed individuals would not be very interesting to the people who compile statistics about crime and criminals. Out of 1,000 men, for example, these persons would be only 0.3 percent of the total number. *In their lives, however, the changes were 100 percent.* They changed completely from persons who had been irresponsible criminals to citizens who could live in peace with themselves and other people in society. How were they able to do it?

All of them reached a point of becoming dissatisfied with their past lives and desired change. Moreover, they realized that the old ways were wrong and that they had harmed other people. They also accepted full responsibility for their own actions. While they knew that they had been driven by wrong impulses and feelings, they did not place responsibility outside themselves. Then they accepted new ideas and beliefs which resulted in change. They seemed to become different persons, and in a way they were. They thought differently, they felt differently, and they acted differently.

Probably none of these men had ever heard of Yochelson and Samenow. But they proved the Yochelson/Samenow thesis: *The criminal chooses his way of life and can change it if he musters the courage or will to do so.*

No Miracles Promised

It would be misleading and thoughtless to say that *every* criminal can be changed by the sparse self-help programs now available in staate and federal prisons. After all, few people in free society make dramatic behavioral changes, so why should criminals be any different from the normal population? Crime is an unsolved problem, but it is not the only unsolved problem.

It also is wrong to say that individuals can be expected to change their lives without help or assistance from others. Actually, all of us are part of society and we owe many of our best ideas and beliefs to others who have helped us, patiently instructed us, and guided us. There is no such thing as a good society without a great deal of human cooperation and voluntary problem-solving.

But this is not the same as saying that society is responsible for our condition or that the proper way to change people is to impose, by coercive means, a certain form of organization on society. The fact is, it works the other way around. People think and act in certain ways, and society becomes a mirror of their beliefs and actions. Criminals are sometimes called the victims of an unjust society. But criminals, like the rest of us, help make society what it is. In fact, the criminal helps destroy the very society that is blamed for his ills.

In dealing with crime and criminals, we still have no answers that promise broad, sweeping changes. We should, however, be very skeptical of any proposals for fighting crime that do not take into account the *individual will* and *motivations* of each person who is or might become a criminal. James Q. Wilson, a Stanford professor who has served on crime and drug commissions, makes an important statement about the general problem of crime in closing his book, *Thinking About Crime:*

... [S]ome persons will shun crime even if we do nothing to deter them, while others will seek it out even if we do everything to reform them. Wicked people exist. Nothing avails except to set them apart from innocent people. And many people, neither wicked nor innocent, but watchful, dissembling, and calculating of their opportunities, ponder our reaction to wickedness as a cue to what they might profitably do. We have trifled with the wicked, made sport of the innocent, and encouraged the calculators. Justice suffers, and so do we all.[5]

Wilson seems to be saying that we should be very humble about our knowledge of crime and its causes. He does say that we still should make distinctions between innocence and wickedness. There are criminals whose actions need to be taken seriously, and who should be locked up in order to protect the innocent. The innocent person should not have to take the rap for the criminal's actions.

One of the crucial questions in thinking about crime is whether or not the criminal is capable of making conscious choices that govern his actions. If he is incapable of making such choices, he should be adjudged insane and dealt with accordingly. If he is capable of choosing right or wrong behavior, then he also can choose a new way of life. Few criminals do make such choices. Perhaps that's why crime still is the great unsolved problem.

---

1. Ramsey Clark, *Crime in America* (New York: Simon and Schuster, 1970).

2. Alvin Karpis, *The Alvin Karpis Story* (New York: Coward-McCann & Geoghegan, Inc., 1971).

3. See "The Criminal Mind: A Startling New Look," *Reader's Digest*, May 1978.

4. See Jonathan Kwitny, "Ford Foundation Mulls Crime Fight," *The Wall Street Journal*, November 18, 1976.

5. James Q. Wilson, *Thinking About Crime* (New York: Basic Books, 1975), p. 209.

Stalking the Criminal Mind

by David Kelley

Crime is a social problem; in a sense it is *the* social problem, because it breaks the bond of trust that makes society possible. But that's about as far as the consensus on the subject goes. On March 3, 1985, for example, the Justice Department released a study showing that 40 percent of the people who entered state prisons in 1979 were on probation or parole for previous crimes—and thus would not have been free to commit new crimes had they served full terms for their earlier ones. The following day, the Eisenhower Foundation issued a report denying the efficacy of punishing criminals and urging that public policy address the "real" causes of crime, such as high unemployment among minority youth.

These two reports neatly illustrate the philosophical dispute that runs through the debate about crime. If our actions are a product of causes outside our control, then it is unfair—and ineffective—to blame criminals for what is really the fault of society, or their parents, or their genes. We must try to alter those causes, and use punishment solely as a means of rehabilitation. If our actions are freely chosen, however, then society can hold us responsible for them and refuse to indulge the kinds of excuses that determinism offers. Punishing wrongdoers is then a form of retribution, and a way of removing them from our midst.

For more than a decade, the public has been moving steadily into the free will camp. Outrage over the trial of John Hinckley led Congress to tighten the insanity defense. Earlier, in the 1960s, the sight of social theorists fiddling with determinism while the cities burned helped elect Richard Nixon on a law-and-order platform. The crime rate, despite a recent dip, is well above the level of two decades ago and remains high on the list of public anxieties. Politicians across the spectrum have long since learned the electoral advantages of being (or seeming to be) tough on crime, and on criminals.

Determinism is more difficult to resist in criminology, however, where the goal is to *explain* criminal behavior. The most powerful models of explanation we have are drawn from the physical sciences. The social sciences have not abandoned the hope of finding laws that govern human action in the way that the law of gravity governs the motion of a stone; and journalists who set out to explain particular crimes, to get behind the "story," are drawn ineluctably into the search for causes. But the search always runs into problems, problems that arise from the very assumption that criminal behavior is solely a product of causes beyond the criminal's control. Thus to solve the social problem of crime, we must first confront a philosophical one. We need to acknowledge the inadequacy of determinism.

The first 610 pages of Joe McGinniss's *Fatal Vision* present two sets of "facts" about Jeffrey MacDonald, the Green Beret doctor who was convicted in 1979 of murdering his wife, Colette, and their two children. The first is the circumstantial evidence against MacDonald, who has never confessed to the crime; the second is a mass of psychiatric testimony, along with McGinniss's own speculations, as to why and how MacDonald could have committed so brutal a crime.

Though the psychological account has many loose ends, its outlines are clear enough. MacDonald was a hardworking, dedicated, and (to all appearances) compassionate doctor. But he had an intense desire to control others and showed great hostility toward anyone who stood in his way, or even disagreed with him. He was remarkably unperceptive about his own behavior, and in several haunting scenes in the book—as when he worries about which uniform he should wear to meet the press after being cleared of murder charges by the military—he reveals an incredible poverty of feeling. McGinniss caught MacDonald in a number of lies, many of them serving no ostensible purpose. And despite MacDonald's protestations that his marriage was happy, he had had a series of casual affairs, apparently fueled by worries about his masculinity.

MacDonald had no history of violence. But if, on the night of the murder, he and his wife had an argument (there is some evidence that they did, and that their relationship had grown increasingly tense in the preceding months); and if the argument reached a pitch of feeling, with Colette stepping out of her usual passive role; and if MacDonald saw her as a threat to his masculinity, to his very sense of self (defined as it was by his ability to control others); and if, having worked for 36 hours straight, he was unable to exert his normal control over his feelings—if all this was so, then perhaps we can begin to understand the murder (of his wife, at least) as a form of self-defense.

On page 610, however, we are given another explanation, a physiological one: MacDonald had been taking diet pills containing amphetamines. McGinniss conjectures that MacDonald took the pills in doses larger than he has admitted—doses large enough, according to the medical literature, to cause psychosis, hallucinations, and delusions of persecution.

Yet neither the psychological nor the physiological explanation of the crime is very satisfying—not, at least, if we are looking for causal explanations. Psychology tends to explain an action by reference to underlying beliefs and goals. The great advantage of this approach is that it can make an action intelligible. If MacDonald believed that his wife was challenging his authority, and if his goal was to avoid such challenges at all costs, then the act of removing the threat follows by a kind of brutal logic. Often, an explanation of this sort is enough. But in the case of a murder it is not. The violent destruction of one's wife and children is not only awful and repellent; it wears its awful and repellent character on its face, visible to anyone not wholly deranged. For most of us, the enormity of such an act would function as a kind of barrier reef: the tides of personality would crash against it and rebound, shaking loose the grip of whatever desires had tempted us.

So we turn with relief to the diet pill hypothesis, not only because it is clear and simple but because it gives us a *real* cause, one that might have compelled MacDonald to act. No one, after all, chooses the way his neurons react to a chemical. But our relief is temporary, for we have purchased causal necessity at the cost of intelligibility. We do not yet understand why or how an amphetamine could trigger an act of violence. We do not even know what *kind* of explanation to look for. The amphetamines did not move MacDonald's arm in the way the wind might move a branch; his arm was guided by his intention to kill. How can a chemical cause an intention?

If the various explanations of the crime in *Fatal Vision* are finally unsatisfying, the problem is not literary but metaphysical. We expect the relation between cause and effect to be both necessary and intelligible. In the case of a human act, physiology can give us the first, and psychology the second, but we cannot put the two together until we understand (and we do not) the causal intercourse between mind and body, matter and spirit.

It has commonly been assumed that science is the natural ally of determinism. Science, after all, trades in causal explanations. Immanuel Kant, two centuries ago, argued that the scientific perspective leads inevitably to determinism, that freedom could be defended only by opposing the authority of science. In *Walden Two*, B.F. Skinner claimed that the increasing success of a science of behavior would make determinism more and more plausible. But the progress of science has not borne out Skinner's prediction. The problem is not that scientists haven't discovered any causal influences on human behavior. The problem is that they have found too many.

No category of human action has been studied in as much depth, or from as many angles, as crime. Here is some of what we have learned from that inquiry:

- Young males are disproportionately responsible for crimes of violence and property crimes. The Baby Boom partly explains the massive rise in crime from the early 1960s to the early 1970s. But only partly. In some areas of the country, the murder rate in those years went up ten times faster than demographic changes alone would have led one to predict.
- Psychologists have found that criminals tend to fall outside the normal range on a number of personality traits. These include some we might expect, such as disrespect for authority and diminished capacity for empathy. But among them are also such unexpected traits as hyperactivity and slower response to aversive stimuli.
- There is a link between poverty and crime, but it is a complex one. Crime rates are higher in poor areas than in wealthy ones (for violent crimes, at least), and poor people are more likely to be arrested and convicted. But the rates are higher in urban slums than in rural areas of equal poverty, and they vary widely among ethnic groups of the same economic status; poverty per se may not be the crucial variable. There is also some evidence that crime rates fluctuate in accordance with the business cycle, suggesting a correlation, if a weak one, between crime and unemployment.

- Delinquents are much more likely to have been abused as children than nondelinquents.
- The incidence of alcoholism—and, especially since the 1960s, of drug use—is much greater among criminals than among the population at large. There is also some evidence that about a third of all serious crimes are committed by people under the influence.
- When a criminal has a twin, that twin is at least twice as likely to be a criminal himself if he is an identical rather than a fraternal twin. And among adopted children who commit crimes, the biological parents are more likely to be criminals than the adoptive parents.

This criminological sampler, brief as it is, shows that no single factor is sufficient to explain criminal behavior. This should not come as a surprise: no social scientist expects to find a single explanation for any human action. It is precisely the job of theory to explain how various causal influences interact. But this raises another, deeper problem. The factors mentioned above are of diverse types: economic, cultural, psychological, physiological, genetic. It is far from clear how one should go about explaining the interaction of causes at such different levels.

The existing theories typically solve this problem by denying it. A good example is E. H. Sutherland's theory of "differential association," which evolved through the ten editions of *Criminology*, by Sutherland and D.R. Cressey (Sutherland, who died in 1950, published the first edition in 1924; the tenth edition was published in 1978). This theory is still perhaps the best known in the field. Sutherland and Cressey hold that criminal behavior is determined by one's participation in a number of groups: family, school, neighborhood clique. We tend to adopt the attitudes of groups we belong to, in proportion to the strength of our ties to these groups. We are all pulled in different directions by competing attitudes toward criminal behavior, by different "definitions" (to use Sutherland's term) of the law as something to be respected or flouted. Thus "a person becomes delinquent because of an *excess* of definitions favorable to violation of law over definitions unfavorable to violation of law" among the groups he belongs to.

The theory of differential association can take into account a number of factors relevant to crime, but only those having to do with social conditions. The theory is essentially a form of environmental determinism, based on the same model of causality as Skinner's behaviorism. To maintain such a reductionist, "single-level" explanation of human action, any causes that are not social must be explained away.

If there is a link between alcohol and criminal violence, for example, Sutherland and Cressey suggest that perhaps the offenders have "learned from associations with others certain ways of acting when intoxicated." There may actually be something to this. It is very difficult to reproduce in the laboratory the types of behavior that alcohol induces; social setting does seem to be a factor. But it is a sign of sociological desperation to claim that it is the only *causal* factor. In some cases, at least, the criminal's intent seems to come first; drinking or taking drugs is a way of nerving himself for the act. It is also likely that alcohol use and crime are related effects of underlying psychological causes. And what of the effect of alcohol on the brain?

Another example: Many social scientists would explain the fact that males commit a higher proportion of violent crimes than females by treating gender as something purely social. Social norms encourage violence in boys, discourage it in girls. That is surely part of the explanation. It is just as surely not the whole explanation; gender is a physiological as well as a social condition. As Melvin Konner points out in *The Tangled Wing*, studies with animals have shown that testosterone levels during key periods in maturation affect the degree of aggressiveness in adults. And an increase in testosterone lowers the threshold of firing in a nerve bundle called the *stria terminalis*, which is part of a neural circuit known to be involved in violent behavior.

Or consider the appalling incidence of child abuse in the families of delinquents. Dorothy Otnow Lewis and her associates divided the youths at a Connecticut correctional school into two groups, according to the severity of their crimes. As she reports in *Vulnerabilities to Delinquency*, 75 percent of the more violent offenders had been abused as children, as against 33 percent of the less violent. And 79 percent of the first group (compared with 20 percent of the second) had witnessed extreme violence: they had seen their mothers slashed, their siblings burned with cigarettes. It would be hard to find more compelling evidence that one's environment can have devastating effects. But it is likely that the violent behavior of these youths flowed from physiological as well as emotional damage they suffered

as children. Virtually all of the more violent offenders had neurological disorders, and 30 percent of them (as against none of the less
violent offenders) had grossly abnormal electroencephalograms and/
or histories of grand mal seizures. Environmental determinists are
aware that between the stimulus and the response lies a very complicated piece of equipment—the human organism. But they regard the
internal properties of that organism as mere "intervening variables,"
to use Skinner's phrase: conduits that pass along, unmodified, the
stream of environmental forces. *The Tangled Wing* is an exhaustive
demonstration that this view is false. Pulling together evidence from
genetics, biochemistry, ethology, and neurophysiology, Konner
shows that the intervening variables are in fact the controlling ones.
An animal's genetic endowment determines which stimuli it can respond to and the kinds of responses those stimuli are most likely to
elicit. Even among humans, action flows in large part from emotions
that have their origins in the interplay of hormones and neural struc-
tures that were shaped by selection pressures over the course of a
million years.

This is not to say, of course, that the environment is irrelevant,
merely that environmental determinism is as narrow and simple-
minded as genetic determinism. As Konner writes, "Any analysis of
the causes of human nature that tends to ignore *either* the genes *or*
the environmental factors may safely be discarded."

But such ecumenism has a cost that Konner does not fully appre-
ciate. The evolution of the nervous system, from the simplest reflex
arc to the human brain, has been a process of interposing longer and
more complex loops between stimulus and response. As control of
behavior moves inward, action replaces reaction, the organism becomes an agent, and we have to consider the possibility that the
whole is more than the sum of its parts.

Despite its sophistication, *The Tangled Wing* is still reductionist,
filled with confidence that a scientific understanding of the parts will
add up to an understanding of the whole. "When we have characterized the biology of moods," Konner suggests, in one of many such
statements, "we will have characterized the major forces behind behavior." But the riches that await us in biological research, and doubtless they are many, will leave Konner's account of human behavior
overdrawn, his confidence in reductionism insufficiently funded by
the evidence. Indeed, a number of prominent biologists, such as

Nobel Prize-winner Roger Sperry, have concluded that behavior will never be understood fully at the neuronal or biochemical level; and they have revived the view that qualitatively new and irreducible properties emerge in a biological system as it becomes more complex.

In the human brain, the massive expansion of the frontal lobes made possible two traits that have always seemed to distinguish man from other animals: the capacities for self-awareness and for abstract, conceptual thought. Konner has almost nothing to say about these capacities, or about the fact that they enable us to modify and override the more primitive responses of evolutionarily older parts of the brain. Yet if Sperry and his allies are correct, these capacities are examples of "emergent" properties beyond the reach of any reductionist explanation. The only hope of understanding them lies in a more holistic approach, one that crosses the mind-body divide and examines them as traits of a conscious self.

The result of such an examination could be merely a more complex deterministic account of human action. But it could also be that the capacities for conceptual thought and self-awareness represent an evolutionary change of kind, not merely degree. They do not, of course, break the bonds of determinism altogether: we are still constrained by our genetic and physiological equipment, and can hardly remain unaffected by our social environment. But if the human agent, the self, is more than the sum of its parts, then our actions may be more than the sum of their antecedents; we may have room to maneuver within the causal net.

Criminology texts routinely denounce the search for criminal man—for a set of personality traits peculiar to criminals. And no doubt a good deal of nonsense has been perpetrated in the course of this search. But there is in fact a personality syndrome that one encounters at every turn in the literature on crime. The type was formerly known as the psychopath or sociopath; in the current edition of the psychiatrists' *Diagnostic and Statistical Manual*, the syndrome goes by the anemic name of "antisocial personality disorder."

The psychopath is not the bug-eyed psychotic who serves as a wild card in Hollywood crime dramas. Psychopathy does not involve any clear psychosis or neurosis; that is why it is classified as a personality disorder. Perhaps the most revealing name for the syndrome is the oldest. Psychologists in the nineteenth century identified a disorder that seemed to involve no cognitive impairment—those who had it were often quite intelligent and clearheaded—but rather a gross deficiency in what used to be called the *moral* faculties: the capacities for deep feeling, working toward goals, living according to standards, cooperating with others. These people seemed profoundly amoral. Despite their intelligence, they were unable to look beyond the impulse of the moment. They seemed constitutionally incapable of empathy and lacked even the most elementary sense of fairness and reciprocity. It was as if human intelligence had been planted in the brain of an innocently predatory animal. The psychologists called these individuals "moral imbeciles."

The classic clinical portrait of the psychopath was drawn by Hervey Cleckley, who was a therapist in private practice, in *Mask of Sanity;* some researchers still use his list of sixteen traits as a diagnostic test. Cleckley's subjects exhibited the normal range of intelligence; many were well informed, many were talented. They were not delusional, and seemed entirely free of anxiety. Yet they seemed unable to learn from experience, making the same mistakes over and over, even after they had recognized them. His subjects were chronic liars, even when no clear gain was involved. Cleckley came to believe that the intelligence they showed in conversation was merely verbal; as he studied them more closely, he was struck by the concreteness and fragmentation of their thinking, reflected in their complete lack of interest in long-range planning for their lives.

Most of his patients, especially those with criminal records, were able to size up people quickly; they were good at manipulating others and mimicking conventional feelings and attitudes when it served their purposes. Yet at other times their actions revealed an inability to anticipate how others would react. (One woman, in applying for jobs, routinely gave as references people whose trust she had repeatedly violated.) Cleckley was most struck by the poverty of feeling these people exhibited. Primitive emotions—spite, vanity, sentimental affection, flashes of violent anger—came and went like New England weather, but there was no indication that they experienced deeper, more complex emotions, such as grief, pride, joy, despair, or love. His patients were often witty, but never revealed any genuine sense of humor. Their egocentricity was so profound as to differ in kind from ordinary self-centeredness. Yet despite their indifference to the suffering they caused others, their obliviousness to moral standards, and their incapacity for feeling shame, humiliation, or regret, they were quick to blame others and to defend themselves when criticized. Moral evaluation mattered to them in a way that belied the appearance of amorality.

Cleckley's patients were not all criminals, nor do all criminals fit the pattern he described.The degree of overlap is hard to estimate. Researchers using the Minnesota Multiphasic Personality Inventory have found that prison inmates score well above the general population on the "psychopathic deviate" scale; however, that scale is a fairly crude measure. The psychopath is perhaps best seen as a prototype to which criminals conform more or less closely.

Any doubts about the existence of a link between crime and psychopathy have been dispelled by the work of Stanton Samenow and Samuel Yochelson, who conducted a fifteen-year study of criminals at St. Elizabeths Hospital, a federal psychiatric facility in Washington, D.C. Their two-volume work, *The Criminal Personality* (summarized in Samenow's more recent *Inside the Criminal Mind*), offers a clinical portrait remarkably similar to Cleckley's. Yochelson and Samenow found the same concreteness in thinking that others have noticed. Their patients' short attention spans made it next to impossible for them to take a long-range view of their lives. They rarely learned from experience. Their non-integrative cognitive style made it difficult for them to see any contradiction between their violent, predatory behavior and the sentimentality they often expressed toward the helpless. The career criminals Yochelson and Samenow studied tended to view "straight" life as a series of concrete acts, most of them boring. These people lived in the moment, and did not see the value of the long-term rewards of a family or a career. These cognitive traits have a common root: an anticonceptual mode of thinking. For it is the power to conceptualize that makes us able to act on principles, to think in terms of long-range goals, and to learn from experience.

The psychopathic syndrome also involves a certain self-conception. The psychopath was traditionally considered less susceptible to fear and anxiety than other people. That, indeed, was the basis for one explanation of the syndrome: psychopaths' insensitivity to punishment hinders the process of socialization. In the course of their interviews, however, Yochelson and Samenow found their subjects to be intensely fearful.

Their greatest fear, Yochelson and Samenow found, was that of "the zero state." This sense of complete and profound worthlessness was something all of their patients had experienced, and went to great lengths to repress. They protected themselves against it by a kind of grandiosity, a conception of themselves as supermen, as effortless heroes able to achieve great ends by unconventional means. Their chief method of sustaining this self-image was to exert control over others. By forcing others to bend to his will—intimidating them, manipulating them through lies and cons—the psychopath makes society affirm a view of his potency that he cannot affirm by looking within.

Conversely, anything that suggests a lack of control over the world threatens to bring on the zero state. According to Samenow, "The threat of being less than top dog, the possibility that he won't achieve unusual distinction, the chance that things will not go as he wants constitute a major threat to the criminal, almost as though his life were at stake. From his standpoint it is, because the puncturing of his inflated self-concept is psychological homicide." Anyone trying to understand the case of Jeffrey MacDonald should find that a chilling observation.

Theories about the causes of psychopathy—like those about the causes of crime—are numerous and varied. Most if not all of the traits of the psychopath have been observed in people with neurological damage. And it is hard to believe that neural damage had nothing to do with the violent behavior of the delinquents studied by Dorothy Otnow Lewis. But as the eminent neurologist Frank A. Elliott has noted, "organic disorders tend to produce a 'partial' psychopath rather than the fully fledged, classical picture."

There are also sociological explanations. In *Criminal Violence, Criminal Justice*, Charles Silberman describes the brutality of crimes committed by juvenile delinquents, often without remorse. Silberman attributes this to the fact that they "have been so brutalized in their own upbringing." More generally, he suggests that crime usually springs from an impoverished self-conception, caused in turn by economic poverty: "In a society that rewards success and penalizes failure . . . to be poor is to live with continual self-doubt." But this cannot be the whole story, unless we assume—and the assumption is often made by social scientists, usually without benefit of evidence—that the individual derives his self-esteem exclusively from the responses of others. That assumption leaves no way to account for the fact that people differ in precisely this respect: the autonomy of their self-estimates.

Cleckley, for his part, held that psychopathy is a deeply rooted disorder, an abnormality more profound even than schizophrenia. Though the psychopath presents a mask of sanity to the world, his actions reveal that the mask "disguises something quite different within, concealing behind a perfect mimicry of normal emotion, fine intelligence, and social responsibility a grossly disabled personality." Yochelson and Samenow maintain that the problem lies much closer to the surface, in patterns of thinking that are accessible to consciousness and—with some effort—subject to conscious control.

They have discovered, for example, a phenomenon they call "cut-off," a severe form of anti-conceptual thinking that allows someone on the threshold of committing a crime to blank out all of his fears and doubts. This act of blanking out is voluntary: "Even though cut-off is so rapid and automatic, it is still a mental process that is under the criminal's control. Whether he invokes the cutoff is his choice." As evidence of volition, they note that criminals learn not to shut off their fears too soon, lest they dull themselves to signs of danger.

By the time of Yochelson's death in 1976, thirteen of the thirty patients in the special therapeutic program at St. Elizabeths were leading responsible lives—a major achievement, given the dismal record of criminal rehabilitation, and a sign that patterns of thinking are amenable to change. The agent of change, as the authors describe it, is the insistence that a patient learn to monitor his thoughts and to prevent his fragile self-image from blocking out his awareness of what he has done, of who he is.

Yochelson and Samenow came to believe that crime is a voluntary act for which the criminal is fully accountable. This is not, to say the least, the majority view in criminology, but it is not surprising that they adopted it. For in tracing the roots of crime to problems in the criminal's ability to think conceptually and to form a self-conception, they arrived at the two uniquely human traits to which anti-determinists in all fields have always appealed.

The conflict between free will and determinism first arose in philosophy, and most of the philosophical arguments for human freedom have been variations on a common theme. Because we are capable of self-consciousness, it is claimed, we can focus attention on an impulse or feeling and examine it from a kind of inner distance that can weaken its aura or grip. Because we are capable of conceptual thought, we can evaluate these impulses and feelings—their consequences, their effects on others, their compatibility with our principles—and choose whether to act on them. We are free agents because those capacities give us veto power over the forces that move us.

Determinists have always found this argument naive: science, they say, will show that behavior is governed by causes beyond the reach of conceptual thought and self-awareness. But in the case of crime, at any rate, the trail of scientific inquiry keeps circling back to those very capacities. It would be too much to say that science can establish human freedom. That will always be a philosophical issue. But the old assumption that science is a witness against free will is not true, either—it will not survive a close look at what scientists have actually discovered. Human beings have turned out to be far more complicated than the sciences of man anticipated. We may just turn out to be as complicated as we always thought.

The Basic Myths About Criminals

by Stanton E. Samenow

In the 1957 musical *West Side Story,* Stephen Sondheim parodied what then was the current thinking about juvenile delinquency in the song, "Gee, Officer Krupke." Delinquents were punks because their fathers were drunks. They were misunderstood rather than no good. They were suffering from a "social disease," and society "had played [them] a terrible trick." They needed an analyst, not a judge, because it was "just [their] neurosis" acting up. In short, their criminal behavior was regarded as symptomatic of a deep-seated psychological or sociological problem. Little has changed since then in terms of deeply ingrained beliefs about the causes of crime. In this chapter, I shall briefly discuss these beliefs. . . . [T]he prevalent thinking about crime has been and still is loaded with fundamental misconceptions resulting in devastating consequences for society.

When a person commits a particularly sordid crime, his sanity may be questioned. Three men pick up two girls who are thumbing a lift. A joyride turns into a nightmare when the teenagers are driven to a desolate mountainous area where they are bound and repeatedly raped. Two of their tormentors dig a hole and tell them to say their prayers. However, the men decide to prolong the torture and spirit the girls off to an apartment and brutalize them again. The girls are saved by a suspicious neighbor who calls the police. Eventually, the court considers the rapists to be "mentally disordered sex offenders" and sends them to a psychiatric hospital, where they spend less than one-third of the time they would have served in prison.

Criminals learn to fool the psychiatrists and the courts in order to serve "easy time" in a hospital with the prospect of getting out more quickly than they would from a prison. From other criminals and from their attorneys, even unsophisticated street criminals learn the ploy of insanity. The game is for the criminal to convince others that he is sick so that he can beat the charge. After he is admitted to the hospital, he plays the psychiatric game of mouthing insights and

47

behaving properly so that he can convince the staff that he is recovering and deserves to be released.

We, the public, may be so revolted by the gruesomeness of a crime that we conclude that only a sick person would be capable of such an act. But our personal reaction is totally irrelevant to understanding the criminal. True, what these men did to the teenagers is not a normal, everyday event. But the key question is, what are these men really like? A detailed and lengthy examination of the mind of a criminal (which is seldom made) will reveal that it is anything but sick. The criminal is rational, calculating, and deliberate in his actions.

Criminals know right from wrong. In fact, some know the laws better than their lawyers. But they believe that whatever they want to do at any given time is right for them. Their crimes require logic and self-control.

Some crimes happen so fast and with such frequency that they appear to be compulsive. A person may steal so often that others are certain that he is the victim of an irresistible impulse and therefore a "kleptomaniac." But a thorough mental examination would show that he is simply a habitual thief, good at what he does. He can size up a situation at a glance and then make off with whatever he wants. A habit is not a compulsion. On any occasion, the thief can refrain from stealing if he is in danger of getting caught. And if he decides to give up stealing for a while and lie low, he will succeed in doing so.

The sudden and violent crime of passion has been considered a case of temporary insanity because the perpetrator acts totally out of character. But again, appearance belies reality.

A man murders his wife in the heat of an argument. He has not murdered anyone before, and statistical trends would project that he will not murder again. It is true that the date, time, and place of the homicide were not planned. But an examination of this man would show that on several occasions he had shoved her and often wished her dead. In addition, he is a person who frequently had fantasies of evening the score violently whenever he believed that anyone had crossed him. He did not act totally out of character when he murdered his wife. He was not seized by an alien, uncontrollable impulse. In his thinking, there was precedent for such a crime. A person with even worse problems might well have resolved them differently.

If criminals are not mentally ill, aren't they nevertheless victims of poverty, broken homes, racism, and a society that denies them opportunities? Since the late nineteenth century, there has been a prevalent opinion that society is more to blame for crime than the criminal.

Sociologists assert that the inner-city youngster responds with rage to a society that has excluded him from the mainstream and made the American dream beyond his reach. Some even contend that crime is a normal and adaptive response to growing up in the soul-searing conditions of places like Watts and the South Bronx. They observe that in correctional institutions there is a disproportionately large number of inmates who are poor and from minority groups. These inmates are seen as casualties of a society that has robbed them of hope and virtually forced them into crime just so they can survive.

Crime knows no social boundaries, as the rising suburban crime rate demonstrates. Suburban delinquents are also regarded as victims—victims of intense pressures to compete, of materialism, of parents who neglect them, push them to grow up too fast, or are overly protective. These adolescents are perceived as rebelling not only against their parents but against middle-class values, seeking meaning instead through kicks and thrills.

Peer pressure is seen as a critical factor in the lives of youngsters from all social classes who turn to crime. Experts point out that among some subcultures the rewards are for being daring and tough, not for good grades and job promotions. Kids learn about crime from one another; they are schooled in the streets and go along with the crowd in order to acquire self-esteem and a sense of belonging. The belief that crime is contagious like a disease is more than a century old.

Every social institution has been blamed for contributing to crime. Schools have been singled out as forcing into crime youngsters who don't fit the academic mold. Churches have been accused of not providing leadership to wayward youth and to the community at large. Newspapers, television, and the movies have been charged with glamorizing crime. American business and advertising have been accused of contributing to distorted values and therefore to crime.

Economic hard times have been associated with an increase in crime. But then so have good times. Financial pressures are said to push despondent people over the edge. But then, when times are booming it has been thought that the gap between the "haves" and "have nots" widens and the latter, out of resentment, turn to crime. Economic troubles are also seen as contributing to crime by forcing mothers to go to work, further weakening the family. Their children have less supervision and guidance than before and are even more vulnerable to peer pressure.

Sociological explanations for crime, plausible as they may seem, are simplistic. If they were correct, we'd have far more criminals than we do. Criminals come from all kinds of families and neighborhoods. Most poor people are law-abiding, and most kids from broken homes are not delinquents. Children may bear the scars of neglect and deprivation for life, but most do not become criminals. The environment does have an effect, but people perceive and react to similar conditions of life very differently. A family may reside in a neighborhood where gangs roam the streets and where drugs are as easy to come by as cigarettes. The father may have deserted and the mother collect welfare. Yet not all the children in that family are in crime. In suburbia, a family may be close emotionally and well off financially, but that is not enough to keep one of the youngsters from using drugs, stealing, and destroying property.

Criminals claim that they were rejected by parents, neighbors, schools, and employers, but rarely does a criminal say why he was rejected. Even as a young child, he was sneaky and defiant, and the older he grew, the more he lied to his parents, stole and destroyed their property, and threatened them. He made life at home unbearable as he turned even innocuous requests into a battleground. He conned his parents to get whatever he wanted, or else he wore them down through endless argument. It was the criminal who rejected his parents rather than vice versa.

Not only did he reject his family, but he rejected the kids in the neighborhood who acted responsibly. He considered them uninteresting, their lives boring. He gravitated to more adventurous youngsters, many of whom were older than he. Crime is not contagious like chicken pox. Even in crime-infested neighborhoods, there are youngsters who want no part of the action. Sure there is the desire to belong to the crowd, but the question is, which crowd? Criminals were not forced into crime by other people. They *chose* the companions they liked and admired.

The school does not reject the antisocial youngster until he is impossible to deal with. Many criminals have no use for school whatsoever. Still some remain in school, then use their education to gain entree into circles where they find new victims. More commonly, delinquent youngsters use the classroom as an arena for criminal activity by fighting, lying, stealing, and engaging in power plays against teachers and other pupils. Basically, for them, school is boring, its requirements stupid, the subjects meaningless. Just as the criminal rejects his parents, he does the same to his teachers. It is neither incompetent teachers nor an irrelevant curriculum that drives him out. In fact, the school may offer him an individually tailored program, but no matter what he is offered, it does not suit him. Finally, he is expelled for disruptive behavior or grows so bored that he quits.

The notion that people become criminals because they are shut out of the job market is an absurdity. In the first place, most unemployed people are not criminals. More to the point, perhaps, is that many criminals do not want to work. They may complain that without skills they can't find employment. (Of course, it was their choice not to remain in school to acquire those skills.) But as many a probation officer will observe, in most areas jobs of some sort are available but criminals find them too menial and beneath them.

Some criminals are highly educated and successful at their work. Their very success may serve as a cover for crime. If a person has a solid work record, he is generally regarded as responsible and stable. But money, recognition, and power are not enough to make a criminal law-abiding. The point is that what a person's environment offers is not decisive in his becoming a criminal.

The media have been criticized for making crime enticing by glorifying both specific crimes and criminals. There has been intense concern about the high incidence of violence in television programs that reach children. Neither scientific studies nor congressional hearings have shed much light on how much the media contribute to crime. Once again arises the erroneous premise that human character is easily shaped by external events. Television does not make a criminal out of a child; nor do movies, comics, magazines, or books. A person already thinking about committing crimes may pick up ideas from the media or become more certain about the feasibility of a particular crime. (Note the rash of skyjackings following extensive publicity about them during the 1970s.) But a responsible person will not be turned into a criminal by what he watches or reads.

Economic adversity affects us all. We may be pushed to work longer hours or to take a second job. Women who prefer to be at home may have little choice but to go to work. Families may have to make do with less and watch goals slip further out of reach, and people on fixed incomes bear a special burden. The responsible person responds to economic pressures by sacrifice and hard work. Even for him, temptation may be stronger to step outside the law as the economic squeeze grows tighter. Ultimately, however, it comes down to how each person chooses to deal with adversity.

What of the observation that a disproportionate number of people incarcerated for crimes are both poor and from minority groups? This is less a commentary on those groups than on the processes by which the criminal justice system arrests, adjudicates, and confines. If a white, upper-middle class youngster is arrested for shoplifting, his parents may hire a lawyer and get the charges dropped by promising that the boy will visit a counselor. He never sees the inside of a courtroom and his record is clean. The black kid may become a criminal justice statistic. He goes to court, is convicted, then sentenced to a term of probation, and has a criminal record. For a more serious crime, the person with money and connections may get probation while the disadvantaged offender is imprisoned. Perhaps we need to examine the system by which people end up behind bars rather than focus on their color or economic status. It is unwarranted and racist to assume that because a person is poor and black (brown, red, yellow) he is inadequate to cope with his environment and therefore can hardly help but become a criminal.

So far, I have contended that criminals are not mentally ill or hapless victims of oppressive social conditions. But the psychiatrists, psychologists, counselors, and social workers still would say that a person is what he is largely because of his early experiences. They regard a man's crimes as "symptoms" of conflicts that are rooted in childhood and remain unresolved.

Too long have the social sciences promulgated the view that a human organism comes into the world like a lump of clay to be shaped by external forces. This view renders us all victims! What it does accomplish is to make explanation of behavior relatively easy. If any of us had taken a criminal path, something could be found in our past to explain why we turned out as we did. If your child has problems, you will be faulted for your child-rearing practices, whatever they were. If you were strict, you will be told that your child has been affected by your harshness. If you were permissive, you will be accused of being too indulgent. If you were relatively democratic, you might be considered wishy-washy or even indifferent. Worst of all, you might be tagged as inconsistent, something that we are all guilty of to an extent. Psychology always has a clever theory about any bit of behavior and offers an explanation, but only *after the fact.* There's the old line that if a patient arrives late for his psychiatric appointment, he's resistant. If he's early, he's anxious. If he's on time, he's compulsive. Although social scientists are sincere in trying to explain why we are the way we are, they are often incorrect.

In varying degrees, all human beings suffer trauma as they grow up. But if a domineering mother or an inadequate father produce delinquent children, why is it that most children who have such parents aren't criminals? Psychologists stress the importance of parents as role models, especially fathers for their sons and mothers for their daughters. Yet many children with weak or irresponsible role models become honest, productive adults. Conversely, some children with strong, positive role models become criminals.

When they are interviewed after being apprehended, criminals invariably relate a tale of horrors about their early lives. They seize upon any hardships in their lives, real or made up, to justify their acts against society. By portraying themselves as victims, they seek sympathy and hope to absolve themselves of culpability.

Some of society's chronic lawbreakers do come from volatile, conflict-ridden families where they have suffered abuse. But that is likely to be only part of the story. In their accounts, they relate only what others did to them, omitting what they did to make a bad situation even worse. A man may describe savage beatings by a maniacal father, but he never tells what he did to provoke such treatment. He conceals the fact that he taunted, deceived, and defied his parents to the point that his frustrated father finally lashed out at him physically. A complete account might reveal that the criminal was the only child in the family to have received severe corporal punishment, whereas his siblings were generally well-behaved. This is not to defend harshness in discipline. It is, however, to suggest that we ought not to limit our inquiries to what parents have done to children but strive to determine what children have done to their parents. A related point is that probably most children who are mistreated suffer long-range effects, but not all are criminals.

Criminals contend that their parents did not understand them and failed to communicate with them. They are often believed, and as usual, the deficiency is attributed almost entirely to parents. If we could be invisible observers in the homes of delinquent youngsters, we might reach a different conclusion. As a child, the criminal shuts his parents out of his life because he doesn't want them or anyone else to know what he is up to. When a teenager skips school, hangs out at a pool hall, joyrides, drinks, smokes pot, and steals from stores, it should be no surprise that he tells his parents little about his day. In fact, he will greet parental interest and concern with accusations that the parent is prying into his business. No matter how hard they try, mothers and fathers cannot penetrate the secrecy, and they discover that they do not know their own child. He is the kid who remains the family mystery.

In short, psychological theory, in its current state, is more misleading than illuminating in explaining why people become criminals. Far from being a formless lump of clay, the criminal shapes others more than they do him.

During the nineteenth century, there was a belief among many experts that people were born criminals. Attempts to identify criminals on the basis of facial or other physical features were discredited. However, the "bad seed" hypothesis never died. In the 1960s, for example, a controversy arose over whether criminals have special chromosome patterns. Evidence for an "XYY" syndrome or other chromosome anomaly remains inconclusive.

Another belief is that perhaps criminals suffer from a physiological dysfunction that may be hereditary or result from trauma. Brain lesions or tumors, temporal lobe epilepsy, blood chemistry changes, glandular abnormality, and hypoglycemia are among the organic factors that have been linked to criminality, but conclusive evidence of such a linkage is still lacking. Of the many people who are afflicted with these conditions, few become criminals.

There has also been a theory that criminals are *inherently* less intelligent than the general population, but this has been laid to rest. Empirical studies of criminals and noncriminals simply did not support such a proposition. Criminals may score low on IQ tests and lack basic information that most people acquire in the primary grades of school. However, their mental acumen and resourcefulness are striking to anyone who is privy to their complex, well-thought-out schemes. Criminals are remarkable in their capacity to size up their environment in order to pursue objectives important to them.

Still the belief lingers, especially among some educators, that criminals have an organically based learning disability. Experts point out that many delinquent youngsters seem *unable* to learn and fall far behind academically They also observe that among prison inmates there is a sizable number who can neither read nor write. Another deficiency noted is that criminals do not seem to learn from past experiences the way most people do.

There are several problems with the learning disability theory. Many criminals who appear learning disabled are highly capable of learning but simply chose not to because school was incompatible with what they wanted to do. Furthermore, most children who are genuinely disabled in their capacity to learn, while experiencing blows to their self-esteem and severe frustration, don't react to their difficulties by becoming criminals. The observation that criminals have an incapacity to learn from experience is inaccurate. They may not learn what parents and teachers want them to learn, but they do utilize the past as a guide when it matters to them. They learn how to become more successful criminals.

No factor or set of factors—sociological, psychological, or biological—is sufficient to explain why a person becomes a criminal. So far, the search to pin down causation has been futile. Far more disturbing is that programs, laws, policies, and decisions about how to deal with criminals have been based upon these theories, and this has resulted in a tremendous waste of resources while crime continues in epidemic proportions.

What is clear is that criminals come from a wide variety of backgrounds—from the inner city, suburbia, rural areas, and small towns and from any religious, racial, or ethnic group. They may grow up in closely knit families, broken homes, or orphanages. They may be grade school dropouts or college graduates, unemployed drifters or corporate executives. In most cases, they have brothers, sisters, and next-door neighbors who grew up under similar circumstances but did not become criminals.

Despite a multitude of differences in their backgrounds and crime patterns, criminals are alike in one way: *how they think*. A gun-toting, uneducated criminal off the streets of southeast Washington, D.C., and a crooked Georgetown business executive are extremely similar in their view of themselves and the world. This is not to deny individual differences among criminals in their aesthetic tastes, sexual practices, religious observance, or favorite sports team. But all regard the world as a chessboard over which they have total control, and they perceive people as pawns to be pushed around at will. Trust, love, loyalty, and teamwork are incompatible with their way of life. They scorn and exploit most people who are kind, trusting, hardworking, and honest. Toward a few they are sentimental but rarely considerate. Some of their most altruistic acts have sinister motives.

More than a half-century ago, the noted psychologist Alfred Adler observed, "With criminals, it is different: they have a private logic, a private intelligence. They are suffering from a wrong outlook upon the world, a wrong estimate of their own importance and the importance of other people." Adler went on to say that the criminal's crimes "fit in with his general conception of life."[1] Implied throughout Adler's writing is the idea that people choose to be criminals, that they are a different breed. Even in 1930, Adler's was a lone voice.

Psychology and sociology long have advanced the view that the criminal is basically like everyone else but has turned antisocial because he has been blocked by others in fulfilling his aspirations. Thus the criminal is perceived as a victim of forces and circumstances beyond his control. Those who hold such a view go a step further, asserting that we are all, in a sense, criminals because we lie, lust, and yield to temptation. But it is absurd to equate the white lie of the responsible person with the gigantic network of lies of the criminal. It is equally absurd to equate a child's pilferage of a candy bar with a delinquent's stealing practically everything that isn't nailed down. At some point, we and the criminal are very different. He is far more extreme in that crime is a way of life, not an occasional aberration. It is misleading to claim that the criminal wants what the responsible person wants, that he values the same things that a responsible person values. Both may desire wealth, but only one will work steadily and earnestly to acquire it and then use it responsibly. The criminal believes that he is entitled to it and grabs it any way he can, not caring whom he injures, and then thirsts for more. Both may desire a family life, but the responsible person shows the give-and-take, the empathy, and the selflessness that family life requires. The criminal pays lip service to love while demanding that his spouse and children place his demands and wishes first.

By taking the position that the criminal is a victim, society has provided him with excuses for crime and thereby supported his contention that he is not to blame. Partly to atone for its alleged injustices to the criminal, society has offered him countless opportunities to "rehabilitate" himself and enter the mainstream. Surprise has given way to despair as the criminal rejects the very opportunities that he rejected before (work, school, counseling) or else shamelessly exploits them while continuing to commit crimes.

Attempts to improve the environment, no matter how worthwhile, have not altered the criminal's personality. Psychological methods have been equally unsuccessful because therapists have mistakenly utilized concepts and techniques suited to patients with a very different character structure. In the more distant past, castration, lobotomy, and drugs were employed in hopes of altering biological forces within the criminal, but to little avail.

The death knell of rehabilitation having sounded, the pendulum is swinging the other way—to "lock 'em up and throw away the key." Given the high recidivism rate of criminals who were considered rehabilitated, such a sentiment is understandable.

What about the function of punishment? Arrest alone or confinement undoubtedly deters some offenders, but contact with the criminal justice system has little lasting impact on habitual offenders. Warehousing a criminal in an institution gets him off the streets for a while, but one day he will be released to wreak havoc again in society. Because prison is expensive—costing the taxpayer more than a year's tuition at an Ivy League college—and because many prisons are dehumanizing, alternatives to incarceration are being developed. In this effort, rehabilitative proposals are once again being heard, but the term is not being used. Instead, it is "community-based corrections," which features a smorgasbord of offerings—vocational training, schooling, counseling, psychotherapy—as well as accountability to a probation officer. In addition, restitution and community service programs have proliferated as society considers finally not just criminals but people who are truly victims.

The more things change, the more they stay the same. The criminal's motivation is to avoid confinement. He sees his probation officer once every couple of weeks for a brief appointment. He may attend some programs if they are mandated by the court. And he may make restitution. But his personality does not change.

And so the criminal comes up against a world that either bleeds for him because he is a victim or else wants to remove him from the earth. Criminals have been imprisoned, educated, counseled, preached to, and even executed. But the policies and programs continue to be ineffective, largely because those conceiving and implementing them do not know with whom they are dealing. Decisions are made on the basis of misconceptions in an atmosphere of "do something now and do it fast."

A surprising number of people who deal with criminals do not know how criminals think. How a person behaves is determined largely by how he thinks. *Criminals think differently.* If we are thoroughly familiar with how they think, we are in a far better position to draft legislation, formulate policies, administer programs, render more informed decisions, and be more effective in direct contacts with criminals both in the institutions and in the community.

There is even a ray of hope that we can help some criminals change and become responsible citizens. But to undertake this task we must see the criminal as the problem, not society. Our approach to change must be to help the criminal radically alter his self-concept and his view of the world. Some criminals can be "habilitated," that is, helped to acquire patterns of thinking that are totally foreign to them but essential if they are to live responsibly.

---

1. Alfred Adler, "Individual Psychology and Crime," *Police Journal*, vol. 17 (1930), reprinted in *Quarterly Journal of Corrections* (1977), pp. 7–13.

Crime in the Welfare State

by David Walter

It is with considerable dismay that one notes the increasing incidence of criminal activities in the United States. After all, do not
people living in the United States have the highest standard of living
in the world and the most opportunity for advancement—thanks to
the operation of the free enterprise system? Why, then, the increase
in crime?

Many persons believe that fear of punishment has a direct effect
on the rate of crime, and that leniency tends to encourage more
crime; whereas others argue that harsh treatment by police or judges
may drive the criminal to more brutal crimes in a desire to "get even"
or "strike back at the oppressors."

Still others contend that crime is committed by those "kept poor
by the system" and that welfare, not punishment, will stem the
causes of crime. However, the record suggests to me that bribery or
blackmail payments in the form of urban renewal, government hand-
outs, and poverty programs unwittingly promote and become the
justification for the commission of crimes. So, I believe we must
examine further the basic causes of crime before prescribing more
punishment as a solution.

The American tradition has been for the people to delegate to
government the responsibility to combat crime through its police and
judicial arms. Citizens supporting these government functions want
a society of individuals content to leave their neighbors in peace.
Police and courts are supposed to deal effectively with those few
individuals who seek to obtain possessions from others by initiating
force and denying rights of ownership.

Government Unbounded

If one is to understand the failure of government to check the
crime wave, one must first recognize that government has taken to
itself or been urged to assume many additional functions which are

difficult to distinguish from outright criminal activity. Government, on all levels, is infringing upon the rights of individuals and taking their property by force. Government is increasingly seeking to control, without permission, those businessmen, entrepreneurs, and hard-working individuals who provide our high standard of living through the free market. If these same interventions were visited upon citizens by private persons, the actions would be clearly identified as crimes. But government, by "legalized" methods, now manages to deprive citizens of some 43 percent of their own earnings. And many persons condone this system; they see the similarity of actions, but feel that coercion for "the right reasons" (to benefit the collective) is permissible while similar action for personal gain is not.

Those who believe in individual rights and the efficacy of the free market should understand why and how the government plunderbund encourages crime. The increasing attacks on private property—by criminals, governments, politicians, activist ministers, welfarists, students, and philosophers—indicate that respect for private property has been replaced or has diminished as a moral value among responsible people. This change in the basic attitude toward private property (which may be defined as the individual's life and all those things one has acquired to sustain it through voluntary transactions) explains the rise in crime. Otherwise, if more and more people were accepting the ideal of private property, surely the remaining criminals could not step up their activities sufficiently to raise the overall level of crime.

The Looter Philosophy

Any society will have its principles reflected in its government, its mores, and its problems. It is not surprising to note an increase in crime in conjunction with an increased acceptance of collectivist principles of human action. For the widespread and popular acceptance of a looter philosophy is bound to bring forth a rash of looters.

Unfortunately for believers in liberty, many of the policies of government in the United States, as in other countries today, are based on the superiority of the group over the individual. We are told that the group (or the "public interest") demands subordination of individuals to the collective will. One might ask where these powers originate, since no individual holds such rights over another. But licensed philosophers of the new faith stand ready to answer that such powers spring like a will-o'-the-wisp from a sufficient grouping of individuals.

Government, under the collectivist philosophy, consists allegedly of the people who have superior insight into the everyday needs of the typical citizen. They decide how to distribute the nation's total output of goods among the masses for the common good. In America, this idea has been most dominant since the New Deal era, though it has governed to some extent every society previously known. Sorrowfully, today's debate concerns only how much to take, at what time, and for what purpose. Whether it is right and proper to take anything at all seems no longer to be questioned. A whole new generation has learned to turn these notions for their own benefit. Labor unions, pressure groups, looter groups such as the Welfare "Rights" Organization, political parties, and even business organizations and industrial concerns are all engaged in organized, sophisticated taking of other people's property. All this has come to be more or less accepted as part of the current political process.

Instant Justice

Nor are people entirely content to play according to the political rules. Why, they ask, should they wait for some greedy bureaucrat to get around to giving them the money "everyone" recognizes as having no rightful owner? Buffeted by government restrictions, or recipients of a poor public education, or unskilled and out of work due to minimum wage laws, or kept in a ghetto by urban renewal and building codes, these people decide to take "what is theirs by right" (or, at the very least, belongs to no one except he who can take it and hold it). So, cutting out the middleman, the thugs take to roaming the streets in search of loot and victims. They read about graft in public construction, war and pillage, inflation, labor union violence, and advice from the thought leaders about redistributing the wealth. Absorbing the society's predilections for violation of private property rights, they decide not to wait their turn in the political process because they have been waiting too long already.

Can the student who, in the morning, devotes his free period to working for a group which urges the workers to seize the factories complain when, in the evening, he is mugged as he leaves the campus? Can the labor union leader or the tariff advocate or the trust buster or the Presidential aspirant deny to criminals the "rights" they themselves demand to the livelihood of others? In a word, no. To be consistent with their own preachings, those who advocate to any degree a collectivist program have no right to complain about criminals trampling the rights of individuals. If they wonder why there are gangs roaming the streets, let them realize that those gangs are only doing what the collectivists piously demanded. The hoodlums do not wear dinner jackets nor do they speak from the podiums of great universities; they do not observe the niceties of "proper" political procedure or claim divine inspiration; they do not ask for the sanction of their victim; and they look upon politicians as fools who preach human liberty while doing everything in their power to enforce conformity and obedience to the welfare state.

Order, stability, and civilization (prerequisites of the free market) require far more than punishment, bribery, and blackmail in an attempt to gain good behavior. It is up to those who believe in private property and individual liberty to set an example for others by living what they preach. Each of us must root out from his own behavior those actions which run counter to voluntary trade among men. We must forswear any attempt to force others to our will. And, if we succeed with applying consistent principles of morality to our own lives, then perhaps others will be inspired to do likewise. Crime will decrease only to the extent that individuals begin to accept the principles of the free society where each man lives his life as he wishes, trades voluntarily with whom he pleases, and respects the right of other men to do the same.

II. THE FLIGHT FROM RESPONSIBILITY

Subverting Justice

by Robert James Bidinotto

The criminal justice system's failure to provide justice was inevitable, given the deterministic premises of its modern architects. Criminologists Wilson and Herrnstein explained, "The modern liberal position on criminal justice is rehabilitative, not retributive, because the offender is believed to have been driven to his crimes, rather than to have committed them freely and intentionally. . . . "[1]

Some "reformers" have even made their antipathy toward traditional conceptions of justice explicit. Here, two of them express acute discomfort with the classical symbol, Justitia—the familiar courtroom figure, robed and blindfolded, holding her scales and sword: "Though excellently symbolizing impartial, even-handed, and effective justice generally, Justitia is ill-equipped to meet our current demands from penal sentences. . . . From her left hand she should drop the scales and put in its place the case history, the symbol of the full psychological, sociological, and criminological investigation of the individual criminal. Her right hand will find very little use for a sword in the modern penal system. . . . Around her knees she would be well advised to gather the adolescent social sciences. . . . Finally, it is essential that she remove that anachronistic bandage from her eyes and look about at the developments in society generally . . . ."[2]

A new kind of justice—"social justice" or "distributive justice"— was to replace the "anachronistic," Justitian sort. Since men were helpless playthings of circumstances, and since circumstances impinged upon men unequally, it was the moral duty of government to intervene and redress the resulting "injustices." Government, according to Excuse-Makers such as John Rawls, was not to be society's impartial umpire, but rather its meddling therapist.

This outlook, largely a legacy of Rousseau's view of human nature,[3] spawned the redistributionist welfare state. "If you are bright, accomplished, famous, well-off, virtuous—you're just lucky, you had nothing to do with it, you didn't deserve any of it. Likewise, if you are stupid, lazy, corrupt, poor, mediocre, even criminal—you can't help that, either. Therefore, 'distributive justice' requires that the government level the playing field."[4]

It also led logically to "a culture of instinctive 'sympathy for the devil,' " as one historian put it, "a feeling that criminals in this society are as much victims as victimizers, as much sinned *against* as sinners—if not more so."[5]

Hence the Excuse-Maker's curious double standard toward crime: "sympathy for the devil," and simultaneous indifference toward crime victims. If no one can help being what he is, then the (usually) "lucky" and "privileged" middle-class crime victim merits only marginal concern. However, the "unlucky" and "underprivileged" criminal is a chronic victim of circumstance, and deserves our full sympathy and compassion. The logic of determinism, then, requires an *inversion* of traditional justice.

This has produced several major social consequences, all mutually reinforcing.

The criminal justice system began supplanting punishment with leniency and "rehabilitation." As early as 1949, the U.S. Supreme Court stated that retribution was "no longer the dominant objective of the criminal law," and was to be replaced by "reformation and rehabilitation."[6] Soon, police were also handcuffed by new court rulings favoring criminal suspects who, even if convicted, were quickly recycled into society. Meanwhile, redistributionist social spending programs abounded, punishing productivity, thrift, honesty, independence, *responsibility*— while rewarding idleness, profligacy, chiseling, parasitism, *irresponsibility*.[7] To make matters worse, such programs also diverted badly needed funds from the criminal justice system.

Today's justice system is an afterthought in governmental spending priorities. According to the American Bar Association, "The entire criminal justice system is starved for resources. Less than 3% of all government spending in the United States went to support all civil and criminal justice activities in fiscal 1985. This compares with 20.8% for social insurance payments, 18.3% for national defense and international relations, and 10.9% for interest on debt. Less than 1% of all government spending went into operation of the Nation's correctional system (including jails, prisons, probation, and parole)."[8]

Thanks chiefly to the Excuse-Making Industry, police are underfunded and undermanned to face the ever-mounting crime wave;

court dockets are flooded with impossible caseloads; jails and prisons are filled to overflowing. This puts pressure on the entire system to incarcerate as few criminals as possible, and to release them as quickly as possible. Thus, the Excuse-Making Industry has undermined the system both morally and practically.

Subverting the Quest for Truth

Since the premise of the Excuse-Makers is that "the criminal is a social victim," they see Constitutional rights *not* as a shield to protect the innocent from predators, but as a buffer between a "victimized" criminal class and the "injustice" of punishment. Byzantine procedural formalities, purportedly to guarantee the "rights" of the accused, now take precedence over the quest for simple truth and justice.

Confessions: The Miranda Decision[9]

On June 13, 1966, by a 5–4 decision, the United States Supreme Court rendered its now-famous *Miranda v. Arizona* decision. Supposedly based on the Fifth Amendment to the U.S. Constitution, which states that "No person . . . shall be compelled in any criminal case to be a witness against himself," *Miranda* twisted these simple words beyond recognition.

The Court held that even *voluntary, uncoerced* confessions by a suspect in police custody would no longer be admissible as evidence, unless the police first warned him that (1) he had the right to remain silent, (2) anything he said might be used against him in court, (3) he had the immediate right to a lawyer, and (4) he could get a free lawyer if he couldn't afford one. The suspect then had expressly to waive those rights before any questioning could proceed. Should police make the slightest omission or error in this ritual, any evidence they get can be thrown out, and the suspect can "walk."

In this single decision, four veteran criminals, convicted after voluntarily confessing to separate crimes, had their convictions overturned. The first was a three-time convict who admitted to a robbery after being identified by two victims. The second forged stolen checks from a purse-snatching in which the victim was killed. The third, a veteran bank robber, confessed after being told of his rights, but didn't *explicitly* waive them first. The fourth, arrested for kidnapping and rape, was identified by his victim, and later confessed "with full knowledge of my legal rights, understanding that any statement I make may be used against me." He hadn't, however, been formally advised of his right to have a lawyer present.

Even though these confessions weren't "involuntary in traditional terms," wrote Chief Justice Earl Warren for the majority, "in none of these cases did the officers undertake to afford the appropriate safeguards . . . to insure that the statements were truly the product of a free choice."

By what convoluted reasoning could such voluntary admissions be construed to be coerced? According to the Court's majority opinion, "In each of the cases, the defendant was thrust into an *unfamiliar atmosphere* and run through *menacing* police interrogation procedures. The *potentiality* for compulsion is forcefully apparent, for example . . . where the *indigent Mexican defendant* was a seriously disturbed individual with pronounced sexual fantasies [author's note: the man had been judged mentally competent to stand trial], and [where] the defendant was an *indigent Los Angeles Negro* who had dropped out of school in the sixth grade." [Emphasis added]

This is the deterministic language of the Excuse-Maker, brimming with thinly veiled editorials about poverty and racism, regarding even a *confessed criminal* as a helpless pawn of social pressures. (By contrast, the rape victim was coldly described as "the complaining witness.")

As for the remark about "menacing police interrogation procedures," the Court admitted that, "To be sure, the records do not evince overt physical coercion or patent psychological ploys." So, what was coercive? Dissenting Justice Byron White angrily noted, ". . . in the Court's view in-custody interrogation is *inherently* coercive. . . . " [Emphasis added] Observe the deterministic premise: we must assume that the suspect had little or no free will, and that his confession was thus involuntary, unless police somehow proved otherwise.

Often a suspect, feeling guilty or anxious, wants to unburden himself. Thanks to *Miranda*, at that point police are obliged to buck up his flagging courage and nagging conscience with repeated reassurances about his right *not* to cooperate. Justice John Harlan, another *Miranda* dissenter, protested that "the thrust of the new rules is to negate all pressures, to reinforce the nervous or ignorant suspect, and ultimately to discourage any confession at all. The aim, in short, is toward 'voluntariness' in a utopian sense. . . . One is entitled to feel astonished that the Constitution can be read to produce this result."

Furthermore—as the Court noted in subsequent cases—*Miranda* not only prohibited direct questioning without the suspect's prior permission, but also banned even indirect comments between police officers in his presence which were "reasonably likely to elicit an incriminating response." Any oblique police "appeal to . . . 'decency and honor'" in the suspect, charged Justice Thurgood Marshall, was "a classic interrogation technique." This is a perfectly logical outgrowth of the determinist premise. Since the suspect is presumed to be powerless in the face of his emotions, any appeal to these omnipotent emotions is itself "coercive." Thus, the Excuse-Makers construe the Constitution as protecting a criminal *even from his own guilty conscience.*

Miranda dissenter Justice White warned at the time, "In some unknown number of cases, the Court's rule will return a killer, a rapist or other criminal to the streets . . . to repeat his crime whenever it pleases him." That, of course, is precisely what has happened.

In late 1968, the suspected murderer of a missing ten-year-old girl was warned five separate times of his *Miranda* rights, and remained silent. Later, on a drive with the police, one officer remarked that the girl's parents would be relieved if they could find her body, and give her a "good Christian burial." The suspect, feeling guilty, then offered to lead them to the child's body, and was later convicted of murder. But the Supreme Court—again by a slim 5–4 vote—ruled that the policeman's statement amounted to unwanted interrogation, and that the case had to be retried. (Thanks to this ruling, the case was not resolved for over 15 years.)[10]

In California, a man beat a college co-ed to death. Read his *Miranda* rights, including his right to have a lawyer present, he waived them all and confessed. Yet a California appeals court threw out his conviction, because when arrested he hadn't been allowed to consult *his mother.*[11]

In Pennsylvania, a man who admitted clubbing to death his mother, sister, and grandmother was set free, because the arresting officer told him that anything he said could be used "for or against" him. The court ruled that the word "for" made the confession inadmissible.[12]

In Texas, a girl was shot dead after agreeing to testify in a drug case. The suspect refused a lawyer, but was assigned one anyway. Read his *Miranda* rights, he again refused a lawyer. He chose to plea bargain, signed a detailed confession, and took police to the murder site. Despite this, a judge, citing Supreme Court decisions, threw out his confession—because *no lawyer had been present.*[13]

The cost of such procedural utopianism is incalculable: it lies not just in convictions dismissed and overturned, but in confessions never made. Forty percent of murder convictions depend upon voluntary confessions by the perpetrator.[14] It is crucial, then, that police be allowed to ask questions without first begging the suspect's permission and encouraging his resistance. Yet *Miranda* equates "questions" with "coercion."

A reconstituted Supreme Court returned partly to its senses in 1984. Its *Quarles* decision exempted police from having to give *Miranda* warnings in situations where there was an immediate danger to the public, and found that confessions obtained under such circumstances could stand in court.[15] But *Miranda* itself remains, an infamous legal legacy of the Excuse-Making Industry and a major impediment to the pursuit of truth.

Evidence: Exclusionary Rules

Not only may confessions be excluded from criminal proceedings: so may any other sort of evidence.

The Fourth Amendment requires that only on "probable cause" may search warrants be issued, specifying the place to be searched, and the evidence sought. However, until 1914, even evidence illegally seized could be used in a criminal trial. That year, the Supreme Court ruled otherwise, and in 1961 *(Mapp v. Ohio)* extended the federal exclusionary rule to the states.[16]

The consequences have been appalling. The Bureau of Justice Statistics and National Institute of Justice estimated in 1983 that up to 55,000 serious criminal cases are dropped annually, thanks to the exclusionary rule. These released criminals are free to prey on innocents again: half of those set loose on exclusionary-rule grounds have been rearrested within two years.[17]

In 1964, a 14-year-old girl was brutally murdered in New Hampshire. Finding the bullet had come from a rifle of the prime suspect, police went to the state attorney general who, under then-existing law, was authorized to issue search warrants. With this warrant, they found further incriminating evidence, and the suspect was tried and convicted. Seven years later, however, the U.S. Supreme Court reversed his conviction, on grounds that the attorney general, as a prosecutor, was not a neutral judicial party. Since his search warrant was invalid, the incriminating evidence from the search had to be thrown out, too. Here, police "erred" due to good-faith obedience to existing law; but—as Supreme Court Justice Benjamin Cardozo had once noted—"The criminal is to go free because the constable has blundered."[18]

As in the case of *Miranda* confessions, the Supreme Court, in 1984, finally allowed some "good-faith" exceptions to search-and-seizure exclusionary rules. But that did not prevent it from allowing the guilty to escape in other cases.

A bullet fired through the floor of a squalid Phoenix apartment struck a man below. Entering the suspect's apartment, investigating officers found three weapons, a stocking mask, and two sets of expensive stereo equipment. Common sense warranted suspicion, and an officer lifted a turntable to get the serial number. Routine checking confirmed that these were, indeed, stolen items, and they were seized as evidence.

However, Arizona courts ruled that, though police had the right to enter when responding to the shooting, they did not have the right to seize the stereos, *since these were unrelated to the gunfire.* Had their serial numbers been in plain view, the evidence would have been admissible; but *touching* them violated the suspect's Fourth Amendment rights. In 1987, the Supreme Court upheld this decision by a 6–3 vote.[19]

Justice Hugo Black once wrote that such decisions seemed "calculated to make many good people believe our Court actually enjoys frustrating justice by unnecessarily turning professional criminals loose to prey upon society with impunity." He had a point.[20] After all, the purpose of the courts is to determine truth and administer *justice.* That can't happen if *facts*—however obtained—are selectively excluded from fact-finding proceedings. Yet because the Excuse-Making Industry regards those "driven" to crime as victims, matters of truth and justice are subordinated to a complex procedural etiquette whose alleged purpose is to "level the playing field." The substantive *ends* of the justice system must be sacrificed to new procedural *means*—means to a new *egalitarian* end.

In this light, exclusionary rules and the *Miranda* decision may be viewed as having the same purpose as "affirmative action" rules: to tip the balance scales of "social justice" on behalf of a class of presumed social victims. And, if the *facts* of a given case interfere with that agenda, every effort must be made to *exclude* them from the courtroom.

Subverting the Quest for Justice

Bail and Release on Recognizance

At his arrest or his initial appearance on charges, a suspect may be released on his own recognizance or on bail (assuming charges aren't dismissed outright). In many jurisdictions, a judge can deny bail if a suspect has a criminal record, or seems to pose a danger to the community. In the rest, he can hold the suspect without bail only if there is substantial doubt he'll return for trial. But due to overcrowded cells—and the protests of Excuse-Making "civil liberties" attorneys—many judges try to minimize the number of criminals held for trial in jail. This often means absurdly dangerous leniency.

Consider a typical case, that of career criminal Philip J. DiCarlo. Wanted on numerous felony warrants in Massachusetts, he was arrested on separate charges in Florida, but freed on only $2,626 bail. He finally surrendered to Massachusetts authorities. In exchange for a guilty plea, DiCarlo bargained fifteen felony burglary charges down to only eight counts, and got a sentence allowing parole eligibility after only two years. Despite being warned of the man's 20-year adult criminal record, the judge then postponed the imposition of the sentence, and freed DiCarlo on his own recognizance *so that he could be with his family for the holidays.* Showing more common sense than the judge, DiCarlo promptly skipped town.[21]

Other bail incidents are no laughing matter. Despite convictions for two murders, two armed robberies, and an assault, Jerold Green of Philadelphia was nonetheless released on bail while appealing the second homicide verdict. After losing his appeal, Green didn't bother reporting to prison. Instead, while being hunted, he committed a third murder.[22]

Or take the case of Steven Judy, imprisoned after three violent crimes involving kidnapping and stabbing during the 1970s. Paroled, he soon committed another robbery—yet was still granted bail. While free, he murdered an Indiana woman and her three children.[23]

Such incidents aren't rare. The U.S. Justice Department reports thirty-five percent of those with serious criminal records, and who are freed on bail, either violate their release conditions, fail to reappear for trial, or are arrested for new crimes during the bail period. And this statistic includes only *known* violations.[24]

Excuse-Making "civil libertarians" argue that the rights of suspects to be freed on bail may be denied based only on "speculation" about their criminal tendencies.[25] But as the examples and statistics show, the danger of releasing career criminals is no matter of mere speculation. Career felons should *never* be released on recognizance, or bail. Bail is *not* a fundamental human right, or an end in itself: it's a means to an end. Like the right to vote, it's only a contextual, *procedural* right, whose purpose is to secure the *substantive* rights of life, liberty, and property.

Everything said about excluding evidence and confessions applies equally here. To defend bail for proven predators as some fundamental right is to subordinate the system's *ends* to its *means*. Judging a man by his past record is both wise and just; and a chronic criminal can claim no "right" to be judged otherwise. This point, however, is lost on those who hold the deterministic, "criminal-as-victim" premise.

Plea Bargaining

In Nevada, a man killed his girlfriend by forcing a large quantity of bourbon down her throat. A good case could have been made for premeditated murder, or at least second-degree homicide. But, in a plea bargain deal, the court allowed the defendant to plead guilty to a reduced charge of *involuntary manslaughter*. In exchange, he received a mere three-year sentence, and was released after only 22 months.[26]

In a 1981 courtroom deal, a Massachusetts man pled guilty to a charge of raping a female jogger. In return, he was sentenced to ten years at Concord Reformatory, a sentence which meant a minimum of only *one year* to be actually served. But by the terms of his plea bargain arrangement, he spent only *three days* in jail before being transferred to a halfway house. That surely taught him an encouraging lesson about the justice system. In 1984, he was arrested for burglary and another rape—and became the prime suspect in seven other attacks on women.[27] Or consider the young Wisconsin man who confessed to three armed robberies of savings and loan companies. A plea bargain deal placed this dangerous, repeat felon on probation for his full sentence, sending him instead to a "work release" program at the Milwaukee House of Correction. While serving this "sentence," he was driven around town by social workers, allegedly trying to find a job. Instead, he brazenly robbed two more savings and loan branches. Four days after being released from the program, he robbed yet another.[28]

These are but a few examples of the thousands of sentencing outrages occurring daily throughout the nation. *If* a criminal is finally arrested after a string of offenses, and *if* the prosecutor decides to accept the case, and *if* police evidence isn't thrown out on "exclusionary rule" grounds—then the criminal's next way to evade justice is to "cop a plea." Today, 80 to 90 percent of all convictions stem from pre-trial guilty pleas, invariably to reduced charges, negotiated between prosecutors and defense attorneys, and rubber-stamped by judges.[29]

Such cynical maneuvers allow criminals to evade the full penalties of their crimes by receiving reduced punishment or probation; permit lazy prosecutors to enhance their political careers by boasting of high "conviction rates"; let defense attorneys quickly handle a large number of clients (and collect a large number of fees) without ever having to prepare for trial; and (allegedly) help harried judges quickly clear clogged court calendars and jammed jails. It's the triumph of expediency over justice. Everyone leaves the courtroom smiling—except for the crime victims, who, ignored in the proceedings, look on in shocked disbelief and rage, realizing that they have just been mugged again.[30]

As Wisconsin Circuit Court Judge Ralph Adam Fine observes, plea bargaining is essentially a bribe to the defendant, a "payoff for a guilty plea,"[31] to entice him not to bother everyone with a trial. As a reward, a rape charge may be reduced (usually without the victim's knowledge or consent) to mere "assault and battery"; and multiple crimes (say, breaking-and-entering, assault, and robbery) may be combined into a single charge (e.g., "assault"). Once the deceit starts, there's no end to it—as in the routine courtroom trick called "swallowing the gun," i.e., reducing an armed-robbery charge to unarmed robbery, by simply *ignoring* the use of a gun in the crime.[32] Finally, even the sentences meted out for the remaining reduced charges are usually softened. Multiple sentences often are allowed to be served concurrently, rather than consecutively, letting the criminal pay only once for several offenses; or, with the complicity of a prosecutor, a "first offender" (i.e., one whose carefully edited record is presented to seem innocuous) may "walk" on a suspended sentence and probation.

The flip side is that the defendant is often made to understand that, should he plead innocent and lose in court, the prosecutor and judge will punish him with *harsher* sentences than he would have gotten if he had "gone along." In this way, even innocent people are sometimes bullied into a guilty plea, and are denied their day in court.

Plea bargaining falsifies the defendant's true criminal record. In the case of the innocent defendant, it gives him the taint of a conviction he doesn't deserve. In the (far more usual) case of a guilty defendant, it makes him look less menacing than he really is, and more worthy of further "breaks" from the next judge he sees.

This, of course, is a clear incentive to criminality. "Should we be surprised," asked former Chief Justice Warren E. Burger, "if the word gets around . . . that you can commit two or three crimes for the price of only one?"[33] The U.S. National Advisory Commission on Criminal Justice Standards and Goals concluded in 1973 that "plea bargaining results in leniency that reduces the deterrent impact of the law." Today, it's also a ruse by which judges and lawyers skirt the tough sentencing requirements of new mandatory sentencing laws for repeat offenders. Prosecutors don't bother telling the judge about a repeat offender's prior record, and the judge doesn't ask. Or, charges are simply reduced in advance, to compensate for the harsher penalties mandated by the actual offense.[34]

In 1971, the U.S. Supreme Court put its imprimatur on this cynical practice, calling plea bargaining "an essential component of the administration of justice. . . . If every criminal charge were subjected to a full-scale trial, the States and the Federal Government would need to multiply by many times the number of judges and court facilities." The practice, echoes the American Bar Association, "saves time and conserves resources which can be applied to other pending cases."[35]

But that is nonsense. In 1975, the state of Alaska's attorney general ordered an end to all plea bargaining. Other jurisdictions, such as New Orleans and Pontiac, Michigan, have also rejected it. They all found that there was no sudden tidal wave of "not guilty" pleas, requiring a trial and swamping the system. In fact, as the National Institute of Justice discovered in a 1980 investigation of the Alaska experiment, "Guilty pleas continued to flow in at nearly undiminished rates. Most defendants pled guilty even when the state offered them nothing in exchange for their cooperation." Contrary to expectations, cases were actually processed *more rapidly* in each major jurisdiction, and sentences were more severe. As one prosecutor put it, "I was spending probably one third of my time arguing with defense attorneys. Now we have a smarter use of our time."[36]

The key was for prosecutors to screen cases carefully *before* defendants were charged. Faced with air-tight cases against them, guilty defendants simply threw in the towel and pled guilty, anyway. In addition, ending plea bargaining put responsibility back into every level of the system: police did better investigating; prosecutors and lawyers began preparing their cases better; lazy judges were compelled to spend more time in court and control their calendars more efficiently. Most importantly, *justice* was served—and criminals began to realize that they could not continue their arrogant manipulation of a paper-tiger court system.

Tough prosecution and sentencing does *not* clog the court system: *it deters crime from occurring in the first place.* Since repeat offenders commit most of the crime, careful case screening and "no-deals" prosecution tend to incapacitate a greater percentage of this group for longer periods—and thus actually *reduce* caseloads in the long run.

That's the practical side. But more basic is the moral issue: Should the victims of these criminals expect anything less from our system of justice? And should the Excuse-Making Industry be allowed to thwart justice by corrupting the system?

Competency Hearings and Insanity Defenses

The hijacker of a New Orleans bus was found incompetent to stand trial, thanks to psychiatric testimony. Instead of incarceration, he was released. Fifteen months later, he was back in court—for dismembering his roommate.

A former Connecticut policeman killed his wife, but, due to "expert" psychiatric testimony, was acquitted of murder charges on the ground of insanity. He spent only three months under psychiatric treatment. Five years later, he was arrested once more—for killing his second wife.[37]

But for irony worthy of Hitchcock, the tale of serial killer Edward Kemper can't be topped. After shooting both his grandparents as a teenager, Kemper spent the next four years in a mental hospital. In 1969, he was returned to the California Youth Authority, whose "experts" disputed the court psychiatrist's diagnosis and paroled him to his mother. Later, Kemper was examined by two parole psychiatrists, who recommended that his juvenile records be sealed to let him live a "normal" adult life. One of them wrote: "I see no psychiatric reason to consider him to be a danger to himself or any other member of society." Yet at that very moment, out in their parking lot, in the trunk of Kemper's car, was the corpse of his third female murder victim that year.

Because of their "expertise," there would soon be five more.[38]

These cases graphically demonstrate that psychiatry cannot really judge the sanity of criminal defendants, let alone predict their future danger to society. Yet psychiatrists play a major role in the criminal justice system. They testify concerning a defendant's "state of mind" at the time of his crime; judge whether he can grasp the charges against him and assist in his own legal defense; decide (if he's committed to a mental hospital) when he's "cured" and "safe" to return to society. By their "expert" testimony in competency hearings, and in "insanity" and "diminished capacity" defenses, they frequently help dangerous criminals escape the wheels of justice.

Criminals found "insane" spend, on average, far less time in custody than do those sent to prison for the same offenses. In New York from 1965–1976, those acquitted of murder by reason of insanity, and subsequently released from mental hospitals, spent an average of less than a year and a half in custody. (One murderer spent just *one day* in a hospital.) Similarly, New Jersey murderers found insane were released, on average, in just two years. In Florida, those released from mental hospitals following first-degree murder acquittals spent fewer than three years in psychiatric custody; by contrast, those convicted and sent to prison spent nearly ten years in confinement. Meanwhile, other studies have found that over a third of released criminal patients are rearrested.[39]

Stories of how clever criminals manipulate psychiatrists are legendary. In *Two of a Kind*—a brilliant, harrowing account of the "Hillside Strangler" case—author Darcy O'Brien shows how cold-blooded serial killer Ken Bianchi fooled three prominent psychiatrists by feigning a "multiple personality" disorder. Had he been successful, he would have been sent to a mental hospital instead of prison, staged a miraculous "recovery," and soon have been released to prey again on young women. But even after a hypnosis expert proved that Bianchi had faked his hypnosis sessions and multiple personalities, the psychiatrists (though not the judge) remained stubbornly convinced that their "insanity" diagnoses had been correct.[40]

Perhaps the most egregious case is that of Thomas Vanda. In 1971, he murdered a 15-year-old girl, but was found "not guilty by reason of insanity" and sent to a mental institution. Released only nine months later, Vanda was soon arrested for the stabbing death of a 25-year-old woman. While in custody, he wrote another jailed murder suspect, advising him how to fake insanity. Vanda told him to offer bizarre interpretations of the famous Rorschach "inkblot test," to feign "hearing voices" that "told you to do your crime," and to "act crazy in front of the staff." A Chicago psychiatrist had already judged Vanda legally insane for the second murder. Shown Vanda's letter, he *still* insisted he had no cause to alter his finding.[41]

After psychiatrist Stanton Samenow and an associate studied dozens of people acquitted under the insanity defense, they concluded that most of them "aren't crazy at all. . . . They were rational, purposeful and deliberate in what they did. But they were very astute at conning the system, the courts, the psychiatrists and the hospital into believing that they were mentally ill, thereby beating the charge."[42]

Samenow, who has spent years studying criminals firsthand, also dismisses the idea that even the perpetrators of ghastly crimes operate under an "irresistible impulse" or compulsion. "What is habitual is not necessarily compulsive and beyond one's control," he warns. "Behind the appearance of uncontrollable impulse lies the stark reality of the offender's *calculating* and proficient method of operating. . . . From my clinical observations, I have concluded that 'kleptomaniacs' and 'pyromaniacs' are simply people who enjoy stealing or setting fires." (As another observer put it, a crime may be sickening, but not necessarily "sick.")[43]

Samenow also cites the example of "Son of Sam" serial killer David Berkowitz. After capture, Berkowitz claimed that demons were talking to him through a dog, and had ordered him to kill. Later, he acknowledged he'd been faking insanity. "There were no real demons, no talking dogs, no satanic henchmen. I made it all up via my wild imagination so as to find some form of justification for my criminal acts against society."[44]

Several courtroom outrages, however have prompted a new look at the validity of psychiatric involvement in the legal system. One was the infamous diminished capacity, "Twinkie" defense of Dan White, who shot San Francisco's mayor and a city superintendent in 1978. Despite abundant evidence of premeditation,[45] the jury accepted psychiatric testimony that (among other excuses) White's mental control was impaired because of eating junk food. They found him guilty only of involuntary manslaughter. The other major outrage was the murder acquittal of would-be presidential assassin John Hinckley "by reason of insanity." This led to a reform of federal law. Before then, prosecutors had *to prove the defendant sane;* now, the defense must prove him insane.

But even this doesn't get to the heart of the matter. Psychiatrist Lee Coleman warns that "psychiatrists do not have the tools that society thinks they have. They have no special way of predicting who will commit a criminal act or of determining when a criminal is cured of antisocial tendencies. They have no tests to determine a person's innermost thoughts, even though the courts assume they do." He argues that "psychiatry should be stripped of its state-given powers," by banning psychiatric testimony in legal proceedings, as well as abolishing the "insanity" and "diminished capacity" defenses.[46]

This does *not* mean that judges and juries would be spared the legal task of determining *criminal intent;* only that "in determining what, if any, criminal intent was present, and in deciding punishment, [they] need no help from psychiatrists .... A decision on intent should be based on the factual evidence surrounding the crime." A defense attorney would still be free to argue that the defendant was in an impaired mental state during his crime. But evidence would be limited to fact-based testimony of witnesses, citing the defendant's bizarre or irrational statements and behavior.[47] It would *not* include fanciful theoretical speculations by Excuse-Making "experts," using inkblots and word-association "tests" to decipher the alleged impact of junk food or an over-possessive mother on the defendant's presumed mental state.

This is a common-sense approach to putting objectivity and responsibility back into criminal proceedings.

Probation and Parole

Parole is the release of a convict, under periodic supervision, after he has served only a portion of his sentence. Probation is the conditional release of an individual found guilty of a crime, as an alternative to incarceration, also usually under periodic supervision. Both are used routinely, and both are progeny of the Excuse-Making Industry.

As one criminology text puts it: "Parole can be considered as an extension of the *rehabilitative (and now reintegrative) program of the prison....* If prisons are, in fact, to be concerned with modifying criminal behavior so that the offender can eventually be reintegrated into society, parole is also supposed to provide the supervision and assistance that makes successful reintegration possible." [Emphasis in original][48]

A measure of that "success" lies in the dismally high rates of inmate recidivism (i.e., percentages of inmates who commit subsequent crimes after release). A RAND Corporation study found that about half of those sentenced to probation in California were convicted of another crime within three years.[49] And "success rates for probation," concede its backers, "are generally considerably higher than for parole."[50] The Bureau of Justice Statistics released a 1985 study showing that 42 percent of inmates arriving at state prisons were on parole or probation for an earlier conviction at their time of arrival. Twenty-eight percent of these would still have been in prison for the earlier offense, had they served out the maximum term to which they were sentenced.[51] This means, of course, that thousands of people were needlessly subjected to robbery, assault, even murder, through the early parole and probation releases of convicted felons.

One example symbolizes them all. Larry Gene Bell had been involved in abnormal sexual incidents since he was a child. In 1975, at age 26, he tried to force a young housewife into his car at knifepoint. Bell plea bargained a deal to avoid prison by undergoing psychiatric treatment. He quit after two visits. Five months later, Bell tried to force a co-ed into his car at gunpoint. A psychiatrist recommended mental hospitalization, but Bell got a five-year prison sentence instead. However, after just 21 months, Bell was released on parole.

Later, on probation, he terrorized a little girl and her mother with obscene phone calls. Result: another plea bargain, and more probation, with orders to see a psychiatrist. He again stopped treatment after a short time. The climax came in 1985, when Bell kidnapped, sexually assaulted, then murdered two young girls. He was subsequently linked to the case of another missing woman, and suspected in the deaths of three more.[52]

Here we see many tools of the Excuse-Making Industry in action: plea bargaining, psychiatric defenses, early parole, suspended sentences, and probation. And we see the terrible price such policies regularly exact.[53]

The ideological origins of parole and probation are obvious. There are also pragmatic, cynical considerations motivating their proponents.

Probation is the routine sentence for any first offender, often regardless of the severity of the crime. As in the example above, it's frequently "imposed" even in subsequent offenses. The reason? To free up overcrowded jail and prison cells. In 1985, for example, there were 503,300 state prison inmates and 255,000 federal prisoners. In the same year, there were 277,400 people out on parole, and a whopping 1,870,100 on probation.[54]

There is an equally cynical reason for parole—namely, control of inmates. Parole is the handmaiden of "indeterminate sentencing"— sentences of indefinite length, with only the maximum and minimum specified. As the previously cited criminology text notes, the main reason underlying the development of parole in America was "shortened imprisonment as a reward for good conduct."[55] By holding out the carrot of an early release, and poising the stick of a full sentence over the inmate's head, prison authorities suppress inmate violence. In short, rather than risk the safety of the guards (and the warden's job) in prison uprisings, the prison bureaucrats prefer to risk the lives and property of the public with early releases.

Neither parole nor probation are justifiable, practically or morally. They are a demonstrable failure in reducing inmate recidivism. They undermine the deterrent impact of the law on criminals, while demoralizing crime victims with their outrageous leniency. Most important, they jeopardize public safety. They amount to playing Russian Roulette with innocent human lives.

---

1. James Q. Wilson and Richard J. Herrnstein, *Crime and Human Nature* (New York: Simon & Schuster, 1985), p. 505.

2. Norval Morris and Gordon Hawkins, *The Honest Politician's Guide to Crime Control* (Chicago: University of Chicago Press, 1970), p. 138.

3. Wilson and Herrnstein, pp. 518–522.

4. Owen Gallagher, "The Only Real Crime is Punishing Criminals," *Conservative Digest*, October 1988, p. 19.

5. Arthur Eckstein, "Revenge of the Nerd," *Chronicles*, March 1988, p. 31.

6. Ralph Adam Fine. *Escape of the Guilty* (New York: Dodd, Mead & Co., 1986), p. 247.

7. Robert James Bidinotto, "Paying People Not to Grow," *The Freeman*, October 1986.

8. American Bar Association, *Criminal Justice in Crisis*, November 1988, p. 5.

9. This section draws heavily from Fine, pp. 119–130, reprinted in this volume as "The Urge to Confess," in Part II.

10. Fine, pp. 126–130.

11. "Why the Justice System Fails," *Time*, March 23, 1981, p. 23.

12. Patrick J. Buchanan, "Children of the Warren Court," *Washington Inquirer*, November 5, 1982, p. 4.

13. Eugene H. Methvin, "The Case of Common Sense vs. Miranda," *Reader's Digest*, August 1987, p. 96.

14. Fine, p. 144.

15. *Ibid.*, p. 148.

16. *Ibid.*, pp. 149–154.

17. Edwin Meese III, "A Rule Excluding Justice," *New York Times*, April 15, 1983.

18. Fine, pp. 154–155.

19. James J. Kirkpatrick column, *Washington Post*, March 24, 1987.

20. Fine, p. 155.

21. *Middlesex* (Mass.) *News*, January 30, 1985, p. 1.

22. "Our Losing Battle Against Crime," *U.S News & World Report*, October 12, 1981, p. 39.

23. *Ibid.*, p. 40.

24. *Boston Herald* and *Boston Globe*, January 28, 1985.

25. "Impact of Uncle Sam's New Crime Law," *U.S. News & World Report*, October 22, 1984, p. 50.

26. Edmund Newton, "Criminals Have All the Rights," *Ladies' Home Journal*, September 1986.

27. *Boston Herald*, December 6, 1984, p. 5.

28. Fine, p. 42.

29. *Criminal Justice in Crisis*, p. 38; "Why the Justice System Fails," *Time*, March 23, 1981, p. 22; Fine, p. 3.

30. Fine offers an excellent summary of the plea bargaining "charade" in chapters 2–5. (See also his "Plea Bargaining: An *Un*necessary Evil," in Part II of this volume.)

31. *Ibid.*, p. 34.

32. *Time*, March 23, 1981, p. 22.

33. *U.S. News & World Report*, October 12, 1981, p. 41.

34. Fine, pp. 17, 47–49.

35. *Criminal Justice in Crisis*, pp. 40–41; p. 67, note 80.

36. Fine, pp. 103–111.

37. Preceding examples from "Turned Loose Too Soon?" *U.S. News & World Report*, June 27, 1983, p. 52.

38. Elliott Leyton, *Hunting Humans* (New York: Pocket Books, 1986), chapter 2, especially pp. 31 and 57.

39. Lee Coleman, *The Reign of Error* (Boston: Beacon Press, 1984), pp. 55–56; reprinted in Part II of this volume as "The Insanity Defense." See also *U.S. News & World Report*, June 27, 1983, pp. 53–54; and Fine, p. 218.

40. Darcy O'Brien, *Two of a Kind* (New York: New American Library, 1985), pp. 229–280, 350–353.

41. Coleman, pp. 55–56.

42. Quoted in *People*, May 14, 1984, p. 79.

43. Stanton E. Samenow, *Inside the Criminal Mind* (New York: Times Books, 1984), pp. 124–125.

44. *Ibid.*, p. 130.

45. For details see Coleman, pp. 65–70.

46. *Ibid.*, p. x; chapters 3–5.

47. *Ibid.*, p. 62.

48. Robert D. Pursley, *Introduction to Criminal Justice* (New York: Macmillan, 1980), pp. 435–436.

49. "Punishment Outside Prisons," *Newsweek*, June 9, 1986, p. 82.

50. Morris and Hawkins, p. 135.

51. *New York Times*, March 4, 1985.

52. Eugene H. Methvin, "Beauty and the Beast," *Reader's Digest*, February 1989, pp. 132–138.

53. For other examples of horror stories specifically concerning parole and probation releases, see: *MacLean's*, July 18, 1988, esp. pp. 42–43; *Time*, March 5, 1984, p. 50; *Redbook*, April 1988, pp. 128, 162; *U.S. News & World Report*, June 27, 1983, p. 52.

54. Bureau of the Census, *Statistical Abstract of the United States* (1988), p. 176, Table 308. (For updated statistics, see data under "Myth Nine" in "Ten Deadly Myths About Crime and Punishment in the United States," in Part II of this volume.)

55. Pursley, p. 435.

Plea Bargaining: An *Un*necessary Evil

by Ralph Adam Fine

I. Introduction

The United States Supreme Court has acknowledged that plea bargaining would not exist in what it called an "ideal world."[1] Similarly, the Wisconsin Supreme Court recognizes that, in the words of the current Chief Justice, Nathan S. Heffernan, the practice does not "offer exact justice to the state and the defendant"[2] and "can tend to subvert the ends of justice rather than to advance them."[3] As I point out in *Escape of the Guilty*,[4] plea bargaining is a double evil: it encourages crime by weakening the credibility of the system on the one hand and, on the other, it tends to extort guilty pleas from the innocent. Nevertheless, an overwhelming majority of those in the criminal justice system accept plea bargaining as an "important component of this country's criminal justice system."[5] The natural question is "Why?" The answer is a combination of "myth" and "expediency."

Most defenders of plea bargaining believe that without it an already overburdened criminal justice system would grind to a halt. Thus, for example, the Wisconsin Supreme Court has recognized that "plea bargaining is accepted pragmatically as a device to speed litigation . . . . "[6] As we shall see, however, this "system would become clogged" rationale is a myth. Plea bargaining has been successfully abolished when those in the system have wanted to make a ban work: in Alaska; in New Orleans, Louisiana; in Oakland County (Pontiac) Michigan; in Ventura County, California; and, in a petri-dish example, in New Philadelphia, Ohio. Stripped of the only reason for which courts have tolerated the practice, plea bargaining stands naked against the winds of justice.

"Plea bargaining" is that bushel basket of practices whereby a prosecutor agrees to:

• charge a crime or crimes less seriously than the facts warrant, and/or

- reduce a charge or charges already issued, and/or
- dismiss a charge or charges already issued, and/or
- not issue additional charges, and/or
- make a sentence recommendation, all in return for a guilty or a no contest plea. It includes what has variously been described as "charge bargaining" and "sentence bargaining" as well as "plea bargaining." Importantly, however, whatever form the leniency takes, the leniency is payment to a defendant to induce him or her not to go to trial. The guilty or no-contest plea *is* the *quid pro quo* for the concession; there is no other reason. Thus, plea bargaining does *not* encompass those situations where the facts of a particular case may justify a lenient sentence, a dismissal, or reduction. Obviously, for example, if a case initially charged as "first-degree murder" is discovered to be, in reality, "manslaughter," reducing the charge to "manslaughter" is *not* plea bargaining but justice. By the same token, consideration to a defendant may be warranted, in appropriate cases, to get his or her help in catching or convicting a "bigger fish" or to avoid the trauma of a trial for a particularly fragile victim.[7] Again, this is *not* plea bargaining but—if appropriate—justice for society and for the victim.

One of the excuses often advanced for plea bargaining is that "half a loaf is better than none" when the evidence is weak, and that it is better to "get a dangerous person off of the streets for a short time" than risk an acquittal. This argument was punctured by Dan Hickey, a chief prosecutor in Alaska both before and after that state abolished plea bargaining in 1975:

> It is, in essence, a *meaningless gesture* to take in a whole lot of bad cases that can't be proved and bargain them out for meaningless dispositions. It is no solution to crime in this country to run someone through the process to get some kind of conviction which, more often than not, is for something much less than they were accused of and which results in something which really doesn't mean anything in terms of real punishment.[8]

Charging a rape as "disorderly conduct,"[9] for example, under the aegis of a "half a loaf is better than none" theory disables justice as the victim wonders, and the criminal gloats, at the law's impotence.

II. The Arguments Against Plea Bargaining

The criminal law protects society in three major ways: deterrence, isolation, and rehabilitation. We attempt to deter persons from committing crimes with the threat of punishment, and rehabilitate those, who for one reason or another, have not been deterred. If deterrence and rehabilitation both fail, there is no alternative but to isolate the offender from the rest of society through long-term incarceration.

A. Plea Bargaining Weakens Deterrence

The very essence of deterrence is credibility. As I point out in *Escape of the Guilty*, we keep our hands out of a flame because it hurt the very *first* time (not the second, fifth, or tenth time) we touched fire. If deterrence is to work, we must, in the words of noted Norwegian law professor and criminologist, Johannes Andenaes, make "the risk of discovery and punishment" outweigh "the temptation to commit crime."[10] Yet, plea bargaining destroys this needed credibility. A good example is what happened in two states with strict gun laws.

Massachusetts and Michigan have both tried to control the unlawful use of guns. Starting in April of 1975, someone carrying a handgun without a license in Massachusetts faced a mandatory one year in jail. Michigan's anti-gun law went into effect in 1977 and required that an additional two years be tacked on to any felony sentence if the defendant was carrying a gun at the time of the crime. Prosecutors and judges in Massachusetts took the law seriously and it worked. However, the Michigan story, as James Q. Wilson relates, was different:

> Many judges would reduce the sentence given for the original felony (say, assault or robbery) in order to compensate for the add-on. In other cases, the judge would dismiss the gun count. Given this evasion, it is not surprising that the law had little effect in the rate at which gun-related crimes were committed.[11]

As a 1973 report of the U.S. National Advisory Commission on Criminal Justice Standards and Goals concluded:

> Since the prosecutor must give up something in return for the defendant's agreement to plead guilty, the frequent result of plea bargaining is that defendants are not dealt with as severely as might otherwise be the case. Thus plea bargaining results in leniency that reduces the deterrent impact of the law.[12]

Deterrence is, of course, further weakened as the criminal brags about his deal and spreads word throughout the community that the law has no teeth. Dean Roscoe Pound of the Harvard Law School, who studied plea bargaining in the 1920s, called it a "license to violate the law"[13] and, over a hundred years ago, the Wisconsin Supreme Court derisively condemned it as "a direct sale of justice."[14]

B. Plea Bargaining Weakens Respect for the Law

An essential component of rehabilitation is a respect for society and its laws. However, plea bargaining teaches the criminal that judges and lawyers can ignore the law when it is expedient to do so. Significantly, many plea bargains result in charges that cannot be sustained by the facts. One common plea bargain in Wisconsin is to reduce a charge of "operating [a] vehicle without [the] owner's consent," a two-year felony,[15] to "joyriding," a nine-month misdemeanor,[16] *even though* the car may have been damaged and return of the vehicle *un*damaged within twenty-four hours is an element of the misdemeanor charge.[17] Prosecutors, of course, should issue only those charges for which the evidence would support a conviction at trial.[18] Milwaukee County District Attorney E. Michael McCann, apparently goes a step further and advocates an even more rigorous screening, at least under some circumstances. Thus, several years ago, although he publicly stated that two Green Bay Packers players accused of sexual assault were guilty of "indecent and immoral sexual overreaching"[19] and that their conduct in connection with the incident was "reprehensible, shameful and depraved,"[20] he declined to prosecute them because he "determined that the state [would] be unable to prove the guilt of the two men beyond a reasonable doubt."[21] This, as Wisconsin Supreme Court Justices Donald W. Steinmetz and Roland B. Day have noted,[22] is an even stricter standard than that recommended by the American Bar Association[23] and would, obviously, preclude many plea bargain arrangements.

Nevertheless, plea bargaining often involves fiddling with the facts.[24] As a prosecutor told two researchers working under a National Institute of Mental Health grant: "A lot of fictions are entered into. For instance, with the elements. In order to get within a lesser included offense, people kind of fudge the facts a bit. I've seen some people plead guilty . . . to attempted possession of narcotics, and I think that is pretty hard to do!"[25]

What is the "spree" criminal to think when it is "bargain day" at the courthouse: four armed robberies for the price of one? What is an impressionable young man to think when, after smashing up a stolen car, he is allowed to plead guilty to the reduced charge of "joy riding?"[26] As one commentator has recently written, plea bargaining "often destroys the integrity of the criminal justice system by allowing defendants to appear to be convicted of crimes different from the ones they actually committed."[27]

One of the biggest fictions connected with plea bargaining is the practice of permitting a defendant to plead "guilty" while simultaneously proclaiming his or her innocence. Although authorized by *North Carolina v. Alford*[28]—which was, significantly, a death penalty case—it is an *Alice in Wonderland* expediency that vitiates public confidence in the criminal justice system. Simply put, if we want defendants to respect the law, we must enforce it with justice and honesty.

C. Plea Bargaining Tends to Extort Guilty Pleas

A 1967 report issued by the President's Commission on Law Enforcement put the issue squarely: "There are also real dangers that excessive rewards will be offered to induce pleas or that prosecutors will threaten to seek a harsh sentence if the defendant does not plead guilty. Such practices place unacceptable burdens on the defendant who legitimately insists upon his right to trial."[29] Six years later, the National Advisory Commission of Criminal Justice agreed:

> Underlying many plea negotiations is the understanding—or
> threat—that if the defendant goes to trial and is convicted he

will be dealt with more harshly that would be the case if he had pleaded guilty. An innocent defendant might be persuaded that the harsher sentence he must face if he is unable to prove his innocence at trial means that it is to his best interest to plead guilty despite his innocence.[30]

The case that sanctions this type of extortion is *Bordenkircher v. Hayes*,[31] where the Supreme Court permitted a prosecutor to "up the ante" in order to obtain a guilty plea on a bad check charge. This is how the prosecutor put it when he questioned Hayes about it at a later hearing:

Isn't it a fact that I told you at [the initial bargaining session] that if you did not intend to plead guilty to five years for this charge and . . . save the court the inconvenience and necessity of a trial and taking up this time that I intended to return to the grand jury and ask them to indict you based upon these prior felony convictions?[32]

An indictment as a repeater would subject Hayes, if convicted on the bad check charge, to a mandatory life term. Nevertheless, Hayes exercised his constitutional right to a jury trial and, true to his word, the prosecutor obtained the repeater indictment. Hayes was convicted and sentenced to the mandatory life term. In affirming the conviction the Supreme Court explained that there was no "punishment or retaliation so long as the accused [was] free to accept or reject the prosecution's offer."[33] The Court wrote:

Plea bargaining flows from "the mutuality of advantage" to defendants and prosecutors, each with his own reasons for wanting to avoid trial. . . . Defendants advised by competent counsel and protected by other procedural safeguards are presumptively capable of intelligent choice in response to prosecutorial persuasion, and unlikely to be driven to false self-condemnation.[34]

Those in the system *do* have "their own reasons for wanting to avoid trial" and, unfortunately, those reasons usually have very little to do with "justice."

1. Advantages for Prosecutors

Prosecutors want to avoid trial for a number of reasons. Perhaps the most important reason in the context of an analysis of plea bargaining is that trials are hard work and many prosecutors have heavy case loads. A case that is "dealt away" is seen as a case that does not have to be tried. An experienced assistant district attorney in Milwaukee County once admitted to me that plea bargaining was a "concession to the burned out" prosecutor that "keeps us on the job for ten or fifteen years when we might otherwise burn out after two to three."[35]

2. Advantages for Defendants

Defendants also want to avoid trial for a number of reasons. Those who are clearly guilty fear that once the judge hears all the grisly details from the victims the resulting sentence will be more severe than if the judge had heard a dispassionate statement of the facts from the lawyers. Additionally, defendants may fear that the prosecutor will recommend, and the judge will impose, a more severe sentence just because—in the words of the *Hayes* prosecutor—they both had to endure "the inconvenience and necessity of a trial." Finally, of course, defendants are usually getting great plea bargained deals. In fact, one excellent and tenacious defense lawyer once told me, on the record, that he was removing his client's case from my court[36] because he had worked out a "great plea bargain" with the prosecutor, which he did not think I would accept. When I asked for specifics, he replied that he did not want to tell me the deal because "[y]ou'd be so grossed out."[37]

3. Advantages for Defense Lawyers

Many defense lawyers in the private bar rarely, if ever, take criminal cases to trial; they plead their clients guilty. That is the only way some of them can earn a living given the fact that they usually represent people who have either very little money or none at all. In the latter case, the lawyers are paid by government programs and the fees are such that taking a case to trial is usually not economical. In the former case, a client and his family may be able to come up with a few thousand dollars. That is a handsome fee for an hour or so of bargaining and a quick guilty plea; it is nothing for a jury trial and the needed investigation and preparation. As Professor Albert W. Alschuler has pointed out:

> There are two basic ways to achieve financial success in the practice of criminal law. One is to develop, over an extended period of time, a reputation as an outstanding trial lawyer. In that way, one can attract as clients the occasional wealthy people who become enmeshed in the criminal law. If, however, one lacks the ability or the energy to succeed in this way or if one is in a greater hurry, there is a second path to personal wealth—handling a large volume of cases for less-than-spectacular fees. The way to handle a large volume of cases is, of course, not to try them but to plead them.[38]

A Boston lawyer he interviewed put it this way: "A guilty plea is: a quick buck."[39] An attorney in Alaska was a little more genteel and told National Institute of Justice researchers: "Criminal law is not a profit-making proposition for the private practitioner unless you have plea bargaining."[40] The simple fact is, as sociologist Abraham S. Blumberg pointed out in a 1967 article entitled *The Practice of Law as Confidence Game,* many criminal defense lawyers find it more advantageous to cooperate with prosecutors and judges who press for guilty pleas than to zealously represent their clients. After all, they must deal with them on a day-to-day basis. The client, on the other hand, is a transitory figure who is usually—and quite literally—gone tomorrow.[41]

4. Defendants Are Vulnerable to Extortion

While the Supreme Court assumed that defendants would be "advised by competent counsel," what advice can even an eager and idealistic lawyer give someone in Paul Hayes' position, assuming the financial aspects of the case did not chill his or her willingness to take it to trial? Simply put, there is little protection for the defendant who maintains his or her innocence in the face of threats from an "up the ante" prosecutor.

Assume, for a moment, that Hayes was innocent. If he had pled guilty because of the prosecutor's threat, that would have been pre-cisely the type of "false self-condemnation" the Court said could not happen. Although the Court opined that defendants were "protected by other procedural safeguards," there are none in any court where the judge permits the prosecutor to "up the ante" on a defendant who refuses to cave in and forgo his constitutional right to a jury trial. Hayes was punished by having his exposure increased to a manda-tory "life" sentence the moment he asserted his innocence and de-manded that jury trial. Indeed, since a guilty person had the choice between a sure five years or a sure life sentence, it can be argued with some success that *only* an innocent person would have rejected the prosecutor's deal.

In my three years of presiding full time over criminal cases (in the Juvenile, Misdemeanor, and Felony divisions of the circuit court), at least three persons later adjudged to be *not guilty* attempted to plead guilty either because their lawyer wanted them to, they feared an "up the ante" recommendation from the prosecutor, or they wished to "get the matter over with." Importantly, the facts fully supported the acquittals. An example of what *Hayes* hath wrought can be seen from an incident I relate in *Escape of the Guilty*.

A Milwaukee county prosecutor initially offered a woman ac-cused of inflicting superficial wounds on her husband a nine-month misdemeanor charge of "battery."[42] When she refused to plead guilty, he—according to affidavits filed in the case—charged her with the five-year felony of endangering safety by conduct regardless of life.[43] When she refused to plead guilty after the preliminary exami-nation, the prosecutor—again, according to affidavits filed in the case—"upped the ante" to the twenty-year felony of attempted first degree murder.[44] When challenged in a "prosecutorial vindictive-ness" motion, the prosecutor dropped the case entirely.[45]

Significantly, when the United States Supreme Court first had an opportunity to discuss the legitimacy of plea bargaining as a tool of criminal justice in 1970, it approved the practice but cautioned against "the situation where the prosecutor or judge, or both, deliber-ately employ their charging and sentencing powers to induce a par-ticular defendant to tender a plea of guilty."[46]

A finely tuned criminal justice system will punish the guilty and leave the innocent unmolested. We have already seen how plea bar-gaining lets many criminals escape a "just" punishment. Since the

1978 decision in *Hayes*, the innocent have been at risk as well.[47] Indeed, in the November 7, 1983, issue of the *National Law Journal*, one legal commentator argued that guilty pleas should not be used as evidence in civil lawsuits because of the tainting effects of plea bargaining: "Since a defendant may plead guilty for numerous reasons unrelated to actual guilt, convictions stemming from such pleas offer little assurance of reliability."[48]

To an innocent person, even probation is a constant reminder of an unfair criminal justice system. To a guilty person, unjustified leniency is a spur to further criminal activity. In short, plea bargaining is an evil that doubly compromises our criminal justice system: the guilty smirk at its impotence; the innocent are rubbed raw by its haste.

III. Plea Bargaining Is Unnecessary

David L. Bazelon, the former Chief Judge for the United States Court of Appeals for the District of Columbia, in a decision written a year before *Brady v. United States*,[49] recognized that plea bargaining was not the imperative that all seemed to assume:

> The arguments that the criminal process would collapse unless substantial inducements are offered to elicit guilty pleas have tended to rely upon assumption rather than empirical evidence. In many jurisdictions lacking sophisticated resources for criminal investigations, a large proportion of suspects apprehended are caught virtually red-handed. The argument "But what if everyone did not plead guilty?" has force only to the extent that a sizable proportion of defendants have some motivation to plead innocent. If the defendant does have some hope of acquittal, the right to a trial assumes overarching importance. If he does not, there is some presumption that most men will not indulge in a meaningless act.[50]

Some six years after Judge Bazelon wrote those words, his prediction was tested when Alaska's Attorney General, Avrum M. Gross, abolished plea bargaining statewide. Appointed Attorney General in December of 1973, Alaska's unique centralized criminal justice system gave Gross control over all of the state's district attorneys. His new policy was announced in a memorandum dated July 3, 1975, and was addressed to "all district attorneys." With exceptions for unusual circumstances, permission for which "will be given sparingly," there was to be no sentence concessions or charge reductions in exchange for guilty pleas. Sentencing recommendations and charge reductions could still be made, but *only if* they were warranted by the facts and were not used "simply to obtain a plea of guilty."

Before Gross' plea bargaining ban in August of 1975, the practice was as endemic in Alaska as anywhere else. As one judge related, it was part of the defense lawyer's job to go to the district attorney "to see what could be worked out"[51] Often, a lot "could be worked out." An assistant district attorney told how one of his colleagues had eleven cases set for trial in one week: "He hadn't even looked at one of the files. He dealt them all out on the last day, and he was proud of himself. I'm afraid we were giving away the farm too often. It was a little difficult to sleep at night."[52] This same prosecutor then put it all in context:

> The whole system became ridiculous. We were giving away cases we plainly should have tried. We often said to ourselves, "Hell, I don't want to go to trial with this turkey; I want to go on vacation next week." We learned that a prosecutor can get rid of everything if he just goes low enough.[53]

In 1980, the National Institute of Justice sponsored a study of the Alaskan experiment. It concluded that, despite all the dire predictions by the naysayers, the plea bargaining ban was successful and "guilty pleas continued to flow in at nearly undiminished rates. Most defendants pled guilty even when the state offered them nothing in exchange for their cooperation."[54]

Additionally, contrary to all expectations, the cases were processed more quickly without plea bargaining than they were before its abolition. The National Institute of Justice report puts it this way: "Supporters and detractors of plea bargaining have both shared the assumption that, regardless of the merits of the practice, it is probably necessary to the efficient administration of justice. The findings of this study suggest that, at least in Alaska, both sides were wrong."[55] Indeed, the disposition times for felonies in Anchorage fell from 192 days to just under ninety. In Fairbanks, the drop was from 164 days to 120, and in Juneau, the disposition time fell from 105 days to eighty-five.

Avrum Gross is no longer Alaska's Attorney General. Yet, his reformation of that state's criminal justice system survives. It survives because those working in the system realize things are better now. An Alaskan prosecutor probably said it best: "Much less time is spent haggling with defense attorneys. . . . I was spending probably one-third of my time arguing with defense attorneys. Now we have a smarter use of our time. I'm a trial attorney, and that's what I'm supposed to do."[56] Another attorney was even more upbeat: "My job is fun now, and I can sleep nights."[57]

Three other jurisdictions have also ended their reliance on plea bargaining: Ventura County, California, a community of 700,000 just north of Los Angeles; Oakland County (Pontiac) Michigan, a community not unlike Milwaukee County; and New Orleans, Louisiana. There, too, the bans have worked. Indeed, in what I have earlier called a "petri-dish example" of how those with resolve can end the plea bargaining habit, Municipal Judge Edward Emmett O'Farrell of New Philadelphia, Ohio, has successfully abolished the practice in his jurisdiction for drunk driving cases. Although the defense bar tried to overwork him with cases during his first year, he stood firm.[58] In 1986, only *ten* persons accused of drunk driving took their cases to a jury: 322 pled guilty even though Judge O'Farrell imposes fifteen days in jail for a first offense, ninety days in jail for a second offense, and a year in jail for a third offense. Alcohol-related traffic fatalities in his community fell from twenty-one in 1982, to three in 1984, two in 1985, and four in 1986, showing that a staunch policy of non-bargained justice does deter crime.

A. We Should Abolish Plea Bargaining

Plea bargaining exists only because it is thought to be essential to the efficient functioning of the criminal justice system: "Whatever might be the situation in an ideal world, the fact is that the guilty plea and the often concomitant plea bargain are important components of this country's criminal justice system."[59]

The experiences of Alaska, Ventura County, Oakland County, New Orleans, and Judge O'Farrell prove that it is *not* essential. Perhaps Judge Stern put it best when he compared the system of plea bargaining to a "fish market" that "ought to be hosed down."[60]

We do not need plea bargaining—we should not tolerate it. Abolition, however, will require work and dedication. As Robert C. Erwin, then Associate Justice of the Alaskan Supreme Court, told Professor Alschuler in a June, 1976 interview:

> A no-plea-bargaining policy forces the police to investigate their cases more thoroughly. It forces prosecutors to screen their cases more rigorously and to prepare them more carefully. It forces the courts to face the problem of the lazy judge who comes to court late and leaves early, to search out a good presiding judge, and to adopt a sensible calendaring system. All of these things have in fact happened here."[61]

They can happen everywhere as well, if those in the system only try. As Judge Stern told me, recalling his days as a federal prosecutor, "It worked for me, and I tell you, it would work for anybody."[62]

B. A Proposal

First, there should be no reduction of a charge unless the prosecutor can demonstrate, and the judge can specifically find on the record, that:

(1) There are facts that were unknown to the prosecutor at the time the charge was issued that make a new charge more appropriate;[63] or

(2) There are other circumstances that may militate against going to trial.[64]

Second, the prosecutor should certify, on the record, that the charging decision was not based on a defendant's willingness to plead guilty but on his or her independent evaluation of the facts, including any circumstances that may militate against going to trial.

Third, the prosecutor should certify, on the record at sentencing, that the recommendation, if any, is based on the prosecutor's independent evaluation of the facts and not a *quid pro quo* for a guilty plea, except where there are other circumstances that may militate against going to trial.

IV. Conclusion

Plea bargaining is a blot on our criminal justice system. It encourages crime and demoralizes victims and society. Abolition will restore a long-absent respect for the criminal justice system.[65] Not long ago, a woman told me how an acquaintance of hers bragged that he was going to beat a serious drug charge. "Did you do it?" she asked. "Sure," was his cocky reply. "Then why," she asked, "do you think you should be able to get away with it?" His response was simple: "Because I can." We teach society a dangerous lesson when people believe that they "should" get away with crime because they "can."

On the average, there is a murder in this nation every twenty-eight minutes, a rape every six minutes, an armed robbery every sixty-three seconds, and a burglary every ten seconds.[66] Millions of Americans are terrorized by crime and the fear of crime. Many—especially the elderly—have become prisoners in their own homes as they hide from the predators who roam our communities with impunity. Abolition of plea bargaining will be a major step in restoring peace and dignity to the lives of our people. We will then have a system that, at the very least, *tries* to offer "exact justice" not only for the prosecution and the defense but for victims and society as well.

Some will say that we cannot afford true justice and that our prisons are already bursting from overcrowding. Yet, on a per-serious-crime basis, we only imprison criminals at two-thirds the rate we did in 1960.[67] Additionally, we spend only .6 percent of our federal, state, and local budgets on court services and only .7 percent of those budgets on corrections.[68] The cost of crime—in tears as well as dollars—is infinitely greater. We short change our citizens when we settle for a criminal justice system that gives them much crime but little justice. The expediency-based practice of plea bargaining has done precisely that. Our people deserve better.

---

1. *Bordenkircher v. Hayes*, 434 U.S. 357, 361–62 (1978); *Blackledge v. Allison*, 431 U.S. 63, 71 (1977).

2. *Armstrong v. State*, 55 Wis. 2d 282, 287, 198 N.W.2d 357, 359 (1972).

3. *Pontow v. State*, 58 Wis. 2d 135, 142, 205, N.W.2d, 775, 779, (1973).

4. R. A. Fine, *Escape of the Guilty* (1986).

5. *Bordenkircher*, 434 U.S. at 361–62; *Blackledge*, 431 U.S. at 71.

6. *Armstrong*, 55 Wis. 2d at 287, 198 N.W.2d at 359.

7. The "spare the victim" excuse for leniency raises difficult questions, some of which the Wisconsin Supreme Court has addressed in the context of a child abuse case:

Were the district attorney to decide not to call the child as a witness, the district attorney may protect the child's emotional interest in not being forced to face the alleged abuser and accuse the abuser of criminal acts, but may inflict a greater harm on the child by allowing the alleged abuser to go free and by demonstrating to the child that the state of Wisconsin does not place a high enough value on the child's suffering to bring to justice the person alleged to have caused the suffering.

State v. Gilbert, 109 Wis. 2d 501, 507, 326 N.W.2d 744, 747 (1982). Prosecutors must avoid the trap of using expressed concern for a victim's sensibilities as a mere rationalization for inappropriate concessions.

Recently, a young woman in California wrote to me of her ordeal. Those in the criminal justice system had used the "spare the victim" excuse as one of the reasons to permit her rapist to escape just punishment:

I was raped in my apartment one night in July of 1986. Although the rapist wore a nylon stocking over his face, I recognized him as the man who had managed the apartment building where I lived some years before. He was arrested two days later, and I picked him out of a line-up without any problems. The police also obtained substantial physical evidence against the man. In fact, the detective in charge of the case told me that out of the approximately 600 rape cases he had investigated, mine was the most "solid" he had come across.

In addition, the rapist had a long history of sexual abuse crime, and at the time he raped me, he was on probation for child molestation. (Actually, he molested his five-year-old daughter, but the charge had been reduced to "Lewd and Lascivious Conduct with a Child under 14," for which the Court placed him on 90 days probation!).

I have provided details because I think they help to explain my shock and anger at what happened next. Two weeks later, I received a subpoena which ordered me to appear in court. . . . I arrived at the courthouse early. I was scared and nervous, and I had no ideas what to expect. I was instructed to sit in a small room until the D.A. had time to see me, and I was informed that the pre-trial hearing was scheduled for 10 a.m. The D.A. "found time" to see me two *very long* hours later. As we were going over my statement, he received a phone call which made him extremely happy, and which infuriated me. In the D.A.'s words, "[the rapist] accepted our deal."

Although I requested him to explain the details of the plea bargain several times, he avoided the question, but he did explain that plea bargaining was necessary because if every case had to go to trial, the courts would be back-logged for years, especially considering the high crime rate in the area (Oakland, California). He also explained that even if we went to trial, and the rapist was found guilty, some liberal judge may sentence him to less than what "we got" from the plea bargain (I found this irrelevant and illogical). Finally, he told me that I should be "happy" that he had "spared me the pain of going to trial." I was amazed that a man whom I had not met at the time this "bargain" was planned, had the extra-sensory power to know that I would be "pained" by going to trial. In short, I felt cheated, and I still am very angry. Not only was I completely ignored, but the rapist got a good deal.

My frustration increased geometrically as I confronted the courts. One judge told me that I should "try to understand the poor guy because he was the product of a broken home, alcoholic parents, and a poor childhood." That same judge told me I should be "grateful that he didn't hurt me!" When I spoke at the sentencing, the judge told me I should "just forget the whole thing," and that I should have no trouble getting my life back together since I'm so young (I'm 25). I find it hard to quantify the contempt I feel for those men.

Letter from Jane Doe to Judge Ralph Adam Fine (March 9, 1987).

I have quoted the woman's letter at some length for two reasons. First, it shows that at least some victims are tougher and have more resolve than many in the criminal justice system believe. Second, I hope its eloquence will sway some of those who may be skeptical of *Escape of the Guilty*'s warning that plea bargaining is rotting the law's integrity.

8. *60 Minutes* (CBS television broadcast, January 18, 1987) (emphasis added).

9. R. A. Fine, *supra* note 4, at 51–54.

10. Andenaes, *Punishment and Deterrence* (1974).

11. Wilson, "Thinking About Crime," *Atlantic Monthly*, September 1983, p. 79.

12. Church, *In Defense of Bargain Justice*, 13 LAW & SOC'Y. REV. 509, 517 (1979) (quoting 1973 U.S. National Advisory Commission Report).

13. R. Pound, *Criminal Justice in America*, 184 (1930).

14. *Wright v. Rindskopf*, 43 Wis. 344, 354–55 (1877).

15. Wis. Stat. §§ 943.23(1), 939.50(3)(e) (1985–86).

16. *Id.* at §§ 943.23(2), 939.51(3)(a).

17. *Id.* at § 943.23(2).

18. *Standards for Criminal Justice* Rule 3–3.9 (2d ed. 1986).

19. State *ex rel. Newspapers v. Circuit Court*, 124 Wis. 2d 499, 502, 370 N.W.2d 209, 211 (1985).

20. *Id.*

21. *Id.*

22. State *ex rel. Unnamed Petitioners v. Connors*, 136 Wis. 2d 118, 154 n.1, 401 N.W.2d 782, 797 n.1 (1987) (Steinmetz, J., and Day, J., dissenting).

23. *See supra* note 18.

24. R. A. Fine, *supra* note 4, at 49–55, 68–71, 101, 107–08.

25. Hagan & Bernstein, *The Sentence Bargaining of Upperworld and Underworld Crime in Ten Federal District Courts*, 13 LAW & SOC'Y REV. 467, 470 (1979).

26. See *supra* notes 15–17 and accompanying text.

27. McDonald, *Judicial Supervision of the Guilty Plea Process: A Study of Jurisdiction*, 70 JUDICATURE 203–09 (1987).

28. 400 U.S. 25 (1970).

29. President's Comm'n on Law Enforcement and Admin. of Just., *The Challenge of Crime in a Free Society* 135 (1967).

30. U. S. National Advisory Comm'n of Criminal Justice, *Courts* 43, (1973).

31. 434 U.S. 357 (1978).

32. *Id.* at 358 n.1.

33. *Id.* at 363.

34. *Id.* (citations omitted).

35. R. A. Fine, *supra* note 4, at 72.

36. Wisconsin is one of the few states that permits a criminal defendant to peremptorily bump a judge from his or her case. *See State v. Holmes*, 106 Wis. 2d 31, 315 N.W. 2d 703 (1982), Wis. Stat. §§ 971.20 (1985–86).

37. R. A. Fine, *supra* note 4, at 109.

38. Alschuler, *The Defense Attorney's Role in Plea Bargaining*, 84 YALE L.J. 1179, 1182 (1975).

39. M. Rubinstein, S. Clarke & T. White, *Alaska Bans Plea Bargaining* 39 (National Institute of Justice 1980) [hereinafter M. Rubinstein].

40. *Id.*

41. *See* Blumberg, *The Practice of Law As Confidence Game: Organizational Cooptation of a Profession*, 1 LAW & SOC'Y REV. 15 (June 3, 1967).

42. Wis. Stat. §§ 940.19(1), 939.51(3)(a) (1985–86).

43. *Id.* at §§ 941.30, 939.50(3)(d).

44. *Id.* at §§ 940.01, 939.32(1)(a), 939.50(3)(a).

45. R. A. Fine, *supra* note 4, at 79–83.

46. *Brady v. United States*, 397 U.S. 742, 751 n.8 (1970).

47. Herbert J. Stern, a former United States District Court Judge in New Jersey and a former United States Attorney has catalogued the horrors:

> We have developed a system of bargain and sale. Defendants are induced to plead guilty by specific promises of benefit or threats of harm. Prosecutors, aided and abetted by judges, are permitted to elicit courtroom confessions by techniques that would turn our stomachs if they were employed in the station house.
>
> Defendants may be threatened with the possibility that more serious charges will be brought against them unless they waive their sixth amendment rights and plead guilty to lesser ones. Wives who refuse to plead may be threatened with increased penalties for their co-defendant husbands. In places like New York, defendants are permitted to plead to hypothetical crimes, to crimes which never occurred, even to "logically impossible" crimes, all to make the sale possible and move the docket along. We have even sunk to the level of permitting defendants to plead guilty while professing their innocence.

Stern, Book Review, 82 COLUM. L. REV. 1275, 1283 (1982) (citations omitted) (reviewing A. Goldstein, *The Passive Judiciary* (1981).

48. Thau, *How Lawyers Can Benefit From Trends in Collateral Estoppel*, NAT'L L.J., Nov., 1980 at 22, 26 n. 5.

49. 397 U.S. 742 (1970).

50. *Scott v. United States*, 419 F.2d 264, 278 (D.C. Cir. 1969) (footnotes omitted).

51. M. Rubinstein, *supra* note 39, at 2.

52. *Id.* at 11.

53. *Id.* at 12.

54. *Id.* at 80.

55. *Id*. at 102–03.

56. *Id*. at 46.

57. Rubinstein & White, *Alaska Bans Plea Bargaining*, 13 LAW & SOC'Y REV. 367, 371 (1979). [Editor's note: after a change in political administration, plea bargaining, regrettably, was reintroduced in Alaska in recent years.]

58. Judge O'Farrell had 179 jury trials in 1982.

59. *Bordenkircher v. Hayes*, 434 U.S. 357, 361–62 (1978); *Blackledge v. Allison*, 431 U.S. 63, 71 (1977).

60. Stern, *supra* note 47, at 1283.

61. Alschuler, Book Review, 46 U. CHI. L. REV. 1007, 1029 n. 81 (1979) (reviewing C. Silberman, *Criminal Violence, Criminal Justice* (1981)).

62. R. A. Fine, *supra* note 4, at 111.

63. *See State v. Kenyon*, 85 Wis. 2d 36, 270 N.W.2d 160 (1978).

64. *Id*.

65. One small step in the right direction in Wisconsin was the Supreme Court's rejection of a proposal that would have, in effect, permitted judges to participate in the bargaining process. In the *Matter of the Amendment of Rules*, 128 Wis. 2d 422, 383 N.W. 2d 486 (1986) (percuriam).

66. U.S. Dept. of Justice, *Uniform Crime Reports for the United States*, 1985, 6 (1986).

67. *Bureau of Just. Statistics Bull., Prisoners in 1984*, 6–8 (U.S. Dep't. of Just. 1985). Indeed, an analysis of the per-serious-crime imprisonment rate over the years shows a chilling relationship between the ferocious explosion of violent crime we have recently experienced and the lenient policies of the mid-1960s and 1970s. In 1960, there were 6.3 prison admissions per 100 crimes. In 1965, the rate fell to 4.5. By 1970, it dipped to 2.3 and remained below 3 per 100 serious crimes until 1981, when it rose to 3.5. *Id*.
Some who advocate a return to leniency point out that our prison populations have risen as of late and the number of prisoners per 100,000 of population has never been higher. The only *meaningful* measure of incarceration however, is that which compares the lock-up rate with the number of crimes being committed. Despite the large number of prisoners in this country, we have yet to reach the rate of incarceration per serious crime we had in 1960.
As I point out in *Escape of the Guilty*, approximately two-thirds of all persons incarcerated for the *first* time learn their lesson and never return to prison. R. A. Fine, *supra* note 4, at 248. Others, however, will remain a danger as long as they are free or until old age has weakened their criminality. Thus, 61 percent of those admitted to prison in 1979 were repeaters and, ominously, 46 percent of them would have *still* been in prison on an earlier sentence at the time of their new crime if they had not been released on parole. *Id*. "The message is clear, deter those who can be deterred, incarcerate those who cannot." *Id*. Sadly, efforts at rehabilitation—the concept that fathered the leniency—have generally not worked to protect society. *Id*. at 40–41, 164–66, 247–249.

68. Bureau of Justice Statistics, *Crime and Justice Facts* 19 (1986).

The Paradox of the Exclusionary Rule

by Caleb Nelson

The right of the people to be secure in their persons, houses, papers, and effects, against unreasonable searches and seizures, shall not be violated, and no Warrants shall issue, but upon probable cause, supported by Oath or affirmation, and particularly describing the place to be searched, and the persons or things to be seized.
— The Fourth Amendment

In 1914, one hundred and twenty-three years after the ratification of the Fourth Amendment, the Supreme Court declared that the Amendment was "of no value" if unconstitutionally seized evidence could be used in federal courts. The Court held all such evidence inadmissible.

This exclusionary rule was entirely the invention of the Court, not the Framers. Indeed, only thirty-five years later the Court confessed that the rule was not a necessary corollary of the Constitution; in 1949, though it decided that the Fourteenth Amendment applies the Fourth Amendment to the states, it nonetheless refused to impose the exclusionary rule on state courts. In 1961, however, the Court again changed its mind, extending the "constitutionally required" rule to the states in the landmark case of *Mapp v. Ohio*.

Much has been made of the extent to which the exclusionary rule frustrates justice by forcing the release of obviously guilty criminals. To all such criticism, civil libertarians have responded that the occasional release of the guilty is the price of liberty, and that the exclusionary rule protects everyone—innocent and guilty alike—from overly intrusive policemen. The debate over the rule has thus centered on how to balance the competing claims of justice and freedom.

But in fact no balance need be struck in order to assess the rule; civil libertarians should join law-and-order advocates in demanding its abolition. Growing evidence suggests that the exclusionary rule, in addition to freeing criminals, also encourages judges to undermine individual rights. As many legal scholars have suggested, a close look

102

at Supreme Court cases of the past two decades indicates that the rule's existence is causing a steady constriction in the effective scope of the Fourth Amendment, as the Court condones questionable police behavior rather than suppress crucial evidence. The irony is unmistakable: just as the 1914 Court twisted the Constitution to invent the exclusionary rule, so the modern Court invents legal theories to circumvent the rule, unintentionally but inevitably eroding the very rights that the rule was created to protect.

The Exclusionary Rule and Crime

The Court's motives are clear. Within ten years of *Mapp*, researchers had begun to argue that the exclusionary rule was responsible for the release of many hardened criminals. The most influential early work was that of University of Chicago professor Dallin Oaks, whose 1970 law-review article summarizing past studies and announcing new data instantly attracted widespread attention. Professor Oaks examined twelve sample days in the proceedings of two Chicago courts, and found that motions to suppress evidence were filed in 34 percent of the narcotics prosecutions and 36 percent of the concealed-weapons prosecutions. Two-thirds of the weapons motions and 97 percent of the narcotics motions were granted. Every single case in which the motion was successful was subsequently dismissed, since crimes of possession cannot be prosecuted when the illegal objects are not available as evidence. Thus the exclusionary rule ensured that a third of Chicago's narcotics cases and a quarter of Chicago's weapons cases were never tried.

Chicago was perhaps atypical—proponents of the exclusionary rule charged that the city's police willfully and routinely violated the Constitution—but researchers in other jurisdictions agreed with Oaks that the exclusionary rule doomed many criminal prosecutions. In California (where at the time the rule was slightly stronger than elsewhere because of provisions in the state constitution) a National Institute of Justice study concluded that many cases involving illegal searches were rejected for prosecution before ever reaching a suppression hearing. Between 1976 and 1979, for instance, almost three thousand felony drug cases in California were not prosecuted because of search-and-seizure problems; what is more, nearly half of the defendants who were not prosecuted in 1976 or 1977 because of such problems were rearrested within two years on new charges. Another analysis of California data estimated that up to 7.1 percent of all felony drug arrestees may have been released because of the exclusionary rule. Other researchers suggested that prosecutors, rather than risk the suppression of their key evidence, often accept lenient plea bargains.

Proponents of the rule responded with a 1979 study conducted by the General Accounting Office, which found that only 1.1 percent of all *federal* criminal defendants were freed by suppression of evidence. But everyone agreed that regardless of percentages, the exclusionary rule frees a large number of criminals. As studies of the rule's effects began to pile up, and as the rule's defenders left the Court, the justices became less willing to apply the rule.

Erosion of the Rule

Dallin Oaks' article quickly attracted the Supreme Court's attention. In a 1970 dissent, then-Chief Justice Warren Burger relied on it extensively to conclude that the Court should reverse direction: "Some clear demonstration of the benefits and effectiveness of the exclusionary rule is required to justify it in view of the high price it extracts from society—the release of countless guilty criminals."

Indeed, as early as 1965, when the Court refused to apply *Mapp* retroactively, the majority arrived at its decision by weighing the social costs of applying the rule against the social benefits. In the following years, the Court used this balancing test extensively, and the scales tipped increasingly against the suppression of evidence. The turning point was the 1974 case of *U.S. v. Calandra*, in which the Court reverted (again) to the position that the exclusionary rule is not mandated by the Constitution. "In sum," the Court concluded, "the rule is a judicially created remedy designed to safeguard Fourth Amendment rights generally through its deterrent effect, rather than a personal constitutional right of the party aggrieved." Notwithstanding the Court's prior rhetoric, the use of illegally seized evidence "work[s] no new Fourth Amendment wrong," and hence the rule is properly "restricted to those areas where its remedial objectives are thought most efficaciously served."

The Court was certainly correct that there is no "personal constitutional right" to the suppression of evidence. The problem is that there *is* a personal constitutional right to be free from unreasonable searches and seizures, and under current practice its scope is largely determined by the scope of the exclusionary rule.

Aside from the rule, there are two major formal checks on policemen: the internal disciplinary apparatus of their departments, and the threat of civil or criminal actions against them. The exclusionary rule's existence hampers both of these mechanisms, but especially the first. If evidence gathered by questionable means might be needed in a trial, police departments have reason to refrain from punishing the investigating officers, or at least to delay for years. To discipline them before the case is conclusively settled would be to admit that the evidence was illegally seized and should be suppressed.

Civil suits and criminal charges can sometimes be brought against offending policemen. But the law is constructed, properly enough, so that policemen who unknowingly overstep their authority in a good cause are not held personally accountable; the threat of direct legal sanctions applies only to willful violations of the Fourth Amendment, and hence such sanctions are almost never imposed. Yet the effectiveness of even this last-ditch measure is currently linked to the exclusionary rule. Under the current system, when courts decide against excluding unconstitutionally seized evidence, juries may be more inclined to absolve the offending policemen.

To at least some extent, then, courts now must choose between condemning police misconduct and punishing criminals. As the principal mechanism to enforce the Fourth Amendment, the exclusionary rule reacts to one injustice by countenancing another; in Cardozo's famous words, "the criminal is to go free because the constable has blundered." Even when the rule is applied, the constable himself rarely suffers any direct punishment—except the guilty knowledge that his misconduct has freed a criminal to prey once more on society.

This system makes little sense, and so since *Calandra* the Court has steadily narrowed the exclusionary rule. It began by holding the rule inapplicable in certain special proceedings such as grand-jury hearings and civil actions, citing the societal costs imposed by a rule that "deflects the truthfinding process and often frees the guilty." And the Court soon began to erode the rule in criminal trials themselves.

In *U.S. v. Ceccolini* (1978), for instance, the Court went against a long history of suppressing evidence gathered on the basis of unconstitutionally obtained information, by permitting the testimony of a witness whose identity was discovered in an unconstitutional search. In December 1974 a police officer had entered the shop of a florist named Ceccolini to chat with the sales clerk. He noticed an envelope on the drawer of the store's cash register, and saw some money protruding from it. For no apparent reason, and without any authorization, he opened the envelope and sorted through its contents, observing that it contained betting slips as well as money. He asked the clerk about the envelope, and she told him that the store's owner had asked her to give it to someone. The policeman notified federal gambling investigators, who obtained the cooperation of the sales clerk; on the basis of her testimony, Ceccolini was convicted of perjury. The lower federal courts invoked the exclusionary rule to set aside the conviction, but the Supreme Court reversed this decision. It reasoned that since the policeman was not investigating gambling offenses when he examined the envelope, suppressing the clerk's testimony "could not have the slightest deterrent effect" on similarly situated policemen.

Despite this claim, under *Ceccolini* policemen have a positive incentive to conduct idle unconstitutional searches. As long as they are not investigating particular crimes or expecting to acquire evidence—in other words, as long as they are merely nosing around instead of acting upon probable cause—they might uncover useful witnesses. It is probably true that the social costs of suppressing testimony in cases like *Ceccolini* would outweigh the benefits. This fact, however, argues for the abolition of the rule and the creation of a more fine-tuned mechanism to deter police misconduct.

Yet rather than reach this conclusion, the Court has simply continued its *ad hoc* use of the balancing test to avoid suppressing evidence. In *Nix v. Williams* (1984), for example, the Court sidestepped abolition by establishing a new exception to the exclusionary rule: "If the prosecution can establish by a preponderance of the evidence that the information ultimately or inevitably would have been discovered by lawful means . . . then the deterrence rationale has so little basis that the evidence should be received."

The Good-Faith Exception

Judicial hostility to the exclusionary rule is sensible, but as long as the rule exists this hostility will lead to reductions in the effective scope of the Fourth Amendment. Consider, for example, the "good faith" exception to the rule, created in *U.S. v. Leon* (1984). The *Leon* majority catalogued the various ways in which the exclusionary rule frustrates justice, paying particular attention to the California studies about the number of criminals freed by the rule. Applying a cost-benefit analysis, the Court held that evidence seized by police acting "in objectively reasonable reliance" on a warrant issued by a "detached and neutral magistrate" should be admissible in trial, even if the warrant later fails judicial scrutiny.

The Court extended the good-faith standard in *Illinois v. Krull* (1987), holding that evidence seized in objectively reasonable reliance on a statute authorizing warrantless searches should not be suppressed even if the statute is later found to be unconstitutional. Again, the Court justified this decision by appealing to the balancing test, citing "the substantial social costs exacted by the exclusionary rule." President Bush subsequently asked Congress to create a general good-faith exception to the rule.

The President and the Court are doubtless correct that society is better served by an exclusionary rule with the good-faith exception than by one without it. But the exception is no panacea. While a policeman who truly believes himself authorized to conduct a search would never have been deterred by the exclusionary rule, the good-faith exception undercuts a broader kind of deterrence: its existence discourages police departments from training their agents in constitutional practice.

As many critics have observed, the good-faith exception is a defense tailor-made for policemen who are not fond of civil liberties. Officers who knowingly violate the law of search and seizure will have few moral scruples against perjuring themselves to convince judges of their good faith. If they succeed, they face no punishment.

In addition, the good-faith exception eliminates any possibility that the exclusionary rule will deter magistrates and legislatures from authorizing unconstitutional searches. Under the current exclusionary rule, the Fourth Amendment no longer protects against searches and seizures that are unreasonable, but only against searches and seizures that are egregious.

Searches of Third Parties

Sometimes it does not even do that.

In 1972 an IRS agent asked private detective Norman Casper to investigate people who had bank accounts at the Castle Bank in the Bahamas. Casper devised a plan, approved by the agent, to get access to bank records. He introduced one of the bank officers to Sybol Kennedy, a female private investigator who had an apartment in Miami. On January 15, 1973, the bank officer went to the apartment, dropped off some baggage, and took Kennedy to dinner. While they were out, Casper entered the apartment with a key given him by Kennedy, took the bank officer's briefcase, and handed it over to the IRS agent. Under the agent's guidance, the papers in the briefcase were photocopied, as an operative kept tabs on the couple to make sure that the briefcase was returned before being missed. Acting on information found in the briefcase, investigators discovered that Jack Payner, one of the bank's American depositors, had falsified his 1972 tax return.

In the ensuing case of *U.S. v. Payner* (1980), the Supreme Court observed that "[n]o court should condone the unconstitutional and possibly criminal behavior of those who planned and executed this 'briefcase caper.'" But it held that Payner had no standing to suppress the illegally seized documents, because his own Fourth Amendment rights had not been violated; it was the bank officer's briefcase, not his, that was rifled. Since the bank officer had committed no crime, he was in no position to benefit from the exclusionary rule. Hence the Court's analysis robbed the rule of any possible value in deterring illegal searches of the possessions of innocent third parties.

The potential for police abuse is obvious. Indeed, according to the lower court in *Payner*, "the Government affirmatively counsels its agents that the Fourth Amendment standing limitation permits them to purposefully conduct an unconstitutional search and seizure of one individual in order to obtain evidence against third parties. . . . "

Even though the erosion of the exclusionary rule, under the current system, reduces the effective scope of the Fourth Amendment, there is a bright side: it paves the way for the rule to be abolished entirely. There is no bright side to the other method that the Court has used to avoid suppressing relevant evidence: eroding the Fourth Amendment itself.

While it is obviously impossible to say how the Fourth Amendment law would have developed in the absence of the exclusionary rule, there can be no denying that the rule's existence gives judges at all levels a powerful incentive to condone questionable police actions. Proponents of the rule, however, counter that without the exclusionary rule, Fourth Amendment claims would never be litigated, and the Fourth Amendment rights that we now enjoy might never have been articulated.

An Alternative to the Exclusionary Rule

The Court's frequent invocation of the balancing test shows its powerful aversion to freeing criminals in order to defend Fourth Amendment rights. But if the exclusionary rule were abolished in favor of a sensible mechanism for directly punishing offending policemen, the Court's present dilemma would be resolved. As long as the sanctions were subject to judicial review, the Court could still pass on Fourth Amendment claims, without the distorting presence of the exclusionary rule.

Perhaps the best alternative to the exclusionary rule that has yet been proposed is the creation of independent boards to review charges of official misconduct and to impose direct punishments. Allegations of police abuses could be brought before these boards by independent prosecutors, since regular prosecutors might hesitate to press charges against the policemen on whom their careers depend. The policemen, in turn, would be represented by lawyers. Although police perjury would still pose problems, good-faith violations would no longer have to go entirely unpunished; the board could fine the offending officers' departments and order them to step up their training efforts. More flagrant offenses could result in direct sanctions against the officers themselves.

Not only would this system end the exclusionary rule's distortion of constitutional law, but it would also improve the deterrence of official misconduct. Under the current system, the punishment for illegal searches falls on society, not the police. Although post-*Mapp* policemen are probably better trained and more aware of the Fourth Amendment than were their counterparts of the fifties, there is no guarantee that offending officers will ever find out about convictions lost because of the suppression of evidence, let alone learn the reasons behind the suppression. Nor, for that matter, is there any guarantee that they would care if they did find out; some police departments still base officers' performance ratings on their arrest totals, and pay less attention to how many of their arrestees are subsequently convicted. The review-board scheme would solve these problems.

In addition, since the boards would be able to consider illegal searches that turned up no evidence, they could extend the protections of the Fourth Amendment to the innocent as well as to the guilty. The boards would also be empowered to deal with police actions aimed solely at keeping the peace or at confiscating weapons and drugs; the exclusionary rule, by contrast, applies only when police are interested in prosecution. Direct sanctions against offending officers or their departments would be much more likely than the exclusionary rule to deter the few rogue policemen who willfully violate the Fourth Amendment.

The vast majority of policemen, who honestly try to follow the Constitution's commands, would also be better served by a system of direct sanctions. Currently, Fourth Amendment law is so convoluted that even experienced lawyers often do not know whether particular searches are likely to be upheld by the courts. Without the incentive to draw fine lines in order to admit evidence, judges could restore some order to their Fourth Amendment rulings. If search-and-seizure law were simpler, well-meaning officers would find it easier to obey the judiciary's Fourth Amendment standards.

There will always be some tension between investigating crime and protecting rights. If reform of the exclusionary rule gives judges less reason to restrict Fourth Amendment rights, it may hinder law enforcement. But to the extent that it makes the system more intelligible, it could both help policemen and make rights more secure. A rational legal system is a goal that both law-and-order advocates and civil libertarians should support.

Yet it is a goal that the exclusionary rule frustrates. Based on the decisions of his colleagues on the bench, D.C. Circuit Judge Malcolm Wilkey once wrote: "If one were diabolically to attempt to invent a device designed slowly to undermine the substantive reach of the Fourth Amendment, it would be hard to do better than the exclusionary rule." There is no reason for the Court to retain an artificial rule that impedes justice and distorts constitutional law when the rule's purpose can be better served by more sensible alternatives.

The Urge to Confess

by Ralph Adam Fine

Although trials are usually described as searches for the truth, the quests are often beset with many detours, hazards, and, indeed, outright barriers. Some of the barriers and detours, such as the rules of evidence, which govern all trials, are necessary. They help, rather than hinder, the pursuit. Others, however, have been placed along the way for reasons unrelated to the search for truth; they permit criminals to escape conviction because, in the late Supreme Court Justice Benjamin N. Cardozo's famous phrase (written when he was the chief judge of New York), a "constable" may have "blundered."

The modern-day trial is a forum for persuasion. Each side presents evidence in an attempt to convince a neutral and disinterested fact-finder (usually a jury, but occasionally a judge sitting alone) that something is true. In a civil case, for example, the dispute may be over which car ran the red light at the corner of Elm and Maple. In a criminal case, the dispute may be whether the defendant robbed Jim's liquor store.

There are essentially two types of evidence: the testimony of witnesses who tell what they have seen, heard, or otherwise personally experienced, and tangible items (called *exhibits*) that have some bearing on the dispute. The rules of evidence operate much like a complex valve. They govern the flow of testimony and exhibits so that the jury hears and sees only those things that are most probative of the issues it has to decide. In the liquor store robbery trial, for example, testimony about Marilyn Monroe and her movies might be interesting to those curious about the actress, but obviously it would have absolutely nothing to do with the case; it would be *irrelevant*.

The rule requiring that evidence be relevant to the issues keeps the trial on track. There are myriad other rules whose rationales are less clear and whose application can be frustrating to lawyers and laymen alike. Nevertheless, these rules also keep the search for the truth uncluttered by inconsequential and potentially misleading facts. Consider, for example, the rule against hearsay, which prevents one person from relating another person's version of an event:

Q: Mrs. Jones, which car went through the red light?

A: Well, I wasn't there, but my husband, Sam, was passing by that very moment and he tells me that it was definitely the black Chevy.

If the other side objects, the judge won't let the well-intentioned Mrs. Jones tell the jury what her husband had to say because that party's lawyer can't effectively test the accuracy of *Mr. Jones's* observations by asking *Mrs. Jones* questions: What was *he* doing at the time of the accident? Did he have a clear view of the scene? Was he distracted? Could *he* actually see the traffic light, or is he relying on what someone else might have told him?

The running-the-red-light example is a fairly straightforward application of the rule against hearsay. The rule itself, however, is exceedingly complex, and not all hearsay is excluded. Rather, in some rough way, the law balances the need for certain evidence, the difficulty in getting eyewitness testimony, and the reliability of the hearsay statement. Thousands of books and articles have analyzed the rule against hearsay and its numerous permutations and exceptions. Two quick examples before we move on: The question "Sir, when were you born?" obviously calls for a hearsay response. The witness does not remember when he was born—he remembers what others have told him. But just think how cumbersome—and often impossible—it would be to require eyewitness testimony on this issue. Similarly, a dying murder victim's accusation against the alleged killer is admissible into evidence as long as the victim knew he was dying because the law considers such statements to be reliable (on the theory that no one will go to his Maker with a lie on his lips) and, since the victim may be the only witness to the murder, his or her last words are often necessary for any prosecution.

* * *

The rules of evidence, as they have evolved over the course of centuries, are an attempt to isolate for the jury information that is both relevant and reliable. On the other hand, the rules of *exclusion*— fashioned by some judges to keep the police from overstepping the bounds of their authority—prevent the jury from learning things even though they may be pertinent and trustworthy.

Daniel Webster once observed that "the guilty soul cannot keep its own secret." Confession is the voice of conscience, and, as any police officer will tell you, men and women generally have a natural compulsion to confess: to tell of their misdeeds, to take their punishment, and to move on, *even though they may realize it is not in their interest to do so*. Dr. Theodor Reik, in a series of lectures given to the Vienna Psychoanalytic Association first published in 1925 and fittingly called *The Compulsion to Confess*, discusses this special dilemma:

> There is the endeavor to deflect any suspicion from himself, to efface all traces of the crime, and an impulse growing more and more intense suddenly to cry out his secret in the street before all people, or in milder cases, to confide it at least to one person, to free himself from the terrible burden.

Of course, there are exceptions to this inner urge. There are persons without consciences to whom an armed robbery is no more significant than a sneeze or a cough. Hardened criminals and those schooled in the ways of the criminal justice system will usually successfully resist the temptation to bare all to the police although they often relieve their urge to confess by confiding in friends, casual acquaintances they meet in taverns, and cellmates. Indeed, law enforcement investigators are frequently able to solve crimes because they learn of these informal confessions.

Many influential judges and law professors have sought to stifle the wrongdoer's natural urge to confess. As a result, they have not only hindered effective and efficient law enforcement, they have—in the area of confession and elsewhere—turned the quest for criminal justice into a boardgame chase in which one false move by the police can result in freedom for the guilty. The seminal Supreme Court decision concerning confessions is, of course, *Miranda v. Arizona*. We will examine *Miranda* in the context of history. Since the decision was designed to prevent what the majority thought was improper police conduct, we must start with those dark days when torture was an accepted law enforcement tool for obtaining confessions.

Apart from its obvious immorality, we reject torture as a crime-solving tool because statements extracted by the forceps of pain are not trustworthy. Throughout history, men and women have confessed to incredible things to spare themselves the rack's agony or the whip's lash. As the late Supreme Court Justice Hugo Black wrote in 1940,

> The testimony of centuries, in governments of varying kinds over populations of different races and beliefs, stood as proof that physical and mental torture and coercion had brought about the tragically unjust sacrifices of some who were the noblest and most useful of their generations. The rack, the thumbscrew, the wheel, solitary confinement, protracted questioning and cross questioning, and other ingenious forms of entrapment of the helpless or unpopular had left in their wake of mutilated bodies and shattered minds along the way to the cross, the guillotine, the stake, and the hangman's noose.

Nevertheless, in ages when investigative techniques were fairly rudimentary, torture was extensively used; it was a fairly easy way of resolving disputed issues. As a British civil servant in India of the 1870s commented, "There is a great deal of laziness in it. It is far pleasanter to sit comfortably in the shade rubbing red pepper in some poor devil's eyes than to go about in the sun hunting up evidence."

Interestingly, torture was once used because it was thought to *enhance* testimonial validity. In ancient Greece, for example, slaves who were witnesses in either civil or criminal cases were routinely tortured because, as one scholar explained, a slave was believed to be so "absolutely at the mercy of his master" that he "would naturally testify in accordance with the master's wishes unless some stronger incentive to speak the truth were brought to bear."

The "judicial" use of torture got its impetus once thirteenth-century Europe had weaned itself from the methods of proof—oath taking and the ordeal—that we discussed earlier. Officially sanctioned torture occurred mainly on the Continent, where the roles of prosecutor and judge merged into one man and where the burden of proof for serious offenses was extraordinarily high: there had to be two unimpeachable witnesses who actually saw the crime. This high burden—"clearer than the noonday sun"—was established in order to instill as much certainty into the verdicts that were to be rendered by man as was thought to have previously been in the verdicts rendered by God.

Since very few persons commit crimes in front of two unimpeachable witnesses, convictions would have been very rare if suspects did not confess. Theoretically, an inquisitor could only use torture to get a confession if he had independent evidence of guilt and its application was strictly regulated in accordance with complex guidelines. Needless to say, these niceties were often ignored in the haste to bring suspected malefactors and heretics to book.

Torture was less pervasive in England. The fulcrum of English procedure was the jury trial, and it remained unhampered by impossible standards of proof. But even there, torture had its moments of prominence, primarily during the sixteenth and seventeenth centuries when inquisition displaced prosecution for certain crimes, especially under the aegis of the infamous Star Chamber. Nevertheless, English procedure eschewed the Continent's extensive reliance on torture, especially after the Star Chamber was abolished in 1641. As one historian explained,

> The torture could not very well take place in the presence of the jury. Such a thing would have been too shocking to men who were, after all, the neighbors of the prisoner; and if it was inflicted upon him in secret beforehand, he would be certain to recant at the trial, and tell how his confession had been wrung from him by suffering, with a strong probability of arousing violent prejudice in his favor; for a jury would be very differently affected by such a scene than a body of magistrates hardened by constantly dealing with criminals.

That ideal, although not completely accurate, explains why torture was never officially part of our Anglo-American system of justice, with the exception of that one dark period in England.

Criminal law serves society by protecting order and property and by preserving each person's right to live unmolested. Law, in essence, should be no more than a codification of the Golden Rule. Of course, in a perfect world, in which everyone's inner gyroscope was attuned to that Golden Rule, we would need no laws. Unfortunately our world is far from perfect: laws are needed to protect us not only from predators who rob and rape but also from those whose law-enforcement zeal or, tragically, sadistic malevolence override the bounds of humanity. Simply put, both lawmen and the lawless are subject to the law. Confessions compelled by torment are rightfully beyond the law's pale.

Raymond Stewart's bludgeoned body was found in his simple Mississippi farmhouse on the afternoon of March 30, 1934. That night, the local deputy sheriff took a suspect, a young black man by the name of Yank Ellington, to the murdered man's home, where a lynch mob had already gathered. When Ellington denied any part in the murder, the mob tried to force a confession. Two times they hung him from a tree and then cut him down. They then tied him to the tree and scourged him until his blood soaked their whips. Still Ellington refused to confess. The mob, now apparently exhausted by its frenzy, permitted the tortured man to limp home. It was a mere respite from his agony. The next day, he was arrested by the deputy sheriff. Ellington was whipped again. Finally, when he could withstand no more, he confessed.

Two other suspects, Ed Brown and Henry Shields, were arrested and tortured until they, too, confessed. This is how two justices of the Mississippi Supreme Court described the whole sorry episode in their opinion dissenting from their colleagues' hands-off refusal to interfere with local justice:

> [T]he same deputy, accompanied by a number of white men, one of whom was also an officer, and by the jailer, came to the jail, and the two last named defendants were made to strip and they were laid over chairs and their backs were cut to pieces with a leather strap with buckles on it, and they were likewise made by the said deputy definitely to understand that the whipping would be continued unless and until they confessed, and not only confessed, but confessed in every matter of detail as demanded by those present; and in this manner the defendants confessed the crime, and as the whippings progressed and were repeated, they changed or adjusted their confession in all particulars of detail so as to conform to the demands of their torturers.

Those responsible for the outrage freely admitted it. Indeed, when he was later asked about the beatings' severity, the deputy sheriff replied, "Not too much for a Negro; not so much as I would have done if it were left for me."

The defendants repeated their confessions the next morning, and two days later, they were charged by the local grand jury. That afternoon, they were arraigned. Although some of them offered to plead guilty, the trial judge refused to accept any guilty pleas. Rather, he appointed lawyers to represent them and set the trial to start the following morning. The confessions were used and, not surprisingly, the defendants were convicted. The sentence was death. Everyone— the trial judge, the prosecutor, the local constabulary—was aware that there had been torture. To the dissenting justices of the Mississippi Supreme Court, the events read "more like pages torn from some medieval account, than a record made within the confines of a modern civilization which aspires to an enlightened constitutional government." Nevertheless, the conviction was affirmed. Later, the United States Supreme Court reversed and recognized that the fundamental principle of due process prevented the use of torture-extorted confessions.

The use of torture to force confessions was not, of course, limited to the South. The so-called third degree was commonplace all over this nation, but courts, to their credit, generally stood firm in striking down criminal convictions based on such patent violations of human rights. Indeed, a decade before the case involving Ellington, Brown, and Shields reached Washington, the Mississippi Supreme Court also condemned the practice with stirring eloquence:

> We know there are times when atrocious crimes arouse people to a high sense of indignation. And this is true especially in cases where an upright citizen is murdered without cause. But the deep damnation of the defendant's crime ought not cause those intrusted with the enforcement of the law to swerve from the calm and faithful performance of duty. Coercing the supposed state's criminals into confessions and using such confessions so coerced from them against them in trials has been the curse of all countries.

The object of these justices' obloquy was the use of "the water cure"—holding a man down and pouring water up his nose until he confessed—which the court described as "a specie of torture well

known to the bench and bar of this country." Prodded by this barbaric practice, one John Fisher had confessed to a murder. He and a
codefendant were separately tried. It was Fisher's conviction that the
Mississippi Supreme Court reversed on due process grounds. The
other fellow was not so fortunate. Although acquitted in his trial, he
was lynched immediately thereafter. The local sheriff, who was supposed to protect prisoners in his custody, was later fined $500 for
"dereliction of duty."

Rejecting coerced confessions is an "exclusionary rule" founded
in history, common sense, and humanity. It was also fair to both the
accused *and* the victim: if voluntary, the confession could be used; if
not voluntary, it was excluded. Unfortunately, this rational approach
has been abandoned. As we shall see, the new rules of exclusion are
mined with elaborate and often artificial barriers to the truth. They
have twisted the criminal law into a series of byzantine mazes, traps
that ensnare even the most knowledgeable policemen, lawyers, and
judges.

On June 13, 1966, five men—justices of the United States Supreme Court—decreed in *Miranda v. Arizona* that perfectly *voluntary*
statements made by a person suspected of criminal activity in response to questions while in police custody would no longer be admissible into evidence unless the police told him four things *before*
asking any questions:

- He has a right to remain silent. If he does decide to answer
  any questions, he can stop whenever he wants and can pick
  and choose among the questions he wishes to answer without his silence being used against him.
- Anything he does say may be used against him in court.
- He has an immediate right to a lawyer.
- He will get a free lawyer if he cannot afford to hire one.

Additionally, the suspect would have to acknowledge that he had
these rights and that he was expressly giving them up (or "waiving"
them).

The decision was "written" by the then-Chief Justice Earl Warren, although Bob Woodward and Scott Armstrong report in their
book *The Brethren* that Warren rarely wrote the opinions to which he
attached his name. Rather, he told his law clerks—recent law school

graduates—how he wanted the cases to turn out. They dug up research to support his view and drafted the opinions. As explained by Warren's biographer, respected law professor Bernard Schwartz, the clerks were given "a great deal of discretion, particularly on the reasoning and research supporting the decision." This decision-first, reasoning-afterward methodology is a *legislative* approach to judging. It breaks with, rather than builds upon, the past of prior legal precedent.

The late Justice Felix Frankfurter—a liberal law professor but a judicial conservative—once observed that "the vagueness of a constitutional command" does not warrant judges' infusing it with their own "private notions" of social policy. Francis Bacon also warned that "judges ought to remember that their office is *jus dicere*, not *jus dare*; to interpret law and not to make law, or give law."

Legislators are elected to make policy decisions and will be replaced by those more in tune with what the people want if they choose wrongly. On the other hand, all federal judges have lifetime appointments and many state court judges, especially those on the appellate level, are also given protected tenures.

Judges are, appropriately, largely immune from the pressures that govern the legislative and executive branches. Alexander Hamilton called the judiciary the "least dangerous branch" precisely because its powers were limited. Without those limitations of self-restraint, however, it becomes the *most* dangerous branch and subjects the nation to the will, and whims, of men and women who are answerable to no one. The *Miranda* decision highlights this danger of law-making by judges. Significantly, it prevailed by the slimmest of margins: the four other justices violently disagreed. Prior to *Miranda*, the law refused to chill a criminal's desire to clear his conscience: the confessions were admissible as long as improper means were not used. The decree was a cataclysmic change in the law.

The *Miranda* case actually involved the appeals of four men who were separately convicted of various crimes. Michael Vignera was arrested for the robbery of a dress shop in Brooklyn, New York. He admitted committing the crime and was identified by the store owner and a saleslady. However, he had not been told that he had a right to a lawyer or that he had a right not to say anything. Convicted, he was sentenced as a third-felony offender to a term of thirty to sixty years.

Roy Allen Stewart was arrested when Los Angeles police discovered that he had endorsed some dividend checks taken in a series of purse-snatch robberies in which one of the women was killed. When asked if they could search his house, Stewart told the arresting officers, "Go ahead." They discovered various things taken from five of the robbery victims. Over the next five days, Stewart was questioned nine different times, and, during the last session, he admitted to robbing the dead woman but contended that he had not meant to hurt her. He was convicted of first-degree murder and robbery. The jury fixed the penalty as death. The California Supreme Court threw out the convictions because he had not been told that he could have a lawyer and that he could refuse to tell the police anything.

Carl Alvin Westover was arrested by the Kansas City police for two local robberies. He was also wanted by federal officials in California for two bank robberies. The Kansas City officers questioned Westover the night of his arrest and the next morning. They did not tell him that he had a right to a lawyer or that he could remain silent. Nevertheless, Westover maintained his innocence. The Kansas City authorities then let the FBI ask him about the California holdups. The federal agents warned Westover that he didn't have to say anything, that whatever he did say could be used against him in court, and that he had a right to a lawyer. After two and a half hours, Westover confessed. He was convicted of two counts of robbery and sentenced to two consecutive fifteen-year prison terms.

Ernesto Miranda was arrested by Arizona authorities for the kidnapping and forcible rape of an eighteen-year-old girl. He was taken to a Phoenix police station, where he was identified by the victim (to whom Chief Justice Earl Warren's decision later artfully referred in euphemistically aseptic legalese as "the complaining witness"). After two hours of questioning, Miranda gave a detailed oral confession and then wrote out and signed a brief summary, which recited that it had been voluntarily made and "with full knowledge of my legal rights, understanding that any statement I make may be used against me." He was not, however, told that he had a right to have a lawyer present during the questioning. Miranda was convicted of kidnapping and rape and sentenced to concurrent terms of twenty and thirty years.

The Supreme Court reversed the convictions of Vignera, Westover, and Miranda and affirmed the California Supreme Court's reversal of Stewart's conviction. From then on, the United States Supreme Court commanded, police officers who question suspects in custody first have to tell them that they needn't say anything, that what they do say will be used against them if they do say anything, and that they can have a lawyer (retained or appointed) present during the questioning. If these *"Miranda* warnings" are not given, and the rights encompassed by them clearly and expressly waived, any statements, either admitting or denying guilt, cannot be used at trial even though they were freely made. In the course of the lengthy opinion, the five justices recognized that the statements given by Stewart, Vignera, Westover, and Miranda were not "involuntary in traditional terms." Nevertheless, the majority's concern was "not lessened in the slightest" because

> In each of the cases, the defendant was thrust into an unfamiliar atmosphere and run through menacing police interrogation procedures. The potentiality for compulsion is forcefully apparent, for example, in *Miranda,* where the indigent Mexican defendant was a seriously disturbed individual with pronounced sexual fantasies, and in *Stewart,* in which the defendant was an indigent Los Angeles Negro who had dropped out of school in the sixth grade. *To be sure, the records do not evince overt physical coercion or patent psychological ploys. The fact remains that in none of these cases did the officers undertake to afford appropriate safeguards at the outset of the interrogation to insure that the statements were truly the product of a free choice.*

I have italicized the last two sentences because I think they emphasize the essential thrust of the decision: criminal investigation was no longer to be an absolute pursuit of the truth (with appropriate due process safeguards to prevent extortion of confessions). It was now to be a contest in which one player, the police, would have to alert the other player, the suspect, if and when he was about to make a bad move and, if so, to make certain he understood the consequences.

One of the significant policy points upon which the majority relied and which has been cited ever since as a measure of the decree's reasonableness was that the FBI had routinely been giving the warnings they were now imposing on state and local law enforcement. Indeed, Bernard Schwartz's highly acclaimed biography of Earl Warren, *Super Chief*, reports that one of the justices present at the March 6, 1966, conference where the *Miranda* case was discussed and voted upon recalled that the FBI argument was "perhaps the critical factor" in persuading some of the fence-sitting justices over to Warren's side. Yet as Justice John Marshall Harlan noted in his dissent, the FBI warning procedures fell "sensibly short of the Court's formalistic rules," which were now being dictated for the entire country. Thus, Harlan wrote, "there is no indication that FBI agents must obtain an affirmative 'waiver' before they pursue their questioning. Nor is it clear that one invoking his right to silence may not be prevailed to change his mind."

The five-to-four decision requiring that suspects be warned of their Fifth Amendment rights against compulsory self-incrimination during pretrial investigations went well beyond its original scope as framed by the provision's language ("No person . . . shall be compelled in any criminal case to be a witness against himself") as well as beyond its history. The dissenting justices were outraged both by the majority's fast and loose interpretation of history and by what they saw as the imposition of unrealistic and totally unwarranted restrictions on police questioning:

> What the Court largely ignores is that its rules impair, if they will not eventually serve wholly to frustrate, an instrument of law enforcement that has long and quite reasonably been thought worth the price paid for it. There can he little doubt that the Court's new code would markedly decrease the number of confessions. To warn the suspect that he may remain silent and remind him that his confession may he used in court are minor obstructions. To require an express waiver by the suspect and an end to questioning whenever he demurs must heavily handicap questioning. And to suggest or provide counsel for the suspect simply invites the end of the interrogation.

Dissenting Justice John Marshall Harlan bitterly called the historical edifice erected by his five brethren a *trompe l'oeil*—an illusion—

and pointed out that, despite a common misconception fostered by the majority's opinion, the new judge-imposed rules were not aimed at police brutality:

> Those who use third-degree tactics and deny them in court are equally able and destined to lie as skillfully about warnings and waivers. Rather, the thrust of the new rules is to negate all pressures, to reinforce the nervous or ignorant suspect, and ultimately to discourage any confession at all. The aim, in short, is toward "voluntariness" in a utopian sense, or to view it from a different angle, voluntariness with a vengeance.

Harlan noted that the conviction of the bank robber Westover (whom he described as "a seasoned criminal") was overturned even though he was "practically given the Court's full complement of warnings" but "did not heed them." The situation involving the rapist Ernesto Miranda was even more frustrating. This is how justice Harlan told the story:

> On March 3, 1963, an 18-year-old girl was kidnapped and forcibly raped near Phoenix, Arizona. Ten days later, on the morning of March 13, petitioner Miranda was arrested and taken to the police station. At this time Miranda was 23 years old, indigent, and educated to the extent of completing half of the ninth grade. He had an "emotional illness" of the schizophrenic type, according to the doctor who eventually examined him; the doctors' report also stated that Miranda was "alert and oriented as to time, place, and person," intelligent within normal limits, competent to stand trial, and sane within the legal definition. At the police station, the victim picked Miranda out of a lineup, and two officers then took him into a separate room to interrogate him, starting at about 11:30 a.m. Though at first denying his guilt, within a short time Miranda gave a detailed oral confession and then wrote out in his own hand and signed a brief statement admitting and describing the crime. All this was accomplished in two hours or less without any force, threats, or promises and—I

will assume this though the record is uncertain—without any effective warnings at all.

Miranda's oral and written confessions are now held inadmissible under the Court's new rules. One is entitled to feel astonished that the Constitution can be read to produce this result. These confessions were obtained during brief, daytime questioning conducted by two officers and unmarked by any of the traditional indicia of coercion. They assured a conviction for a brutal and unsettling crime, for which the police had and quite possibly could obtain little evidence other than the victim's identifications, evidence which is frequently unreliable. There was, in sum, a legitimate purpose, no perceptible unfairness, and certainly little risk of injustice in the interrogation. Yet, the resulting confessions, and the responsible course of police practice they represent, are to be sacrificed to the Court's own finespun conception of fairness which I seriously doubt is shared by many thinking citizens in this country.

The keystone of the *Miranda* majority's logic was, as we have seen, that "the unfamiliar atmosphere" into which an arrested person is thrust is so inherently coercive that the warnings are required to guarantee that any statements made in response to questioning are "truly the product of a free choice." If no questions are asked, of course, the suspect is free to say anything he or she wishes. The majority explained:

> The fundamental import of the privilege while an individual is in custody is not whether he is allowed to talk to the police without the benefit of warnings and counsel, but whether he can be interrogated.

With this critical issue in mind, Justice Byron R. White's dissenting opinion illumined the inherent flaw in the Court's "bright line" test (either the warnings are given and the rights waived or they are not):

> Although in the Court's view in-custody interrogation is inherently coercive, the Court says that the spontaneous prod-

uct of the coercion of arrest and detention is still to be deemed to be voluntary. An accused, arrested on probable cause, may blurt out a confession which will be admissible despite the fact that he is alone and in custody, without any showing that he had any notion of his right to remain silent or of the consequences of his admission. Yet, under the Court's rule, if the police ask him a single question such as "Do you have anything to say?" or "Did you kill your wife?" his response, if there is one, has somehow been compelled.

There was nothing wrong, the dissenters argued, with the former standards, which required the pretrial statements to pass the due process muster of voluntariness. As Harlan pointed out, the Supreme Court, over the years, had "devised an elaborate, sophisticated, and sensitive approach" for assessing whether confessions met that standard. By contrast, under *Miranda*, if no warnings were given or if the rights were not clearly waived, no response by a suspect can be used as evidence of guilt *even though the response was clearly voluntary*. Application of this mechanistic approach has led to the escape—or near escape—of many guilty persons from the clutches of justice.

On the afternoon of Christmas Eve, 1968, ten-year-old Pamela Powers was with her family at the Des Moines, Iowa, YMCA watching her brother compete in a wrestling tournament. She went to the restroom but never returned.

A recent mental hospital escapee by the name of Robert Williams had been living at the Y. Soon after Pamela's disappearance, Williams was seen carrying a bundle through the Y's lobby. A fourteen-year-old boy who helped him open his car door later told authorities that Williams's bundle had two skinny white legs sticking from it. Williams drove off; the car was found, abandoned, 160 miles away in Davenport. Though the authorities suspected Pamela had been killed, they had no direct proof that she was dead. Williams was charged with abduction, and a warrant was issued for his arrest.

A day and a half later, on December 26, a lawyer told the Des Moines police that he had just received a call from Williams and had made arrangements for Williams to turn himself in to the Davenport authorities. When Williams surrendered in Davenport, he was arrested, advised of his *Miranda* rights, and booked.

Williams was brought before a judge in Davenport for his arraignment. The judge again told him of his rights under the *Miranda* decision. After the brief court session, Williams consulted with a Davenport lawyer who also told him not to talk to the police until he was able to discuss his case with the lawyer in Des Moines.

Two police officers from Des Moines picked Williams up for the return trip. Before they left, one of them reminded Williams that he had a right to have a lawyer present at any questioning. The officer also told Williams that he wanted to make sure that Williams understood that he did not have to say anything because it would be a long trip to Des Moines and they would "be visiting" along the way. Williams again consulted with his Davenport lawyer, who repeated that he was not to say anything to the police during the trip. The lawyer also told the officers not to ask Williams any questions.

The weather was bad, and, before they had been on the road very long, Captain Cletus Leaming, the officer in the back seat with Williams, began to "visit" with him. Leaming knew Williams considered himself to be a very religious person. Among the things Leaming told Williams was that he thought the girl's body had been left near Mitchellville, a town between Des Moines and Davenport. This was his testimony at a pretrial hearing in response to interrogation by Williams's lawyer:

Q: You didn't ask Williams any questions?
A: No sir, I told him some things.
Q: You told him some things?
A: Yes, sir. Would you like to hear it?
Q: Yes.
A: All right. I said to Mr. Williams, I said, "Reverend, I'm going to tell you something. I don't want you to answer me, but I want you to think about it when we're driving down the road." I said, "I want you to observe the weather. It's raining and it's sleeting and it's freezing. Visibility is very poor. They are predicting snow for tonight. I think we're going to be going right past where that body is, and if we should stop and find out where it is on the way in, her parents are going to be able to have a good Christian burial for their daughter. If we don't and it does snow and if you're the only person that knows where this is and if you have only been there once, it's very possible that with snow on the ground you might not be able to find it. Now

I just want you to think about that when we're driving down the road." That's all I said.

Q: About where were you when you said that?

A: Well, not very far out of Davenport. This is on the freeway.

Q: And now when you got to Mitchellville, did you ask him if he thought about it?

A: No. As we were coming towards Mitchellville, we'd still be east of Mitchellville a ways, he said to me, "How do you know that would be at Mitchellville?" And I said, "Well, I'm an investigator. This is my job, and I just figured it out." I said, "I don't know exactly where, but I do know it's somewhere in that area." He said, "You're right, and I'm going to show you where it is."

They found the body. The little girl had been raped and murdered.

At his trial, Williams sought to exclude all his statements as well as the evidence gathered as a result of those statements. The trial judge denied the motion on the ground that by voluntarily taking the officers to the body, he had given up his right not to talk without his lawyer being present.

Williams was convicted of murder, and the Supreme Court of Iowa affirmed the conviction. Williams then sought release from a United States district court judge via the ancient remedy of *habeas corpus*, alleging that his constitutional rights had been violated.

Habeas corpus is Latin for "thou have the body." Although it began as a device to bring a reluctant defendant to court to answer *civil* charges by a plaintiff seeking damages or the return of property, it was frequently used by our early English forebears to compel the many lords who exercised private criminal jurisdiction to produce their prisoners at the King's court so that the prisoners could find out why they were being locked up. Soon expanded to permit a challenge to any detention claimed to be unlawful, *habeas corpus* is such an important predicate of liberty that our Constitution prohibits its suspension except when "in cases of rebellion or invasion the public safety may require it," and then only by the Congress.

The federal judge agreed with Williams that his rights had been violated and granted the writ of *habeas corpus*. A federal appeals court agreed. The United States Supreme Court, on a five to four vote, affirmed and remanded the case back to the Iowa trial court for a retrial.

Writing for the slim majority, Justice Potter Stewart believed that what Williams's appellate lawyers derisively called the "Christian burial" speech had been a ruse to overcome the multiple warnings. In effect, he believed it denied Williams his right to have a lawyer's help. He quoted Leaming's trial testimony:

Q: In fact, Captain, whether he was a mental patient or not, you were trying to get all the information you could before he got to his lawyer, weren't you?

A: I was sure hoping to find out where that little girl was, yes, sir.

Years later, Leaming told a Des Moines newspaper reporter that he "was just being a good old-fashioned cop" and didn't see anything wrong in what he had done. Five Supreme Court justices disagreed. Even the majority recognized that that crime "was senseless and brutal, calling for swift and energetic action by the police to apprehend the perpetrator and gather evidence." Nevertheless, they tossed out the conviction so as not to condone what they called a "clear violation" of Williams's constitutional rights.

Chief Justice Warren Burger's angry dissent called what the majority had done "intolerable" and condemned the way the Court "mechanically and blindly keeps reliable evidence from juries." One can almost taste the venom in the Chief Justice's words:

Williams is guilty of the savage murder of a small child; no member of the Court contends that he is not. While in custody, and after no fewer than *five* warnings of his rights to silence and counsel, he led police to the concealed body of his victim. The Court concedes that Williams was not threatened or coerced and that he spoke and acted voluntarily and with full awareness of his constitutional rights. In the face of all this, the Court now holds that because Williams was prompted by the detective's statement—not interrogation but a statement—the jury must not be told how the police found the body.

The other dissenting justices criticized the majority's opinion in equally strong language and concluded, in the words of Justice White, that the officers "did nothing 'wrong,' let alone 'unconstitutional.'"

Williams was retried for the murder of Pamela Powers. Although the prosecution was forbidden to use his statements or tell the jury how they found Pamela's body, they did persuade the trial judge to let the jury know where, and in what condition, the body had been found on the theory that a large search party combing the area would have discovered it anyway. Williams was convicted and sentenced to a life term in the penitentiary.

The case later returned to the Supreme Court, and on June 11, 1984, fifteen and a half years after Pamela had been raped and murdered, it was finally put to rest. This time on a seven-to-two vote, the Court agreed with the state trial judge and upheld Williams's second conviction, thereby affirming the "inevitable discovery" exception to the exclusionary rule.

The divergence of judicial thought in *Williams* highlights the essential artificiality of the *Miranda* rules. Nowhere was this made more clear than in an angry exchange between Justices John Paul Stevens and Byron R. White in the second appeal. Stevens wrote that he agreed that Williams's conviction should be affirmed, but he criticized Captain Leaming for deciding to "dispense with the requirements of law." "Thanks to" him, wrote Stevens, "the State of Iowa has expended vast sums of money and countless hours of professional labor in his defense. That expenditure surely provides an adequate deterrent to similar violations; the responsibility for that expenditure lies not with the Constitution, but rather with the constable."

Justice White disagreed. Captain Leaming, he explained, was "no doubt acting as many competent police officers would have acted under similar circumstances and in light of then-existing law. That five Justices later thought he was mistaken does not call for making him out to be a villain or for a lecture on deliberate police misconduct and its resulting costs to society." Neither does it make the police officer "wrong" or, for that matter, the state courts of Iowa "wrong" in upholding Williams's original conviction. Rather, as the late Supreme Court Justice Robert H. Jackson (who also served as this nation's chief prosecutor at the Nuremberg war crimes trial) observed in the early 1950s, the varying views reflect "a difference in outlook found between personnel comprising different courts" and that "reversal by a higher court is not proof that justice is thereby better done."

> There is no doubt that if there were a super Supreme Court, a substantial proportion of our reversals of state courts would also be reversed. We are not final because we are infallible, but we are infallible, because we are final.

Williams was ultimately brought to justice—a claim that cannot be made in many of the cases in which the prosecution is forbidden to use an accused's statements. But the question of whether his first conviction should have been overturned and, indeed, whether the exclusionary rule's application to voluntary confessions should be modified persists. Any analysis of this issue must be made in the light of *Miranda's* underlying rationale: that it is improper for the police to elicit perfectly voluntary statements unless they first do all they can to discourage the statements from being made.

As we have seen, most people voluntarily confess because they *want* to, just as most people who smoke first started because they wanted to. The late Chief Justice Earl Warren's implicit intent in fashioning rules to prevent juries from hearing defendants' statements that are not "involuntary in traditional terms" was to place all criminals on an equal level in dealing with law enforcement:

- The hardened recidivist offender whose experience with the system gives him a "cops get nothing for nothing" attitude. He won't tell the police anything unless he gets a deal in return.
- The socially secure person (wealthy or knowledgeable) who is already aware of his rights to remain silent and to have a lawyer and is able to claim those rights without prompting.
- The socially insecure person (poor or unknowledgeable) who, ignorant of his rights, will *voluntarily* confess for all of the reasons we have already discussed.

Since the first two categories of criminals may be able to avoid the siren lure of confession unassisted, Warren contended that the third category of criminals must be prevented from doing what they instinctively want to do (short, perhaps, of taping their mouths shut). The *Miranda* warnings must therefore be given, and once a suspect indicates in the least way that he doesn't want to talk or that he wants a lawyer, all questioning must stop. Although the suspect may waive or relinquish any of the *Miranda* rights even after they have been invoked, the prosecution has a heavy burden of showing that any waiver was voluntary and untainted by police conduct. To return to the smoking analogy, it would be as if the government required an affirmation by everyone seeking to buy a pack of cigarettes that he or she has read the surgeon general's warning, has understood that warning, and has nevertheless decided to make the purchase. Furthermore, before he could make the sale, the merchant would have to demonstrate that the customer's decision was unaffected by tobacco company advertising or by any other form of persuasion. (To those who think that this analogy makes trivial the important issues at stake, I ask, Why do you elevate the right of a smoker to harm his own body over the right of a criminal to voluntarily confess his crime?) To see how heavy some judges would make the "waiver" burden, we look to the Supreme Court of North Carolina.

Willie Butler was convicted of kidnapping, armed robbery, and felonious assault for the holdup of a Goldsboro, North Carolina, gas station, which left the attendant paralyzed. Arrested by the FBI in New York on a fugitive warrant, Butler was orally advised of his *Miranda* rights and then, while at the FBI office, was given an "advice of rights" form to read and sign. Butler told the agents that he understood his rights but would not sign; he said, "I will talk to you but I am not signing any form." He did not ask for a lawyer, and he freely told the agents about the robbery. Nevertheless, the North Carolina Supreme Court reversed his conviction because he had never *specifically* waived his right to counsel by saying, for example, "I hereby don't want a lawyer," or words of similar import.

The United States Supreme Court, on a close five to three vote (one justice did not participate in the decision), reversed and reinstated Butler's convictions. The Court held that Butler's actions clearly indicated a knowing and voluntary waiver and that an *explicit* statement of waiver was not needed. However, the dissenting justices strongly criticized the majority for permitting trial courts in similar circumstances "to construct inferences from ambiguous words and gestures." They argued that "*Miranda* requires that ambiguity be interpreted against" law enforcement. Again, the law enforcement officer was criticized by the dissenters not only for not doing everything he could to discourage the defendant from talking but apparently also for his failure to read the entrails of judicial precedent: "Had agent Martinez simply elicited a clear answer from Willie Butler to the question, 'Do you waive your right to a lawyer?' this journey through three courts would not have been necessary."

Of course, had the FBI agent used those words, Butler might have finally gotten the hint that he should not talk even though he wanted to, and perhaps another serious crime would have gone unpunished. On the other hand, had Butler still confessed in the face of the words suggested by dissenting justice William Brennan, there might have been a dispute as to whether Butler—who went through the eleventh grade—understood what was meant. Indeed, there are some who argue that since very few criminals of the third type discussed above—the socially insecure person ignorant of his rights—can understand the full import of the *Miranda* rights even when they *are* explained, *no confessions should be taken at all.* For example, a study conducted under the aegis of the *California Law Review* shows that only some 42 percent of adults tested "adequately" understood the warnings. Thus, highly respected liberal law professor Yale Kamisar has suggested that public defender lawyers be placed at every police station to advise all suspects upon arrest and to keep police from questioning them.

Willie Butler almost escaped justice because some appellate judges thought his decision to talk without first consulting a lawyer was not articulated with sufficient specificity. Thomas J. Innis also almost escaped justice, despite waivers that were clear and unambiguous, because some judges thought the police had made an unfair appeal to his conscience.

Innis was arrested for murder and armed robbery. His arrest was triggered by the complaint of Gerald Aubin, a Providence, Rhode Island, taxi driver. Aubin told the police that he had just been held up by a man with a sawed-off shotgun, and that he had let him off in an area near a school for handicapped children. The police were especially interested in Aubin's report because the body of another cab driver, killed by a shotgun blast to the back of the head earlier that week, had been found in a shallow grave the day before. While he was at the police station, Aubin saw the robber's picture on a bulletin board. He later fingered the same man from a different picture he picked out of a group of photographs presented to him.

Police searched the area where Innis had been let off. At 4:30 a.m., they saw him. He was unarmed. Innis was arrested and advised of his *Miranda* rights. In a few minutes, a police sergeant arrived. He too gave Innis the required warnings. A police captain showed up just after the sergeant, and he also repeated the *Miranda* litany. In response to this third set of warnings, Innis finally got the hint and said he wanted to speak to a lawyer. The captain told the other officers to take Innis to police headquarters, and he instructed them not to question or intimidate him.

During the ride downtown, two of the officers talked. This is how one of them, Joseph Gleckman, related it later in court:

> At this point, I was talking back and forth with Patrolman McKenna stating that I frequent this area while on patrol and there's a lot of handicapped children running around in this area, and God forbid one of them might find a weapon with shells and they might hurt themselves.
>
> **Q:** Who were you talking to?
> **A:** Patrolman McKenna.
> **Q:** Did you say anything to the suspect Innis?
> **A:** No, I didn't.

Innis overheard the conversation. "Turn around," he told them. "I'll show you where the weapon is." One of the officers radioed the captain, who met them where Innis had told them to stop. The captain *again* reminded Innis of his *Miranda* rights. Innis replied that he understood but that he "wanted to get the gun out of the way" because of the children. The shotgun was found under some rocks in a nearby field.

At his trial, Innis sought to have his statements and the shotgun excluded. The trial judge refused, noting that the officers' concern was "entirely understandable" and that Innis had voluntarily agreed to show them the gun. Innis was convicted. The Rhode Island Supreme Court, voting three to two, reversed. They reasoned that by telling the officers he wanted to speak to a lawyer, Innis had exercised his right to be left alone. The dialogue concerning the shotgun and the children, they contended (drawing an analogy from the so-called "Christian burial" speech in *Williams*), was merely a subtle attempt to coerce a confession. Recognizing that "most of the other evidence against the defendant was circumstantial in nature," they ruled that the prosecution should not benefit from "the improper remarks of Officer Gleckman."

Although the United States Supreme Court later reinstated Innis's conviction, the vote was again close, six to three. In a decision written by Justice Potter Stewart, the Court recognized that *Miranda's* prohibition of custodial interrogation applies to comments "reasonably likely to elicit an incriminating response" as well as to direct questioning, but that since there was nothing "to suggest that the officers were aware" that Innis "was peculiarly susceptible to an appeal to his conscience concerning the safety of handicapped children," there had been no violation.

Justice Thurgood Marshall, joined by Justice William Brennan, bitterly dissented:

> One can scarcely imagine a stronger appeal to the conscience of a suspect—*any* suspect—than the assertion that if the weapon is not found an innocent person will be hurt or killed. And not just any innocent person, but an innocent child—a little girl—a helpless, handicapped little girl on her way to school. The notion that such an appeal could not be expected to have any effect unless the suspect were known to have some special interest in the handicapped verges on the ludicrous. As a matter of fact, the appeal to a suspect to confess for the sake of others, to "display some evidence of decency and honor," is a classic interrogation technique.

In a separate opinion, Justice Stevens also objected to the reinstatement of Innis's conviction. He argued that the distinctions drawn by the majority were disingenuous:

> The difference between the approach required by a faithful adherence to *Miranda* and the stinted test applied by the Court today can be illustrated by comparing three different

ways in which Officer Gleckman could have communicated his fears about the possible dangers posed by the shotgun to handicapped children. He could have:

(1) directly asked Innis:

Will you please tell me where the shotgun is so we can protect handicapped schoolchildren from danger?

(2) announced to the other officers in the wagon:

If the man sitting in the back seat with me should decide to tell us where the gun is, we can protect handicapped children from danger.

or (3) stated to the other officers:

It would be too bad if a little handicapped girl would pick up the gun that this man left in the area and maybe kill herself.

In my opinion, all three of these statements should be considered interrogation because all three appear designed to elicit a response from anyone who in fact knew where the gun was located.

The comments of Justices Marshall and Stevens are instructive on two levels. First, was the murdered cab driver not *innocent*? Was *he* not entitled to life, and was *his* family not entitled to *his* love and companionship? And what about the safety, lives, and families of those who might be *future victims* if Innis were permitted to escape justice? It is interesting that the rights of victims or potential victims are rarely discussed by those who would tie the police to an etiquette well beyond the Marquis of Queensberry as a precondition to the admission of perfectly reliable evidence.

Second, I fail to see the harm in permitting the police to provide an avenue for voluntary confessions. In this regard, I agree with Justice Stevens that there is little difference between the three hypothetical statements. The appeals to "decency and honor" which Justice Marshall so decried are appropriate methods to "catch the conscience" of a suspect. Indeed, such appeals might even generate conscience formation in a person otherwise bereft of feeling. Dr. Theodor Reik has passionately described the underlying dynamics:

To the criminal, confession means that his conscience has acquired its voice. He becomes, through the spoken repetition, conscious of the significance of his deed. . . .

In his confession, the criminal has admitted his misdeed to the community, as the child once admitted his naughtiness to his real father or to his substitute. As the confession of the child unconsciously represents a new wooing for love, an attempt at regaining the lost object, the criminal shows in his confession his intention to reenter society by declaring himself deserving of punishment. The outsider is on his painful detour back to the family of man.

The *Miranda* exclusionary rule often blocks that return. In many instances, it and the search and seizure exclusionary rule permit those who are clearly guilty to avoid their rendezvous with justice.

The Insanity Defense

by Lee Coleman

John Hinckley's acquittal on grounds of insanity made us angry, but it also woke us up. Feelings of outrage and confusion over the insanity plea and courtroom psychiatry in general burst forth. After watching on television Hinckley's attempt to kill President Reagan on March 30, 1981, few people believed that either justice or common sense had prevailed when the jury brought in its verdict. What is more difficult to understand is how and why findings like this one continue to occur. How did psychiatry come to play a crucial role in criminal trials? Why do defense and prosecution psychiatrists often disagree drastically in their expert conclusions? What good, if any, does psychiatry do in our courts? To begin to answer these questions, we must first look at how the insanity defense operates.

Once the defense lawyer decides with the client to enter a plea of not guilty by reason of insanity (known as NGI, sometimes NGRI), the attorney calls in one or more psychiatrists to examine the defendant. Even though the psychiatrists may question the accused weeks or months after the act was committed, they are expected to determine exactly what the defendant was thinking during the moments surrounding the crime. Most particularly, did the accused know what he or she was doing was against the law? If so, was a choice made to commit the crime anyway, or was the behavior beyond the defendant's control? Was he or she driven to it by mental disorder?

Psychiatrists have no tests to reconstruct a past state of mind, but they nonetheless offer an opinion, because they are convinced that their "clinical skills" allow them to expertly determine questions of legal sanity. If they decide the defendant was legally insane at the moment of the crime, the defense lawyer has reason to go forward with an insanity plea. If they decide differently, the defense attorney may decide to start over by hiring another psychiatrist to examine the defendant. A psychiatrist who will reach the desired conclusions can usually be found. Neither judge nor jury learns of the prior psychiatrists, only of those the defense lawyer calls to testify that the defendant was legally insane at the moment of the crime.

If the judge or jury favors the defense psychiatrists' claims of legal insanity over the prosecution psychiatrists' claims of legal sanity, the defendant is found not guilty by reason of insanity and is then sent to a mental institution for an indefinite period of confinement, until at some later date he or she is released as "restored to sanity."

To avoid such an outcome, the prosecutor must try to convince the judge or jury that the defendant indeed understood the criminal nature of the act and also had the capacity to refrain from it but nonetheless chose to commit the crime. Faced with the experts for the defense, the prosecutor also hires one or more psychiatrists, who frequently reach the opposite conclusion: The accused knew right from wrong and had the capacity to refrain from committing the crime.

At the trial, the facts of what actually happened will be presented, but when it comes to whether the person is legally sane and responsible for his behavior, or legally insane and not responsible, the competing claims of the psychiatrists will predominate. Everyone will assume that the psychiatrist is the most qualified to determine such questions. Individual judges or jurors may have some skepticism about psychiatric testimony, but frequently courts are swayed by the very fact that psychiatrists testify as experts and are the only persons allowed to offer opinions on the defendant's innermost thoughts.

In the trial of John Hinckley, the prosecution had to prove beyond a reasonable doubt that Hinckley acted with free will, whereas in most states the defendant is presumed to be legally responsible until proven legally insane. Free will, or the capacity to control one's behavior, can never be proven scientifically, because it is a metaphysical concept rather than a scientific fact. Free will is an *idea*, not a tangible substance to be measured or "examined." To ask a prosecutor to prove that a crime was committed with free will is to ask the impossible. When this question becomes the focus of psychiatric testimony, a fiasco is all too likely.

What's Going Wrong?

Trials like John Hinckley's have at least raised public consciousness about courtroom psychiatry. Many people are angry about psychiatric testimony and feel basic reform is needed, but are unsure what is required. The leaders of forensic (legal) psychiatry agree that problems abound, but they certainly do not acknowledge that these problems stem from a lack 'of true scientific tools available to the psychiatrist. They argue instead that courtroom psychiatrists need *better training* in the skills that forensic psychiatry already has. Seymour Pollack, a leader in forensic psychiatry, put it this way in testimony before a California legislative committee investigating "the role of psychiatry in determining criminal responsibility."

> I would like to stress how necessary it is for there to be support by the state for training and educational programs in this field . . . because at the present time these skills are not taught nor are they developed by the average psychiatrist or psychologist . . . And that's one of the reasons we have such terrible results.[1]

If Pollack is correct, trials featuring the most highly qualified psychiatrists, rather than the average psychiatrist, should avoid "such terrible results." Yet the testimony of the best psychiatrists in forensic psychiatry does not differ from that of their less famous colleagues. The trial of Robert Kennedy's killer, Sirhan Sirhan, can serve as an example.

With no real question that Sirhan was the killer, a mental defense was entered on his behalf. His lawyers argued that when he killed Kennedy and wounded several others, on June 4, 1968, Sirhan was suffering from a mental disorder that prevented him from being capable of deliberately planning a murder. The featured witness for the defense was Bernard Diamond, professor of law and criminology at the University of California's prestigious Boalt Hall of Law, professor of psychiatry at the University of California Medical School in San Francisco, and one of the world's foremost forensic psychiatrists.

Diamond spared no effort. In an interview after the trial, he estimated that he had "worked with him [Sirhan] twenty to twenty-five hours."[2] In addition to talking with Sirhan, Diamond tried hypnosis and liquor in hopes of prying loose Sirhan's intent when he shot Kennedy. The results of these investigations led Diamond to conclude that Sirhan had trained himself to go into a hypnotic trance with the help of mirrors and candles. And these trances supposedly explained Sirhan's notebooks in which he had written "R.F.K. must die" and "Robert F. Kennedy must be assassinated before June 5, 1968."

How did the alleged trances relate to these death threats? The threats, Diamond asserted, came from Sirhan's *unconscious* mind, not his conscious mind. And Sirhan should not be held responsible for behavior that sprang directly from the unconscious mind. Diamond explained it this way:

> After going into a trance thinking of love and peace, he would emerge to find his notebook filled with incoherent threats of violence and assassination. He would have no recollection of having written anything but knew that it was his handwriting . . . In his unconscious mind there existed a plan for the fulfillment of his sick, paranoid hatred of Kennedy and all who might want to help the Jews. In his conscious mind there was no awareness of such a plan or that he, Sirhan, was to be the instrument of assassination.[3]

Yet despite Sirhan's unconscious impulses, Diamond claimed, Kennedy's death was still more a matter of terrible coincidence than a deliberate political assassination.

> Sirhan ended up half-drunk on gin—Tom Collinses—at the hotel late on the night of June 4, when Kennedy won the primary. By the least likely accident of all he blundered into an alcove lined with mirrors and wall lights, which trapped him into his dissociated state. A few more blunders took him by a circuitous route into that pantry shortly before Kennedy happened to come through.[4]

This was, supposedly, courtroom psychiatry at its "best." The great amount of time spent examining Sirhan and Diamond's impeccable credentials were just what the leaders of psychiatry said were necessary in every case.

Why *do* courtroom psychiatrists so frequently offer such farfetched testimony? Because psychiatrists do not have the tools to find out what an accused person was thinking at the time of the crime. The psychiatrist can and does talk to the defendant and sometimes reads information gathered by police. But when it comes to deciding whether at the moment of the crime the accused knew right from wrong, the psychiatrist can do this no better than anyone else. There are no tests to determine the past state of mind of another human being, and there is no expert way of distinguishing truth from lies. Psychologist William Winslade, in *The Insanity Plea*, put it this way:

> We ask the expert in this area, a psychiatrist, to rescue us from this troublesome area of judging our fellow citizens and their actions. And the psychiatrist has responded to this impossible request. He has obligingly provided us with his own confusion—no different from our own—but he presents it in an appealingly expert way, with special language and special tests to validate his special knowledge. Unfortunately, it takes more than tests and fancy language to create special, expert knowledge.[5]

Defining Insanity

The term *insanity* is used in the courtroom to mean something very different from what it has meant over the years, both medically and popularly. Medically, *insanity* used to refer to those symptoms that we now label *psychotic* or *schizophrenic*, such as delusions (irrational thoughts) or hallucinations. Today *insanity* is no longer a medical term. But it is still a legal term.

In about half the states *insanity* is legally defined as the inability to understand the wrongful or criminal nature of the act committed.[6] This use of the term emerged in 1843, when Daniel M'Naughten attempted to kill British prime minister Robert Peel. He did not succeed, but killed Peel's secretary instead. M'Naughten's attorney successfully argued that at the time of the shooting M'Naughten had a mental disorder that prevented him from understanding that his actions were wrong.[7] Although this was by no means the first time an "insanity" defense had been used in England, the trial was unusual for *the role of expert testimony* in determining the state of mind of the accused.[8] M'Naughten's lawyer heavily relied on the book *A Treatise on the Medical Jurisprudence of Insanity*, in which the American physician Isaac Ray argued that doctors should play a key role in any trial in which legal insanity was an issue.[9] Before this time, the testimony of eyewitnesses or acquaintances was the principal basis upon which a judge or jury rendered a verdict.

Today the insanity defense relies almost exclusively on the testimony of psychiatrists. When they offer opinions about whether or not an accused person knew right from wrong at the time of the crime, this is called the M'Naughten test, and in many states this "right-wrong" test still defines legal insanity. For many years psychiatrists expressed discomfort with this test, saying that it failed to take account of unconscious and irresistible impulses. What they wanted was a new test, and they got it in 1954 when a federal court expanded the definition of legal insanity.

The "Product" Test

Psychiatrists pointed out that the "right-wrong" test for insanity was hopelessly out of date because the psychoanalytic revolution had deepened our understanding of how the mind works. Freud had demonstrated that behavior was not merely the result of conscious decisions based on rational thinking. The unconscious mind was a powerful, if hidden, influence on behavior. Furthermore, it was the ability to understand how the unconscious workings of the mind controlled a person's behavior, especially deviant behavior, that set the psychiatrist apart from everyone else. It was here that the psychiatrist could make a real contribution to an insanity trial. If a psychiatrist's talents were wasted on merely determining whether a person knew right from wrong, both science and justice would suffer. A person might know right from wrong but be unable, because of mental disorder, to control his or her specific acts.

A well-known authority described the general discontent psychiatrists felt with the M'Naughten "right-wrong" test of insanity.

We have reached a place where there is a consensus that the M'Naughten test of responsibility in the defense of insanity is no longer useful. The Royal Commission on Capital Punishment conceded that "the test of responsibility laid down by the M'Naughten rule is so defective that the law on the subject ought to be changed." In this country [U.S.] the Criminal Law Advisory Committee of the American Law Institute has likewise viewed the M'Naughten rule. To these views now expressed from the side of the law may be added an almost unanimous expression of dissatisfaction on the part of the profession of psychiatry.[10]

Psychiatry was quite capable of bringing "modern thinking" into the insanity trial if only the legal definition of insanity were modernized. Let the psychiatrist inform the court not only whether the defendant knew the act was wrong but also whether the defendant was capable of restraint; then the confusion would end.

In 1954 this reasoning culminated in the *Durham* rule, written by the highly respected federal appeals court judge David Bazelon.[11] It said, "An accused is not criminally responsible if his unlawful act was *the product* of mental disease or mental defect" (emphasis added). A person could, in other words, know his behavior was wrong yet still be driven to it by mental disorder.

This ruling was what the psychiatrists had long been waiting for. What made them particularly happy was the key phrase "the product of mental disease." Far from restricting the psychiatrists, as the M'Naughten test had done, this phrase allowed them much greater leeway to testify about unconscious forces acting at the time of the crime. These hidden forces were, of course, precisely why psychiatrists were needed in trials on legal insanity. Not surprisingly, the response from the psychiatric community was enthusiastic. Law professor Alexander Brooks explains,

> Articles were written in both psychiatric and legal journals by psychiatrists unstintingly praising the new test as a revelation of enlightenment. . . . Karl Menninger, for instance, acclaimed the *Durham* rule as "more revolutionary in its total effect than the Supreme Court decision regarding segregation." Judge Bazelon was awarded a certificate of commendation by the American Psychiatric Association.[12]

Despite this early enthusiasm, the *Durham* rule was not widely accepted by the courts. Other judges quickly realized that instead of bringing psychiatric testimony under control, *Durham* only allowed it to get out of hand. If *all* behavior was, as Freud taught, the result of predetermined unconscious forces, it was easy for any crime to be interpreted as the result of hidden mental forces and thus the "product" of mental disorder. The result of *Durham* was a huge increase in findings of legal insanity in the District of Columbia, something no one really desired.

Irresistible Impulse Test

Lawyers and leading forensic psychiatrists accepted the unworkability of the *Durham* rule and tried to find another definition of legal insanity. In 1962 the American Law Institute (ALI) came up with this:

> A person is not responsible for criminal conduct if at the time of such conduct as a result of mental disease or defect, he lacked substantial capacity either to appreciate the criminality (wrongfulness) of his conduct or to conform his conduct to the requirements of law.[13]

This definition, commonly called the ALI test, was supposed to avoid the ambiguities of the *Durham* rule. Psychiatrists would now determine whether the defendant either was incapable of knowing right from wrong, *or could not help himself* and was compelled to commit the crime because of mental illness. This was the "irresistible impulse" test, in truth no different from the "product of mental disease" test of *Durham*. In 1972 the Supreme Court gave the new definition of legal insanity its stamp of approval, setting the stage for its eventual adoption by the states.[14]

Have these changes in the legal definition of insanity made any real difference in what happens when psychiatrists are called to testify? By general agreement, they have not. Insanity trials still come down to a battle between expert opinions that seem more the product of speculation than science. A recent case in a state that accepts the ALI test for legal insanity will illustrate this point.[15]

A well-established psychiatrist testified that when the accused, "Tony," stabbed and killed his wife, he was temporarily insane. The wife had threatened to leave Tony many times, and he had threatened to kill her rather than let her go. These threats had worked in the past, but this time she was determined to leave. As she packed her things, he stabbed her repeatedly until she died. After a neighbor alerted the police, Tony confessed to the crime in a coherent and rational manner. He did not appear delusional or out of touch with reality in any way, either to the police or to his co-workers, friends, and neighbors.

The psychiatrist testifying for the defense nevertheless explained that the threatened loss of his wife caused Tony to experience a temporary loss of contact with reality. The psychiatrist called this a dissociative reaction. While in this state Tony killed his wife; after the deed he immediately returned to reality.

When he was later questioned by cross-examination, the psychiatrist made the claim that Tony remained sane until one second before he made the first stab wound. Then, he remained insane until one second after he made the last stab wound. Then he regained his sanity and has been lucid ever since.

For most people, common sense alone dictates that we reject such fanciful speculations. Yet the fact remains that incredible psychiatric testimony of this sort is not at all unusual, and in this case Tony was pronounced legally insane by the judge. Once again, William Winslade, in *The Insanity Plea*, explains in part why this testimony occurs:

> When psychiatrists are not allowed to testify about whether or not the defendant actually understood what he was doing, they begin to testify about whether he had the capacity to understand what he was doing. If that is forbidden, they start testifying about whether he had the capacity to intend harm. The focus of their testimony changes slightly, but the testimony is no more precise, no less misleading, and no more likely to avoid injustice.[16]

The Hidden Purpose of the Insanity Defense

Despite our difficulties with the insanity defense, it continues, for it serves an unspoken function. The insanity defense exists not to excuse the mentally disordered offender from criminal responsibility, as legal theory teaches, but to make all of us feel safer. The irrational offender frightens us more than the rational offender; we have therefore made provisions whereby certain offenders, labeled legally insane, are sent to a mental institution rather than to a prison. We assume that psychiatrists at the mental hospital will treat the person until he is "sane" once more and no longer dangerous. In essence, we rely on the insanity defense not because we wish to excuse some offenders, but because we believe it offers us, through the role of the psychiatrists, better protection from future crimes than an ordinary prison sentence offers.

This conclusion is admittedly a speculation, but it is the result of listening to people's reactions when I recommend that all criminal offenders, even those suffering from mental disorders, be given determinate (fixed) rather than indeterminate sentences. I recommend that offenders be released at the expiration of this definite sentence, with no opportunity for society to extend confinement on the basis of alleged dangerousness. It is this recommendation, rather than my call for a ban on psychiatric testimony, that many people find frightening. They respond, "What if the offender is still dangerous?" I then remind them that neither psychiatrists nor anyone else can tell who is still dangerous, so the sentence should be based on what the offender *has done*, not on what he *might do*.

At this point a crucial thing happens. Despite my arguments about the lack of any way to predict dangerousness, listeners *nonetheless want psychiatric evaluations to continue.* In one way or another they say, "Well, there must be *some* way." Or, "Probably no one can do it any better than the psychiatrists." Or, "We can't simply release insane killers just because a definite sentence has expired."

Although we have to some extent succumbed to emotion in the case of ordinary (legally sane) offenders, and adopted indeterminate sentences for them too, the fear of adopting a policy of definite release is far greater in the case of legally insane offenders. This special fear of the "mad killer" prompts us to retain the insanity defense, a device that seems to guarantee us protection from the irrational criminal.

Safety Through Psychiatry

To win release from the mental hospital, a legally insane offender must go through a second sanity trial. Now it is the state's attorney who uses psychiatric testimony to argue that the person is very sick. The inmate is, in fact, dangerous and must not be released. The defense lawyer counters with psychiatrists who say the person is restored to sanity and is no longer dangerous.

The outcomes of these trials are varied. By relying on psychiatric pronouncements on dangerousness, instead of passing sentences based on the seriousness of the crime committed, courts may release a murderer after just a few months or perhaps a year or two.[17] Meanwhile, the same courts may confine for much longer terms other offenders whose crimes did not involve death or bodily injury. Our reliance on psychiatry is thus hardly making us safer.

Let us consider the record in New York state, for example. Murderers found legally insane between 1965 and 1976 were released, on the average, in less than eighteen months. One murderer spent just *one day* in the hospital, whereas another person whose crime was possession of a weapon was held nearly two and a half years.[18] In New Jersey, murderers found insane were released in just two years, on the average.[19]

The root cause of this injustice is the fact that psychiatric speculations on "dangerousness" are the determining factor in how long the person is held. This practice leads to situations that violate common decency and justice.

An excellent example is Thomas Vanda, a man who profited from the insanity defense and may one day write a book about it. He has already written a letter on the subject, and demonstrated considerable knowledge of its subtleties. In 1971, Vanda murdered a fifteen-year-old girl, but was found not guilty by reason of insanity and sent to a mental institution. Released only nine months later, he was subsequently accused of another murder, the fatal stabbing of twenty-five-year-old Marguerite Bowers. While in custody, he sent a letter to a friend who was also in jail on charges of murder. Vanda entitled his letter "How to beat a murder rap by insanity."[20]

1. Get a psychiatric examination such as: "inkblot test" and come up with some way out things to say as to what those inkblots look like to you.

2. Tell doctors you are hearing voices and what those voices were saying to you, such as, say those voices told you to do your crime.

3. Make it look convincing. Do not give any indication that you are faking.

4. Act crazy in front of the staff.

Vanda even offered his friend some examples of how to carry it off.

1. Say the inkblots look like two men having sex with each other.
2. Tell doctors the voices say to break out in hysterical laughter.
Then break out in hysterical laughter.
3. Masturbate in front of the staff members.

Vanda was pleading legal insanity for the second offense and Edward Keller, chief of Chicago's Cook County Psychiatric Institute, had already concluded that Vanda was legally insane. When Vanda's letter was discovered, Keller was asked if this would change his opinion. The letter, the doctor responded, was no cause for altering his earlier finding.[21]

Events that took place on Thanksgiving Day 1976 offer yet another example. On that day, a white New York police officer, Robert Torsney, shot and killed black fifteen-year-old Randolph Evans. Evans was not armed. Charged with murder, Torsney entered a plea of not guilty by reason of insanity, claiming that at the moment of the crime he blacked out. Defense psychiatrists then testified that Torsney had been suddenly overtaken by an epileptic seizure. They said that epilepsy of the psychomotor type predisposes one to violence, a claim with no scientific basis.[22] Torsney, moreover, had no previous history of epilepsy. Nevertheless, the all-white jury accepted the story. Found not guilty by reason of insanity on November 26, 1976, Torsney was sent to the Creedmoor Psychiatric Center in Queens. After one year, he was allowed to spend most of his nights and weekends at his nearby home. By July 1978, after eighteen months, he was released. The doctors at Creedmoor never found any evidence of epilepsy, either on the night Torsney killed Randolph Evans or at any other time. They declared that Torsney was no longer dangerous. According to law, he therefore had to be released.[23]

The case of Clara Gordon illustrates just how far justice may be perverted by our current policies. She confessed to killing Sharon Reid by stabbing her sixteen times. Two out of three psychiatrists testified that Gordon was insane at the time of the crime, and Judge Kenneth Wendt of the Circuit Court of Cook County found her not guilty by reason of insanity. Sent to Chicago's Reed Mental Health

Center, Gordon was observed by a psychiatrist, who decided she was no longer dangerous. After only one week of confinement, she was released.[24]

We have no national statistics on how often these things happen, but the New York and New Jersey studies indicate that murderers found insane may be released from a mental institution in a year or two—a much shorter time than they would have spent in prison. Because psychiatry has officially proclaimed its inability to predict dangerousness, it is a cruel hoax on society to release murderers on the word of a psychiatrist. A confinement of a year or two, moreover, hardly seems adequate punishment for a person who has brought to an end the life of another.

It is equally unfair when nonviolent offenders found legally insane are locked up until a psychiatrist declares them safe. These persons may remain locked up for years.

Psychiatry Responds

The Hinckley verdict was an embarrassment to psychiatry, for the kind of courtroom speculations that usually go unnoticed were brought before the entire nation. Forced to save face, the American Psychiatric Association (APA) decided to issue a special report on the insanity defense.[25] A brief look at its recommendations will help us decide whether the leaders of psychiatry can get us out of our current mess, or whether we should look elsewhere for truly progressive reform.

The APA's first recommendation is that we return to the M'Naughten "right-wrong" test for legal insanity, and abandon the attempt to decide if a defendant had the "capacity to conform" his or her behavior:

> Many psychiatrists . . . believe that psychiatric information relevant to determining whether a defendant understood the nature of the act, and whether he appreciated its wrongfulness, is more reliable and has a stronger scientific basis than . . . psychiatric information relevant to whether a defendant was able to control his behavior. The line between an irresistible impulse and an impulse not resisted is probably no sharper than that between twilight and dusk.[26]

The leaders of psychiatry are thus saying that their recommendation *during the past one hundred years,* right up to the Hinckley trial, was misguided, even though it was the lobbying of psychiatrists that convinced lawmakers and judges to abandon the M'Naughten "right-wrong" test in favor of the "irresistible impulse" test. "Get rid of M'Naughten," psychiatry said, "and the insanity defense will work fine." Now psychiatry says, "Give us back M'Naughten and the insanity defense will work fine." What official psychiatry will not say, of course, is that *any* test that relies on psychiatric testimony about *anything* will continue to produce the same courtroom circus.

The other major recommendation of the APA report concerns what should happen to the person found legally insane. The APA suggests conditional release, or parole, when there is "a coherent and well structured plan of supervision, management, and treatment" available, one that is "highly likely to guarantee public safety" and that includes "a procedure to reconfine the insanity acquittee who fails to meet the expectations of the plan."[27] This plan, already adopted in Oregon and highly touted in the media, would offer us the worst of both worlds. That is, release would still be based on unreliable predictions of dangerousness, and once released these persons would be subjected to the tyranny of unchecked psychiatric power. They would be forced to take powerful tranquilizing drugs indefinitely and to face reconfinement whenever they were "uncooperative," or whenever they would not "accept treatment." Society, moreover, would receive violent offenders back into its midst because a "treatment plan" was felt to justify release, not because a sentence fitting the crime had been completed. Once again the advice of psychiatry will lead us down the path of injustice and confusion. Something very different is clearly needed.

Ending the Insanity Defense

Experts from psychiatry and law have failed to define adequately the relationship between these two professions because they fail to acknowledge the hypocrisies of the insanity defense. In summary, these hypocrisies are:

1. The justification for the insanity defense—that legally insane persons should neither be blamed nor punished: These persons *are* punished, by incarceration in a mental institution.

2. The mode of determining legal insanity—through psychiatric testimony: The psychiatrist has no special way of telling what a person was thinking, or of evaluating capacity, when that person committed a crime.

3. The reliance on psychiatric predictions to protect society: Indefinite psychiatric confinement is unjust, both to society when the confinement is too short for the crime committed, and to the offender when the confinement is too long for the crime; furthermore, confinement based on psychiatric guesswork about dangerousness neither protects society nor allows real therapy for criminals who happen to have psychological problems.

Abolition of the insanity defense would *not* mean that courtroom decisions on criminal intent (*mens rea*) would be eliminated from the criminal law, as is often assumed by even highly sophisticated legal scholars. On the contrary, courts of law will inevitably need to decide the intent behind many kinds of crime. Negligent homicide secondary to drunk driving, for example, is hardly the same crime as premeditated murder, even though both are major crimes and call for serious punishment. But in determining what, if any, criminal intent was present, and in deciding punishment, our judges and juries need no help from psychiatrists.

How should intent be determined? A decision on intent should be based on the factual evidence surrounding the crime. For the evidence surrounding a crime is really no different from the evidence surrounding our daily lives. And each day we make many inferences about a person's mental intent. We do so by judging what he does and how he does it, what he says and how he says it. If, for example, I am standing in the checkout line at the supermarket and I feel myself pushed from the side, I will turn and by virtue of what I see and hear I will decide the intent of the person who has bumped me. If the person apologizes and motions me to go ahead, I conclude that it was an accident. If the person insists that he or she was ahead of me, or simply looks straight ahead and inches forward, I conclude something very different. I may be wrong in my conclusion, or someone else standing in line may have seen and heard the same things and put the information together differently. But neither of us is an "expert," even if one of us happens to be a psychiatrist.

We make judgments like this every day outside the courtroom, and there is no reason that a judge or jury cannot do the same inside the courtroom. Although the stakes are much higher in court, the fact remains that we have no better way to determine mental intent other than by simply examining the factual evidence concerning what the accused person did and how he or she did it. The judge and jury are already given responsibility to be the "trier of fact," that is, to make the final decisions. Our current laws, thus, say that expert testimony is not the final word in deciding the issue of mental intent. The judge or jury gives expert testimony a little weight or a lot, depending on how credible the testimony seems. If we were to eliminate psychiatric testimony, the task of the judge or jury would not be more difficult; rather it would be *easier* because the real evidence of mental intent—the behavior of the accused person—would no longer be confused by psychiatric speculation.

If we exclude psychiatry, how do we deal with those offenders who, defense lawyers say, committed their crimes while in a state of major mental breakdown? There would be, first of all, no recourse to legal insanity as a criminal defense. During the trial, the defense attorney could present evidence showing that the defendant was in a compromised mental state at the time of the crime. The evidence, however, could not include the testimony of psychiatrists or psychologists. Instead, witnesses present during the crime or in contact with the defendant around the time of the crime could testify about what they saw and heard. Any evidence of the defendant's bizarre or irrational behavior would be the subject of proper testimony.

On the basis of this, the judge or jury might decide that even though the individual was seriously impaired, he or she nonetheless intended to kill the victim and is therefore guilty of murder. In another case, the judge or jury might conclude that the defendant's irrational behavior shows he or she had no intent to kill. The person would be guilty of manslaughter, not murder.

The approach to punishment would also be different. No offenders would be indefinitely incarcerated, as they are now. Instead they would be given the definite sentence assigned to their crime, *no more and no less than the person with no mental disorder*. When their sentences expire, they would be released, with no possibility of confinement being extended because of alleged dangerousness. Neither could persons be released sooner than the release date because of alleged restoration of sanity, or because of any "plan of supervision, management, and treatment."

This requires of society the courage to admit that while the plan appears to be "taking a chance" on the mentally disordered offender, definite sentences for all offenders are no more risky (and probably less risky) than what we do now. All along we have been "taking a chance" on psychiatry, believing that its expert examinations would protect us. If we have lived with this false prophecy for so long, certainly we can do as well and probably better without it.

1. California State Senate, and California State Assembly, Joint Committee on Revision of the Penal Code, *Hearings on the Role of Psychiatry in Determining Criminal Responsibility*, April 11 and April 12, 1979, pp. 24–25.

2. T. George Harris, "Psychiatrist Bernard L. Diamond Tells of the Bizarre Paranoia He Found in Sirhan B. Sirhan: A Conversation with T. George Harris," *Psychology Today*, September 1969, p. 48.

3. *Ibid.*, p. 50.

4. *Ibid.*

5. William Winslade, *The Insanity Plea: The Uses and Abuses of the Insanity Defense* (New York: Charles Scribner's, 1983), p. 3.

6. For an overview of the different approaches to defining legal insanity, see Alexander Brooks, *Law, Psychiatry, and the Mental Health System* (Boston: Little, Brown, 1974), pp. 111–319.

7. For a description of this trial, by a leading advocate of psychiatric testimony, see Bernard Diamond, "Isaac Ray and the Trial of Daniel M'Naughten," *American Journal of Psychiatry* (February 1956), p. 651.

8. Anthony Platt and Bernard Diamond, "Origins of the 'Right and Wrong' Test of Criminal Responsibility and Its Subsequent Development in the United States: An Historical Survey," *California Law Review* 54 (1966), p. 1227.

9. Isaac Ray, *A Treatise on the Medical Jurisprudence of Insanity* (Boston: Little, Brown, 1838).

10. Philip Roche, *The Criminal Mind* (New York: Grove Press, 1958), pp. 176–177.

11. *Durham v. United States* 214 F.2d 862 (D.C. Cir. 1954).

12. Brooks, p. 177.

13. American Law Institute, *Model Penal Code* (1962).

14. *United States v. Brawner* 471 F.2d 979 (D.C. Cir. 1972).

15. Court-martial of "Tony," U.S. Air Force File #8019D6–508.

16. Winslade, p. 200.

17. For data on length of incarceration see Henry Steadman, "Insanity Acquittals in New York State, 1965–1978," *American Journal of Psychiatry* 137 (March 1980): 321. Also Anne Singer, "Insanity Acquittals in the Seventies: Observations and Empirical Analysis of One Jurisdiction," *Mental Disability Law Reporter* 2 (1978): 406.

18. Steadman, p. 325.

19. Singer, p. 407.

20. *Chicago Tribune*, April 18, 1978.

21. *Ibid.*

22. Lee Coleman, "Perspectives on the Medical Research of Violence," *American Journal of Orthopsychiatry* 44 (October 1974), p. 675. See also Alan Scheflin and Edward Opton, *The Mind Manipulators* (New York: Paddington Press, 1978), pp. 266–324, for a critical assessment of psychosurgical procedures sometimes advocated for alleged "violence-producing epilepsy." See also Antonio V. Delgado-Escueta, *et al.*, "Special Report: The Nature of Aggression during Epileptic Seizures," *New England Journal of Medicine* 305 (September 17, 1981), p. 711.

23. Torsney's case has now been extensively covered. See Susan Sheehan, "The Patient: Part I—Creedmoor Psychiatric Center," *The New Yorker* May 25, 1979, p. 75. See also Winslade, pp. 133–158.

24. *National Enquirer,* December 9, 1977.

25. American Psychiatric Association Insanity Work Group, *Statement on the Insanity Defense* (Washington, D.C.: American Psychiatric Association, 1982).

26. *Ibid.*, p. 11.

27. *Ibid.*, p. 16.

Ten Deadly Myths About Crime and Punishment in the U.S.

by Charles H. Logan and John J. DiIulio, Jr.

False ideas can have tragic consequences. For the last quarter-century, a network of anti-incarceration, pro-prisoner analysts, activists, lawyers, lobbyists, journalists, and judges has perpetuated a number of false ideas about crime and punishment in the United States. For average law-abiding American citizens, if not for predatory street criminals and elite penal reformers, the consequences of these false ideas have been quite tragic indeed. As these ideas have been carved into federal, state, and local penal codes, they have succeeded in making it easier for the criminals to hit, rape, rob, burglarize, deal drugs, and murder with impunity. Worse, they have succeeded in concentrating such criminal mischief in economically distressed inner-city neighborhoods, inviting the criminal predators of these areas to repeatedly victimize their struggling underclass neighbors.

In this essay, we propose to identify and rebut ten deadly ideas about crime and punishment in the United States. Before we do so, however, three cautions are in order.

First, we refer to these ideas as "myths." In *The American Heritage Dictionary*, myth is defined in four ways, including a "fiction or half-truth, especially one that forms part of the ideology of a society"; for example, "the myth of racial superiority." The false ideas about crime and punishment in the United States that we wish to challenge are myths in that sense. As we will show, in some cases the ideas are flatly untrue; in other cases, they are more or less skillful, more or less well-publicized exaggerations of half-truths. But, in all cases, they are byproducts of an ideological vision in which punishing all save the most vicious chronic criminals is considered either morally illegitimate, or socially counterproductive, or both. For the purposes of the present essay we shall confine ourselves to the discussion of ten particular myths about crime and punishment in the United States, driving our points through the gaping empirical and other

156

holes in each of them, and suggesting what a truer, or at least a more balanced, vision of the realities in question might be.

Second, our list of ten is by no means exhaustive. There are other myths that could as easily come in for critical scrutiny, such as the myth that building new prisons encourages the courts to fill them up, while a moratorium on prison construction will prevent that outcome. Tempted though we are to try and clean up each and every myth, data availability, interpretive range, and space have limited us to rounding up the ten "worst offenders" below.

Third, we do not believe that most of those who have perpetrated these myths have done so with any sort of malicious intent. Instead, we believe that their intentions have been good, but that they have been blinded by ideology to the connection between the false ideas they have pushed, and the dire human and financial consequences that have resulted.

Myth One: *Crime in the United States is caused by poverty, chronic unemployment, and other socio-economic factors.*

Many academic criminologists, most of whom are sociologists, believe that capitalism produces pockets of poverty, inequality, and unemployment, which then foster crime. The solution, they believe, is government intervention to provide jobs, stimulate the economy, and reduce poverty and other social ills. There certainly is a correlation between the geography of crime and the geography of certain socio-economic factors, but to interpret the correlation as evidence that poverty causes crime is to get it just about backwards.

As James K. Stewart, former Director of the National Institute of Justice, has pointed out, inner city areas where crime is rampant have tremendous potential for economic growth, given their infrastructure of railways, highways, electric power, water systems, and large supply of available labor.[1] There is every reason for these areas to be wealthy and, indeed, many of them have been rich in the past. But crime takes a terrible toll on physical, fiscal, and human capital, making it difficult to accumulate wealth and break out of the cycle of poverty. Criminals steal and destroy property, drive away customers and investors, reduce property values, and depreciate the quality of life in a neighborhood. Businesses close and working families move away, leaving behind a vacuum of opportunity. As Stewart says, crime "is the ultimate tax on enterprise . . . . The natural dynamic of the marketplace cannot assert itself when a local economy is regulated by crime."[2] What these areas need most from government is not economic intervention but physical protection and security. The struggling inner-city dwellers whom sociologist William Julius Wilson has dubbed "the truly disadvantaged" deserve greater protection from their truly deviant neighbors.

People who are poor, uneducated, unskilled, and unemployed may need and deserve help, but not because of their alleged propensity toward crime. In high crime urban areas, most poor people do not commit serious crimes. Fighting poverty and other problems only where, when, and because they are associated with crime would be an injustice to those who are neediest. It also would not succeed; that was the lesson of the 1960s and '70s, when the Great Society and its massive War on Poverty stemmed neither inner-city poverty nor crime.[3]

Economists, like sociologists, see a relation between economic conditions and crime, but the connection they make is much more straightforward. They see criminal behavior, like all behavior, as a rational response to incentives and opportunities. Statistical analyses have provided only mixed and limited evidence that levels of arrest and imprisonment may have deterrent effects, but as a matter of both theory and common sense, the belief that criminal behavior is responsive to reward and punishment has considerable strength.

Crime rates rose during the '60s and early '70s, then fell during the '80s. In contrast, imprisonment rates as a percentage of crimes fell during the '60s and early '70s, then rose during the '80s.[4] A deterrence-minded economist looking at these mirrored trends would say that crime rose and fell in response to its expected cost in terms of punishment.[5] An interpretation more favored by sociologists is that crime rose and fell as the "baby boom" cohort of young men in the population moved through their most crime-prone years. Economist Bruce Benson notes, however, that this "alternative" interpretation still requires some further explanation of why it is that young men are more prone to commit crimes. He provides an economist's answer: the opportunity costs of crime are lower for this group than for others. "Wages for young people are low, and their unemployment is always substantially higher than for the older population. In addition, punishment for young criminals tends to be less severe, particularly for those under eighteen who are prosecuted as juveniles. Even for those over 18, punishment may be less severe in a relative sense."[6]

Myth Two: *In the 1980s, the U.S. enacted all sorts of "get tough on crime" legislation and went on an incarceration binge.*

Prison populations have risen sharply over the last decade; that much is true. The myth is that this is due to an unprecedented and purely political wave of punitivity sweeping the nation, as epitomized by the War on Drugs and by legislative demands for longer and mandatory sentences. Several elements of this myth are shattered by a meticulous and authoritative article published recently [1991] in *Science* by Patrick A. Langan, a statistician at the Bureau of Justice Statistics.[7]

Langan examined the tremendous increase in state prison populations from 1973 to 1986. He determined that the growth was due to increases in prison admissions, rather than to (alleged but nonexistent) increases in sentence length or time served. He estimated that about 20 percent of the growth in admissions could be accounted for by demographic shifts in age and race. Increases in crime were offset by decreases in the probability of arrest, with the result that combined changes in crime and arrest rates accounted for only 9 percent of admissions growth. Increased drug arrests and imprisonments contributed only 8 percent.[8] By far the strongest determinant, explaining 51 percent of growth in prison admissions, was an increase in the post-arrest probabilities of conviction and incarceration.[9] Prosecutors convicted more felons, judges imposed more prison sentences, and more violators of probation or parole were sent or returned to prison. The data suggest that the system may have gotten more efficient but not harsher.

A column in the *Washington Post* captures well the form and spirit of the "imprisonment binge" myth.[10] In "The Great American Lockup," Franklin E. Zimring, a professor of law at Berkeley, claims that we are more punitive now than ever before in history, that the rising tide of imprisonment is a matter of over-zealous policy rather than a response to need, and that we must come to our senses and reverse an essentially irrational imprisonment policy.

When Professor Zimring says that we are experiencing a "100-

year peak in rates of imprisonment," he does not inform the reader that this is true only when you measure imprisonment on a crude per capita basis. If, however, you wish to describe the *punitivity* of our imprisonment rate, you need to measure the amount of imprisonment relative to the number of crimes for which people may be sent to prison. To get an even more complete measure of punitivity, you should multiply this probability of imprisonment by the length of time served. When just such an index is examined for all the years in which it is available, 1960 through 1986, it becomes clear that we have not been marching steadily forward to an all-time high in punitivity. Instead, this index of "expected days of imprisonment" fell steadily from its high in 1959 (93 days) to about one-seventh of that figure in 1975 (14 days). From 1975 through 1986 it returned to about one-fifth (19 days) of its 1960 level.[11] Even if we ignore the factor of time served and look only at prison commitments divided by crimes, we see much the same pattern. In 1960 there were 62 prison commitments per 1,000 Uniform Crime Index offenses; that number fell to 23 in 1970, remained relatively stable during the 1970s, then climbed from 25 back to 62 between 1980 and 1989.[12]

Thus, when we look at imprisonment per crime rather than per capita, and over 30 rather than 10 years, we see that our punishment level is not rocketing to a new high but recovering from a plunge. The myth of the imprisonment binge requires that we focus only on punishment and not on crime, and that we ignore all data prior to about 1980.

Myth Three: *Our prisons hold large numbers of petty offenders who should not be there.*

Tom Wicker, writing in *The New York Times*, asks: "Why does our nation spend such an exorbitant amount of money each year to warehouse petty criminals?"[13] He takes his question, and its underlying assumption, from a study by the National Council on Crime and Delinquency (NCCD), which he summarizes as finding "that 80 percent of those going to prison are not serious or violent criminals but are guilty of low-level offenses: minor parole violations, property, drug and public disorder crimes." Neither Wicker's account nor the NCCD's own summary, however, is supported by the data.[14]

The NCCD study involved interviews with 154 incoming prisoners in three states.[15] Based primarily on "facts" related by these new convicts, their crimes were classified as "petty," "medium serious," "serious," or "very serious." While the NCCD claims in its summary that the "vast majority of inmates are sentenced for petty crimes," we discover in the body of the report that "inmates" refers to just the entering cohort and not all inmates, that "vast majority" refers to 52.6 percent, and that "petty crimes" refers to acts that most Americans believe it is appropriate to punish by some period of incarceration.

Since more serious offenders receive longer sentences (and therefore accumulate in prison), the profile of incoming offenders differs significantly from that of the total population. The NCCD study is based on this distinction, but obscures it by referring always to "inmates," rather than "entering inmates."

A careful reader will find buried in the NCCD report sufficient information to calculate that 25.4 percent of the sample were men whose conviction offense was categorized by the researchers as "petty" but who revealed to the interviewers that they were high-rate offenders who were committed to a criminal lifestyle. If that fact was revealed also to the judge, in the form of a prior criminal record, it would have been a valid factor in sentencing. In any case, shouldn't these 25.4 percent have been added to the 47.4 percent whose crimes were in some degree "serious" (i.e., more than "petty")? Then the study would show that nearly three-quarters of new admissions are either serious or high-rate offenders. And that does not even count 21 percent of the sample who, while not identified as high-rate offenders, were described as having been on a "crime spree" at the time of their commitment offense.

The major fallacy in the NCCD study, however, was in concluding that certain property crimes are "petty"—and therefore undeserving of punishment by imprisonment—merely because they score low on a scale of "offense severity" developed in 1978. For example, burglary of a home resulting in a loss of $1,000 received a relatively low score on the severity scale, albeit higher than some descriptions of robbery, assault requiring medical treatment, bribery, auto theft for resale, embezzlement of $1,000, and many other offenses. A severity score, however, does not tell us what punishment is proper for any particular crime. In a recent survey, an overwhelming majority (81 percent) of Americans said that some time in jail or prison was a proper punishment for a residential burglary with a $1,000 loss. A clear majority (57 percent) thought jail or prison was appropriate even for a nonresidential burglary resulting in only a $10 loss.[16]

What the American public seems to understand, but NCCD does not, is that it is not just the amount of money or other material harm that makes a property crime like burglary or robbery serious rather than petty. It is the breach of an individual's security and the violation of those rights (to property and person) that form the foundation of a free society. Moreover, the NCCD dichotomy of crimes into "serious" and "petty" omits several factors that are very important both legally and morally. These include the number of counts and the offender's prior record, both of which the law recognizes as legitimate criteria in determining the culpability of offenders and the gravity of their acts.

Comprehensive national data from the Bureau of Justice Statistics show that U.S. prison populations consist overwhelmingly of violent or repeat offenders, with little change in demographic or offense characteristics from 1979 to 1986.[17] There may be individuals in prison who do not deserve to be there, and there may be some crimes now defined as felonies that ought to be redefined as misdemeanors or decriminalized altogether (some would argue this for drug crimes). But most people now in prison are not what most of the public would regard as "petty" offenders.

Myth Four: *Prisons are filthy, violence-ridden, and overcrowded human warehouses that function as schools of crime.*

There are two popular and competing images of American prisons. In one image, all or most prisons are hell holes. In the other image, all or most prisons are country clubs. Each image fits some prisons. But the vast majority of prisons in the U.S. today are neither hell holes nor country clubs. Instead, most American prisons do a pretty decent job of protecting inmates from each other, providing them with basic amenities (decent food, clean quarters, recreational equipment), offering them basic services (educational programs, work opportunities), and doing so in a way that ensures prisoners their basic constitutional and legal rights.

It is certainly true that most prison systems now hold more prisoners than they did a decade ago. The Federal Bureau of Prisons, for example, is operating at over 160 percent of its "design capacity";

that is, federal prisons house 60 percent more prisoners than they were designed to hold. When the federal prison agency's current multi-billion dollar expansion program is complete, it will still house about 40 percent more inmates than its buildings were designed to hold. That is by no means an ideal picture, and much the same picture can indeed be painted for dozens of jurisdictions around the country.

Contrary to the popular lore and propaganda, however, the consequences of prison crowding vary widely both within and between prisons systems, and in every careful empirical study of the subject, the widely-believed negative effects of crowding—violence, program disruption, health problems, and so on—are nowhere to be found. More broadly, several recent analyses have exploded the facile belief that contemporary prison conditions are unhealthy and harmful to inmates.

For example, in a study of over 180,000 housing units at 694 state prisons, the Bureau of Justice Statistics reported that the most overcrowded maximum-security prisons had a rate of homicide lower than that of moderately crowded prisons and about the same as that of prisons that were not crowded.[18] By the same token, a recent review of the prison crowding literature rightly concluded that, "despite familiar claims that crowded prisons have produced dramatic increases in prison violence, illness, and hostility, modern research has failed to establish any conclusive link between current prison spatial and social densities and these problems."[19] Even more compelling was the conclusion reached in a recent and exhaustive survey of the empirical literatures bearing on the "pains of imprisonment." This conclusion is worth quoting at some length:

> To date, the incarceration literature has been very much influenced by a pains of imprisonment model. This model views imprisonment as psychologically harmful. However, the empirical data we reviewed question the validity of the view that imprisonment is universally painful. Solitary confinement, under limiting and humane conditions, long-term imprisonment, and short-term detention fail to show detrimental effects. From a physical health standpoint, inmates appear more healthy than their community counterparts.[20]

Normally, those who for ideological or other reasons are inclined to paint a bleaker portrait of U.S. prison conditions than is justified by the facts respond to such evidence with countervailing anecdotes about a given prison or prison system. Perhaps because good news is no news, most media pundits lap up these unrepresentative prison horror stories and report on "powder keg conditions" behind bars. And when a prison riot occurs, it is now *de rigueur* for "experts" to ascribe the incident to "overcrowding" and other "underlying factors." For selfish and short-sighted reasons, some prison officials are all too willing to go along with the farce. It is easier for them to join in a Greek chorus about the evils of prison crowding that it is for them to admit that their own poor leadership and management were wholly or partially responsible for the trouble (as it so often is).

Indeed, recent comparative analyses of how different prison administrators have handled crowding and other problems under like conditions suggests that the quality of life behind bars is mainly a function of how prisons are organized, led, and managed.[21]

Overwhelmingly, the evidence shows that crowded prisons can be safe and humane, while prisons with serious problems often suffered the same or worse problems before they were crowded. In short, the quality of prison life varies mainly according to the quality of prison management, and the quality of prison life in the U.S. today is generally quite good.

More specifically, contrary to the widely-influential "nothing works" school of prison-based criminal rehabilitation programs, correctional administrators in a number of jurisdictions have instituted a variety of programs that serve as effective management tools, and appear to increase the probability that prisoners who participate in them will go straight upon their release. Recent empirical studies indicate that prisoners who participate in certain types of drug abuse counseling, and work-based programs may be less likely than otherwise comparable prisoners to return to prison once they return to the streets, as over 95 percent of all prisoners eventually do.[22]

Unfortunately, the recent spate of analyses that support this encouraging conclusion remain empirically thin, technically complex, and highly speculative. Moreover, each of the successful programs embodies a type of highly compassionate yet no-nonsense management approach that may be easier to describe in print than to emulate in practice or export widely. But, taken together with the more general facts and findings mentioned above, these studies—and the simple reality that most of those released from prison never return there—rebut the notion that most or all prisons in the U.S. are little better than crowded human warehouses that breed crime and other ills.

Myth Five: *The U.S. criminal justice system is shot through with racial discrimination.*

Most law-abiding Americans think that criminal sanctions are normally imposed on people who have been duly convicted of criminally violating the life, liberty, and property of their fellow citizens. Many critics, however, harbor a different, ostensibly more sophisticated view. They see prisons as instruments of "social control." To them, America is an oppressive, racist society, and prisons are a none-too-subtle way of subjugating the nation's poor and minority populations. Thus are roughly one of every nine adult African-American males in this country now under some form of correctional supervision—in prison, in jail, on probation, or on parole. And thus in the "conservative" 1980s was this "net of social control" cast over nearly a quarter of young African-American males in many jurisdictions.

There are at least three reasons why such race-based understandings of the U.S. criminal justice system are highly suspect at best. First, once one controls for socio-economic and related factors, there is simply no empirical evidence to support the view that African-Americans, or the members of other racial and ethnic minorities in the U.S., are far more likely than whites to be arrested, booked, indicted, fully prosecuted, convicted, be denied probation, incarcerated, disciplined while in custody (administrative segregation), or be denied furloughs or parole.

In one recent study, for example, the RAND Corporation found that a "defendant's racial or ethnic group bore little or no relationship to conviction rates, disposition times" and other adjudication outcomes in 14 large urban jurisdictions across the country.[23] Instead, the study found that such mundane factors as the amount of evidence against a defendant, and whether or not a credible eyewitness testified, were strongly related to outcomes. This study echoed the findings of several previous empirical analyses.[24]

Second, the 1980s were many things, but they were not a time when the fraction of African-Americans behind prison bars skyrocketed. In a recent report, the Bureau of Justice Statistics revealed that the number of African-Americans as a percentage of the state prison population "has changed little since 1974; 47 percent in 1974; 48 percent in 1979, and 47 percent in 1986."[25] It is certainly true that the imprisonment rate for African-Americans has been, and continues to be, far higher than for whites. For example, in 1986 the rate of admission to prison per 100,000 residential population was 342 for African-Americans and 63 for whites.[26] But it is also true that crime rates are much higher for the former group than for the latter.

Finally, it is well-known that most crime committed by poor minority citizens is committed against poor minority citizens. The typical victims of predatory ghetto criminals are innocent ghetto dwellers and their children, not middle- or upper-class whites.[27] For example, the best available data indicate that over 85 percent of single-offender crimes of violence committed by blacks are committed against blacks, while over 75 percent of such crimes committed by whites are committed against whites.[28] And if every credible opinion poll and victimization survey is to be believed, no group suffers more from violent street crime, "petty" thefts, and drug dealing, and no group is more eager to have courts, cops, and corrections officials crack down on inner-city criminals, than the predominantly minority citizens of these communities themselves.

The U.S. criminal justice system, therefore, may be biased, but not in the way that elite, anti-incarceration penal reformers generally suppose. Relative to whites and more affluent citizens generally, the system now permits poor and minority citizens to be victimized readily and repeatedly: The rich get richer, the poor get poorly protected against the criminals in their midst. The system is thus rigged in favor of those who advocate community-based alternatives to incarceration and other measures that return violent, repeat, and violent repeat offenders to poor, drug-ravaged, minority communities far from the elites' own well-protected homes, offices, and suites.

Myth Six: *Prisons in the U.S. are prohibitively expensive.*

Certainly, no sane citizen relishes spending public money on prisons and prisoners. A tax dollar spent to confine a criminal is a tax dollar not spent to house the homeless, educate the young, or assist the handicapped. There are many intrinsically rewarding civic ventures, but the imprisonment of wrongdoers is hardly at the top of anyone's list.

Nevertheless, it is morally myopic, and conceptually and empirically moronic, to argue that public money spent on prisons and prisoners is public money wasted. That, however, is precisely what legions of critics have argued.

To begin, nobody really knows how much the United States now spends each year to construct, renovate, administer, and finance prisons. Widely cited estimates range from $20 billion to over $40 billion. Corrections expenditures by government have been growing rapidly of late; in New Jersey, for example, the corrections budget has increased five-fold since 1978, and corrections threatens to become the largest single item in many state budgets. But viewed as a fraction of total government spending, in the 1980s the amount spent on corrections was trivial; for example, despite enormous growth in the Federal Bureau of Prisons, less than one penny of every federal dollar went to corrections. Just the same, estimating the costs of corrections in general, and of prisons in particular, is an exceedingly complex business to which competent analysts have given only scant attention.[29] Still, it is possible to get a conceptual and empirical handle on the financial costs and benefits of imprisonment in the U.S. today.

When critics assert that we are spending "too much" on imprisonment, we must ask "too much relative to what?" Is it the case, for example, that the marginal tax dollar invested in low-income housing, inner-city high schools, or programs for the disabled poor would yield a greater social benefit than the same dollar invested in constructing or administering new prison cells? The heart says yes, but the answer is far from obvious. Meaningful benefit-cost analyses of such competing public purposes are hard to conduct, and great difficulties attend any serious effort to quantify and compare the costs and benefits of this versus that use of public money. It is somewhat easier, but still problematic, to ask what benefits we would forgo if we did not use public money for a given purpose. For example, U.S. taxpayers now spend somewhere between $14,000 and $25,000 to keep a convicted criminal behind bars for a year. What would they lose if they chose instead to save their money, or apply it elsewhere, and allowed the criminals to remain on the streets rather than paying to keep them behind bars?

At least one thing they would lose is personal and property protection against the criminals. In simplest terms, if the typical street criminal commits X crimes per year, then the benefit to society of locking him up is to be protected against the X crimes he would have done if he were free. Thus, if the typical offender committed only one petty property crime per year, then paying thousands and thousands of dollars to keep him confined would be a bad social investment. But if he committed a dozen serious property or violent crimes each year, then the social benefits of keeping him imprisoned might well exceed the social costs of doing so.

Is imprisonment in the U.S. today worth the money spent on it? While critics assert that it is not, only a few serious efforts have been made to grapple with this question.[30] The first such effort was made in 1987 by National Institute of Justice economist Edwin W. Zedlewski.[31] Zedlewski surveyed cost data from several prison systems and estimated that the annual per prisoner cost of confinement was $25,000. Using national crime data and the findings of criminal victimization surveys, he estimated that the typical offender commits 187 crimes per year, and that the typical crime exacts $2,300 in property losses and/or in physical injuries and human suffering. Multiplying these two figures (187 times $2,300), he calculated that, when on the streets, the typical imprisoned felon was responsible for $430,000 in "social costs" each year. Dividing that figure by $25,000 (his estimate of the annual per prisoner cost of confinement), he concluded that incarceration in prison has a benefit-cost ratio of just over 17. The implications were unequivocal. According to Zedlewski's analysis, putting 1,000 felons behind prison bars costs society $25 million per year. But not putting these same felons behind prison bars costs society about $430 million per year (187,000 crimes times $2,300 per crime).

There were however, some flaws in Zedlewski's study. For example, he used dated data from a RAND prisoner self-report survey of prison and jail inmates in Texas, Michigan, and California. The inmates in the survey averaged between 187 and 287 crimes per year, exclusive of drug deals. He opted for the lower bound of 187. But the same RAND survey also found that half the inmate population committed fewer than 15 crimes per year, so that the median number of crimes committed was 15. There are plenty of good analytical reasons for using the median rather than the average in a benefit-cost study of this type. Making this one adjustment (using 15 rather than 187 for the number of crimes averted through incapacitation of an offender) reduces the benefit cost-ratio to 1.38—still positive, but more credibly and realistically so.

Last December one of us published a report on corrections in Wisconsin that featured an analysis of the benefits and costs of imprisonment.[32] The analysis was based on one of the largest and most recent scientific prisoner self-report surveys of inmates in a single system ever conducted. Among a host of other interesting results, the survey indicated that the prisoners committed an average of 141 crimes per year, exclusive of drug deals. The median figure was 12. Using the median to calculate, the study estimated the benefit-cost ratio to be 1.97.

In an attempt to satisfy the more reasonable critics, the Wisconsin data were reanalyzed and the results of the reanalysis were published in a recent edition of *The Brookings Review*, journal of The Brookings Institution.[33] But even after factoring in a host of assumptions that would be likely to deflate the benefits of imprisonment, the study reported a benefit-cost ratio of 1.84. This does not prove that "prison pays"; indeed, the Brookings study suggested that, for the lowest-level offenders, imprisonment probably is not a good social investment. But it does indicate that the net social benefits of imprisonment could well meet or exceed the costs.

At a minimum, the studies discussed above cast grave doubts over the notion that prisons clearly "cost too much," either in absolute terms or relative to alternate uses of the public monies that now go to build and administer penal facilities. What we simply do not know at this point is whether any given alternative to incarceration yields as much relative to costs as imprisonment apparently does. Recent studies have put question marks over several strictly supervised community-based correctional programs that might well represent a better investment than imprisonment for certain categories of low-level offenders.[34] Still, further research on the costs and benefits of imprisonment and other correctional sanctions is badly needed.

Myth Seven: *Interventions by activist judges have improved prison and jail conditions.*

In 1970, not a single prison or jail system in America was operating under judicial orders to change and improve. For most of our legal and constitutional history, prisoners were "slaves of the state," and judges followed the "hands-off" doctrine by normally deferring to the policies and practices of legislators and duly appointed corrections officials.

Today, however, over three dozen correctional agencies are operating under "conditions of confinement" court orders; many have class action suits in progress or population limits set by the courts; and several have court-mandated early release programs that put dangerous felons right back on the streets before they have served even one-tenth of their sentences in confinement. Despite the proliferation of Reagan- and Bush-appointed judges on the federal bench, activist federal judges continue to be the sovereigns of the nation's cellblocks, issuing directives on a wide range of issues, including health care services, staff training procedures, sanitation standards, food services, and the constitutionality of conditions "in their totality." Indeed, in some prison systems, the texts of court orders and consent decrees are now used as staff training manuals and inmate rulebooks, and everything from inmate disciplinary hearings to the exact temperature of the meat served to prisoners at supper is governed by judicial fiat.

There are at least three general points that can be safely made about the course and consequences of judicial intervention into prisons and jails. First, especially in the South, but in many jurisdictions outside the South as well, judicial involvement has substantially raised the costs of building and administering penal facilities.[35] Second, many of the most significant expansions in prisoners' rights, and most of the actual improvements in institutional conditions, made over the last two decades were conceived and implemented by professional correctional administrators, not coerced or engineered by activist judges.[36] Third, in the small but significant fraction of interventions that have succeeded at a reasonable human and financial cost, judges have proceeded incrementally rather than issuing all-encompassing decrees. In conjunction, they have vacated the serenity of their chambers for the cellblocks to get a first-hand understanding of things, working with and through the professionals who must ultimately translate their orders into action, rather than relying solely on self-interested special masters and neatly-typed depositions.[37]

Even taking into account the human and financial accidents caused by judges driving at breakneck activist speed through the intersection of corrections and the Constitution, the net of judicial involvement in this area is arguably positive. But there is at least as much evidence here for the thesis, articulated well by Nathan Glazer, Lon Fuller, and other scholars, that judges should limit themselves to doing what they are schooled to do; namely, to gather and weigh legal evidence, to analyze factual and legal issues, and to apply precedent standards in resolving disputes between parties.[38] At most, the idea that activist judges have helped to make prisons and jails more safe and humane is a half-truth.

Myth Eight: *The United States has the most punitive criminal justice system in the world.*

Over a decade ago, the National Council on Crime and Delinquency foisted on the media a statistic it produced in a 1979 report: in terms of severity of punishment, as measured by the number of prisoners per capita, only two countries in the world—the Soviet Union and South Africa—were more ruthlessly repressive than the United States. The media have been parroting this claim ever since, never asking the NCCD why they were so willing to accept Soviet figures at face value, nor why they did not include the four or five million prisoners held captive in the forced labor camps that have been indispensable to the Soviet economy.[39]

Well, maybe a sloppy attitude toward data didn't matter before; we merely would have been a more distant third. But now the NCCD, the Soviets, and the South Africans have all been trumped. According to The Sentencing Project, a Washington-based research group, the U.S. has moved into first place, with 426 prison and jail inmates per 100,000 population, compared to 333 in South Africa and 268 in the Soviet Union.[40] The media, including commentators as diverse as Tom Wicker and William Raspberry, have reacted just as uncritically to the new figures as they did to the old ones.

While gullibility toward Soviet statistics is the most glaring, it is not the most fatal flaw in this comparison, which also shows American incarceration rates to be much higher than, say, those of European countries, for which we have more reliable figures. The fatal flaw is very simple and very obvious: to interpret incarceration as a measure of the punitivity of a society, you have to divide, not by the population size, but by the number of crimes.

More competent comparative studies have discovered that when you control for rates of serious crime, the difference between the United States and other countries largely, and for some crimes completely, disappears.[41] For example, after controlling for crime rate and adjusting for differences in charge reduction between arrest and imprisonment, the U.S. in the early 1980s had an imprisonment rate virtually identical to Canada and England for theft, fell between those two countries in the case of burglary, and lagged well behind each of the others in imprisonments for robbery.[42]

In addition to the myth of the United States as the world's most punitive nation, The Sentencing Project perpetuates in its report several of the other myths we discuss in this essay. It notes that African-American males are locked up at a rate four times greater than their counterparts in South Africa. A fleeting reference to the very high crime rate among black males is immediately buried in an avalanche of references to root causes, poverty, diminished opportunities, the gap between rich and poor, and the failure of schools, health care, and other social institutions—all wrapped up as "the cumulative effect of American policies regarding black males." The report calls for increased spending on supposed "prevention policies and services" such as education, housing, health care, and programs to generate employment. In a truly wacky expression of faith in social engineering, the report urges the General Accounting Office "to determine the relative influence of a range of social and economic factors on crime."

Most of all, the Sentencing Project advocates the expanded use of alternatives to incarceration, but with a unique twist: they recommend racial quotas in the distribution of criminal justice. Independent of any preceding reduction in criminal behavior, the "Justice Department should encourage the development of programs and sanctions designed specifically to reduce the disproportionate incarceration rate of African-American males."[43] The Sentencing Project endorses the language of one such program designed to reduce the incarceration "of ethnic and minority groups where such proportion exceeds the proportion such groups represent in the general population." Methods recommended for such reduction include diversion from prosecution, intensive probation, alternative sentencing, and parole release planning, among others.

That crime rates are very high in this country, particularly among Black males, is an unhappy fact. When that fact is taken into account, it exposes as a myth the argument that we are excessively punitive, relative to other countries, in our imposition of imprisonment. A related myth is that we have failed to consider sanctions other than incarceration.

Myth Nine: *We don't make enough use of alternatives to incarceration.*

According to this myth, we could reduce prison crowding, avoid new construction, and cut our annual operating costs if we would just take greater advantage of intensive probation, fines, electronic monitoring, community service, boot camps, wilderness programs, and placement in nonsecure settings like halfway houses.

It is important to distinguish the myth of a supposed need for "alternative" sanctions from the more valid assertion of a need for "intermediate" sanctions. Norval Morris and Michael Tonry, among others, argue that, for the sake of doing justice and achieving proportionality between crime and punishment, we need a greater variety of dispositions that are intermediate in punitivity between imprisonment and simple probation.[44] Most people will find that argument perfectly sensible, even if they disagree about what crimes deserve which intermediate punishments.

The myth that we need more sanctions to use as *alternatives* to imprisonment is based on the false premise that we do not already make the maximum feasible use of *existing* alternatives to imprisonment. Consider, however, the following figures for the most recent available years:[45]

2,356,486	(63%)	on probation
407,977	(11%)	on parole
771,243	(21%)	in state and federal prisons
195,661	(5%)	in jails, post-convicted
3,731,367	(100%)	TOTAL

It is true that about two-thirds of convicted felons are sentenced to at least some period of incarceration.[46] (A felony, by definition, is punishable by a year or more in prison.) However, at any time after sentencing and prior to final discharge from the criminal justice system, the great majority of those under correctional supervision (74 percent in the figures above) will be in the community and not incarcerated. In other words, they will be experiencing an "alternative sanction" for at least some part of their sentence.

If one-third of convicted felons receive no incarceration at all, and three-quarters receive at least some time on probation or parole, how much room is left for expanding the use of alternatives to imprisonment? Some, perhaps, but probably not much, especially if you look at offenders' prior records when searching for additional convicts to divert or remove from prison. Two-thirds of inmates currently in state prisons were given probation as an alternative sanction one or more times on prior convictions, and over 80 percent have had prior convictions resulting in either probation or incarceration.[47] After how many failures for a given offender do we say that alternatives to imprisonment have been exhausted?

In sum, the idea that we have not given alternatives to imprisonment a fair chance is a myth. Any day of the week you will find three times as many convicts under alternative supervision as you will find under the watchful eye of a warden. And most of those in the warden's custody probably are there at least partly because they did not do well under some prior alternative.

Myth Ten: *Punishment is bad.*

Underlying all the myths we have discussed so far, and motivating people to believe in them, is the biggest myth of all: that punishment itself is inherently wrong. It is largely because they are opposed to punishment generally and to imprisonment in particular that many people argue so strongly that we must address the root causes of crime, that our criminal justice system discriminates, that we are overly punitive and haven't considered alternatives, that prisons are too costly and overcrowded, and that we must look to the courts for reform.

The "Big Myth" is that punishment has no value in itself; that it is intrinsically evil, and can be justified as a necessary evil only if it can be shown to be instrumental in achieving some overriding value, such as social order. Even retributivists, who argue that the primary purpose of the criminal sanction is to do justice by imposing deserved punishment (rather than to control crime through such strategies as rehabilitation, deterrence, or incapacitation), can find themselves caught up in utilitarian terminology when they speak of the "purpose"—rather than the "value"—of punishment.

Andrew von Hirsch provides the major contemporary statement of the justice model in his book, *Doing Justice*.[48] Following Immanuel Kant, von Hirsch calls for penal sanctions on moral grounds, as the "just deserts" for criminally blameworthy conduct. Unlike Kant, however, von Hirsch sees deservedness only as necessary, but not sufficient, to justify punishment. There is supposedly a "countervailing moral consideration"—specifically, "the principle of not deliberately causing human suffering where it can possibly be avoided."[49] Accepting this principle, von Hirsch argues that for punishment to be justified, it must also be shown to have a deterrent effect. A utilitarian element has been added.

Von Hirsch's compromise is internally inconsistent, and this is weaker than a purely retributivist justification. The principle that punishment for wrongdoing is deserved, and the principle against all avoidable suffering, are logically incompatible. To say that *some* suffering (i.e., punishment) is deserved is to say that we do *not* believe that *all* avoidable infliction of pain *should* be avoided. The justice model is stronger when the utilitarian requirement of deterrence is dropped.[50]

The best defense of punishment is not that it upholds the social order, but that it affirms important moral and cultural values.[51] Legal punishment is a legitimate and, if properly defined and administered, even a noble aspect of our culture. Imprisonment, in order to be respectable, does not need to be defined as "corrections," or as "treatment," or as "education," or as "protection of society," or as any other instrumental activity that an army of critics will forever claim to be a failure.

We must reject the false dichotomy between punishment and "humanitarianism." It is precisely within the context of punishment that humanistic concepts are most relevant. Principled and fair punishment for wrongdoing treats individuals as persons and as human beings, rather than as objects. Punishment is an affirmation of the autonomy, responsibility, and dignity of the individual.

Punishment in the abstract is morally neutral. When applied in specific instances and in particular forms—including imprisonment—its morality will depend on whether or not it is deserved, justly imposed, and proportionate to the wrongfulness of the crime. Where these conditions are met, punishment will not be a necessary evil, tolerable on utilitarian grounds only when held to the minimum "effective" level. Rather, under those conditions, it will have positive moral value.

---

1. James K. Stewart, "Urban Crime Locks People in Poverty," *Hartford Courant*, July 15, 1986.

2. *Ibid.*

3. See Charles Murray, *Losing Ground: American Social Policy, 1950–1980* (New York: Basic Books, 1984); and James Q. Wilson, *Thinking About Crime* (New York: Basic Books, 1975).

4. See Myth Two, below.

5. Morgan Reynolds, *Crime in Texas*, NCPA Policy Report No. 102 (Dallas: National Center for Policy Analysis, February 1991).

6. Bruce Benson, *The Enterprise of Law: Justice without the State* (San Francisco: Pacific Research Institute, 1990), p. 258.

7. Patrick A. Langan, "America's Soaring Prison Population," *Science*, March 29, 1991, Vol. 251, pp. 1568–1573.

8. The war on drugs probably had a greater effect on state prisons after 1984 and undoubtedly has had a great effect on federal prisons, where over half of last year's admissions were for drug offenses.

9. *Ibid.*, p. 1572.

10. Franklin E. Zimring, "The Great American Lockup," *The Washington Post*, February 28, 1991.

11. Mark Kleiman *et al.*, *Imprisonment-to-Offense Ratios* (Washington, D.C.: Bureau of Justice Statistics Report, November 1988), p. 21; we are using his figures without adjustment for under-reporting by the UCR, since that adjustment is only possible from 1973 on.

12. Robyn L. Cohen, *Prisoners in 1990* (Washington, D.C.: Bureau of Justice Statistics, 1991), p. 7.

13. Tom Wicker, "The Punitive Society," *The New York Times*, January 12, 1991, section 1, p. 25.

14. James and Austin and John Irwin, *Who Goes to Prison?* (San Francisco: National Council on Crime and Delinquency, 1990). The discussion here draws on Charles H. Logan, "Who Really Goes to Prison?" *Federal Prisons Journal*, Summer, 1991, pp. 57–59.

15. See Logan, *op. cit.*, for a critique of the study's methodology, including the sample.

16. Joseph E. Jacoby and Christopher S. Dunn, *National Survey on Punishment for Criminal Offenses* (Bowling Green, Ohio: Bowling Green State University, 1987).

17. Christopher A. Innes, *Profile of State Prison Inmates*, 1986 (Washington, D.C.: Bureau of Justice Statistics Special Report, 1988).

18. Christopher A. Innes, *Population Density in State Prisons* (Washington, D.C.: Bureau of Justice Statistics, December 1986).

19. Jeff Bleich, "The Politics of Prison Crowding," *California Law Review*, Volume 77 (1989), p. 1137.

20. James Bonta and Paul Gendreau, "Reexamining the Cruel and Unusual Punishment of Prison Life," *Law and Human Behavior*, Volume 14 (1990), p. 365.

21. For example, see Bert Useem and Peter Kimball, *States of Siege: U.S. Prison Riots, 1971–1986* (New York: Oxford University Press, 1989), and John J. DiIulio, Jr., *Governing Prisons: A Comparative Study of Correctional Management* (New York: Free Press, 1987).

22. For an overview, see John J. DiIulio, Jr., *No Escape: The Future of American Corrections* (New York: Basic Books, 1991), chapter 3.

23. Stephen P. Klein *et al.*, *Predicting Criminal Justice Outcomes: What Matters?* (Santa Monica, Calif.: RAND Corp., 1991) p. ix.

24. For example, see Stephen Klein *et al.*, "Race and Imprisonment Decisions in California," *Science*, volume 247, February 1990, pp. 769–792.

25. Patrick A. Langan, *Race of Prisoners Admitted to State and Federal Institutions, 1926–1986* (Washington, D.C.: Bureau of Justice Statistics, May 1991), p. 8.

26. *Ibid.*, p. 7.

27. See Stewart, *op. cit.*, and John J. DiIulio, Jr., "The Impact of Inner-City Crime," *The Public Interest*, No. 96, Summer 1989, p. 28.

28. Joan Johnson, *et al.*, *Criminal Victimization in the United States, 1988* (Washington, D.C.: Bureau of Justice Statistics, December 1990), p. 48.

29. For a good overview, see Douglas C. McDonald, *The Cost of Corrections: In Search of the Bottom Line* (Washington, D.C.: National Institute of Corrections Research in Corrections Report, February 1989).

30. In addition to the efforts to be described in the remainder of this section, see the following: David P. Cavanagh and Mark A. R. Kleiman, *Cost-Benefit Analysis of Prison Cell Construction and Alternative Sanctions* (Cambridge: Mass.: BOTEC Analysis Corp., June 1990); Tara Gray *et al.*, "Using Cost-Benefit Analysis to Evaluate Correctional Sentences," *Evaluation Review*, Volume 15 (August 1991), pp. 471–481; and Peter W. Greenwood *et al.*, *The RAND Intermediate-Sanction Cost Estimation Model* (Santa Monica, Calif.: RAND Corp., September 1989).

31. Edwin W. Zedlewski, *Making Confinement Decisions* (Washington, D.C.: National Institute of Justice Research in Brief, 1987). The material in the remainder of this section is adapted from John J. DiIulio, Jr., *Crime and Punishment in Wisconsin: A Survey of Prisoners* (Milwaukee, Wisc.: Wisconsin Policy Research Institute, December 1990), and John J. DiIulio, Jr. and Anne Morrison Piehl, "Does Prison Pay?," *The Brookings Review*, Fall 1991.

32. See DiIulio, *Crime and Punishment*, *op. cit.*

33. DiIulio and Piehl, *op. cit.*

34. For example, see Joan Petersilia and Susan Turner, *Intensive Supervision for High-Risk Probationers: Findings from Three California Experiments* (Santa Monica, Calif.: RAND Corp., December 1990).

35. Malcolm M. Feeley, "The Significance of Prison Corrections Cases: Budgets and Regions," *Law and Society Review* (1990).

36. Clair A. Cripe, "Courts, Corrections, and the Constitution: A Practitioner's View," in John J. DiIulio, Jr., ed., *Courts, Corrections, and the Constitution: The Impact of Judicial Intervention on Prisons and Jails* (New York: Oxford University Press, 1990), chapter 10.

37. DiIulio, *Courts, op. cit.*, especially chapter 11.

38. Nathan Glazer, "Towards an Imperial Judiciary," *The Public Interest*, (1978); Lon Fuller, "The Forms and Limits of Adjudication," *Harvard Law Review*, (1978).

39. See Ludmilla Alexeyeva, *Cruel and Unusual Punishment: Forced Labor in Today's U.S.S.R.* (Washington, D.C.: AFL-CIO Department of International Affairs, 1987; see also various editions throughout the 1980s of the State Department's annual *Country Reports* on human rights practices of governments around the world.

40. Marc Mauer, *Americans Behind Bars: A Comparison of International Rates of Incarceration* (Washington, D.C.: The Sentencing Project, January 1991).

41. James Lynch, *Imprisonment in Four Countries* (Washington, D.C.: Bureau of Justice Statistics Special Report, February 1987); see also Alfred Blumstein, "Prison Populations: A System Out of Control?" in Michael Tonry and Norval Morris, *Crime and Justice: A Review of Research*, vol. 10 (Chicago: University of Chicago Press, 1988).

42. Lynch, *op. cit.*, p. 2.

43. Mauer, p. 12.

44. Norval Morris and Michael Tonry, *Between Prison and Probation: Intermediate Punishments in a Rational Sentencing System* (New York: Oxford University Press, 1990).

45. Figures are taken from the following Bureau of Justice Statistics Bulletins: *Probation and Parole 1988* (November 1989); *Prisoners in 1990* (May 1991); *Jail Inmates, 1990* (June 1991).

46. Jacob Perez, "Tracking Offenders, 1988" *Bulletin* (Washington, D.C.: Bureau of Justice Statistics, June 1991); a study of offenders convicted of felonies in 14 states.

47. Christopher A. Innes, *Profile of State Prison Inmates, 1986* (Washington, D.C.: Bureau of Justice Statistics Special Report, January 1988), combining information from Tables A and 8.

48. Andrew von Hirsch, *Doing Justice: The Choice of Punishments* (New York: Hill and Wang, 1976).

49. *Ibid.*, p. 553.

50. Charles H. Logan, *Private Prisons: Cons and Pros* (New York: Oxford University Press, 1990), pp. 243, 298.

51. This discussion draws on Charles H. Logan and Gerald G. Gaes, "Meta-Analysis and the Rehabilitation of Punishment," *Justice Quarterly*, vol. 10, no. 2, June 1993, pp. 245–263.

III. RESTORING RESPONSIBILITY

Crime and Moral Retribution

by Robert James Bidinotto

What is justice?

Since man's beginnings, we have been trying to define what justice means, and to implement it in our laws and social institutions. Yet today, our criminal justice system is torn by clashing philosophical premises, to the point where justice has been largely obliterated.

Consider a single illustration: the modern prison.

Is This Punishment?

The Mercer Regional Correctional Facility in western Pennsylvania looks like a small college campus, with tidy brick buildings scattered across expansive, manicured green yards. The prison superintendent, a self-described "liberal," told me he tries to make the prison experience for inmates "as much like the street as I can." At one point, he referred to them as his "clients," adding: "Inmates aren't evil, by and large. Many just did not have good life circumstances, and have reacted inappropriately." He concluded: "The public needs to know that modern corrections is not like a Jimmy Cagney movie."

That is an understatement.

The only building with actual *cells* is the Restricted Housing Unit, where a handful of troublemakers are locked up all day. But the rest of the inmates wander freely among the two-story, brick dormitories. One holds rapists, child molesters, and HIV-positive inmates. Though small, it has two separate recreation rooms, so that inmates watching TV don't distract those who wish to play cards. Individual inmate rooms are about 8 X 10 and have no bars—just doors with glass windows. In one, the only occupant lounges comfortably on his bunk, reading a book. Around him are a desk, bookshelves, lots of magazines, and his own TV.

Mercer's thieves, rapists, and killers are indulged with a very good library, a separate law library, and a beautiful chapel. The prison offers them GED and art classes, electrical and mechanical

181

training, even night college courses in classrooms filled with books and computers—all for free. Inmates can visit the infirmary and dentist offices for free medical care on demand, while those with emotional problems have access to four staff psychologists and ten counselors—again, at no charge.

One of three "activities directors" leads me from a commissary stocked with amenities to the gymnasium. A volleyball net bisects the gleaming floor of the full-size basketball court. At one end, nine cycling machines and four "stepper" aerobics machines face a TV. These, he explains, are for the inmates' "leisure fitness program." Two rooms are jammed with weightlifting equipment; from another, current movie videos are broadcast nightly to the TVs in the inmates' rooms. "Nothing cheap here," my guide says proudly.

Outside, there is a softball field with bleachers, and a running track circling an outdoor weightlifting pavilion, exercise stations, five horseshoe pits, two bocci courts, a handball area, and more basketball hoops. My guide rattles off some of the other pastimes available: tennis, racketball, ping-pong, football, chess, checkers. . . . Inmates even have their own leagues for basketball, softball, volleyball, and power lifting. Teams of felons are squired around in prison vans, by guards and activities directors, to compete at other state prisons.

Contrary to the claim of Mercer's superintendent, this does *not* mirror life on the outside. For most housed in modern prisons, life is far *better* than it is on the streets.

Since that visit, I have toured other prisons. Some look more like the ones depicted in the movies, but all of them shower felons with amenities. Today's correctional facility is an expensive, even enticing, hybrid of camp, clinic, and community college.

True, inmates aren't free to leave at will. But looking at the strolling felons on Mercer's sun-licked lawns, I wondered: Why would they want to? In fact, few American taxpayers could afford all the programs and "perks" that they are forced to provide, without charge, to those who rob, rape, or kill them.

Is this, then, justice?

Not according to the typical outraged citizen, who thinks that prisons exist to punish wrongdoers. He bases his view on the premise that criminals are morally responsible for the harm they do. But today's intellectual counters that nobody is responsible for what he does—that crime is the result of "root causes" beyond the perpetrator's control. The answer to crime, he concludes, is not to punish, but to alter the conditions which forced the felon into a life of crime.

These clashing premises have created an incoherent criminal justice system that tries to deter yet forgive, punish yet reform, incapacitate yet rehabilitate. As everyone now acknowledges, this irrational system is a dismal failure in all of its objectives, and needs to be reformed. But where to begin?

A first step would be to analyze the warring theories which shape the institutions of justice, and which define the various strategies being employed against the crime problem.

Utilitarian Strategies

The dominant philosophy in today's criminal justice system is *utilitarianism*—the view that the ultimate end of a policy ought to be "social utility," or "the greatest good for the greatest number." Utilitarian strategies of crime control aim not to obtain justice for any individual victim, or to punish any individual criminal, but rather to prevent or suppress crime *generally*, to levels deemed to be "socially tolerable." Utilitarian strategies include:

Prevention. During debate on the 1994 Federal Crime Bill, U.S. Attorney General Janet Reno argued that money spent on a variety of social programs—"Head Start" classes for pre-schoolers, remedial education for teenagers, midnight basketball leagues for inner-city youths—would prevent today's youngsters from turning to crime in the future.

However, since the onset of the Great Society, the federal government alone has spent several *trillion* dollars on social welfare programs, many addressing the alleged "root causes" of crime. Yet the failure of these programs may be gauged by the simple fact that, despite all this spending, per capita crime rates today remain more than triple what they were in 1960.

Restitution. Of all utilitarian strategies, making the criminal "restore" his victim by paying back the costs of the harm done is closest to the principle of justice. But in practice, it has proved to be hard to enforce. Thanks to their irresponsible lifestyles, criminals often remain poor and infrequently employed. Outside of a prison work environment, it is difficult to compel them to pay back their victims. In addition, it is hard to translate damages for some kinds of crimes into dollar terms.

Rehabilitation. These strategies aim to transform a criminal's character or behavior by educational, therapeutic, and self-improvement programs. However, rehabilitation efforts have been a dismal failure. Studies of hundreds of rehab programs, inside and outside of prisons, for problems ranging from drug abuse to sex offenses to anti-social behavior, have shown no evidence of any effectiveness in changing criminal behavior.[1] Even prisons specifically designed to provide inmates with every rehabilitation program known to man—such as the facilities in Butner, North Carolina and Patuxent, Maryland—have utterly failed to reduce the rates at which criminals return to crime.

Deterrence. Some utilitarians argue that type and severity of punishments ought to be calculated and adjusted so as to discourage people from committing crimes in the future. "Succinctly stated," writes economist Morgan O. Reynolds, "economists have developed strong evidence that if greater costs are imposed on criminals, there will be fewer crimes. . . . Only if the anticipated subjective benefits (self-gratification) of an illegal act exceed the anticipated sacrifice does the person commit a crime, by definition; he does not commit a crime if the perceived costs outweigh the perceived benefits."[2]

Clearly, the threat of punishment works on many would-be criminals. Yet it does not always work, because most criminals are present-oriented and impulsive. The prospect of future punishment for current crime has little reality to them, hence limited power to deter.[3] There is mounting evidence that for the most serious criminals—those labeled "psychopaths"—the threat of punishment poses virtually no deterrent.[4]

Deterrence may work at the margins; but for amoral, conscienceless criminals, we need a different strategy. The most effective is . . .

Incapacitation. This means depriving criminals of the ability to commit crimes. The most common method is to remove them from society by incarcerating them. While locked up, a criminal cannot harm anyone except other prisoners and guards.

Incapacitation makes no assumptions about the capacity of social programs to prevent crime, the ability of treatment programs to rehabilitate, or the power of prospective punishment to deter. It simply makes crime virtually impossible for the duration of confinement. Given that the typical state prison inmate, while free, commits over a dozen serious felonies annually,[5] the public safety impact of locking up hundreds of thousands of chronic criminals is very considerable. And since the damages caused by the typical inmate, while not incarcerated, vastly exceed the annual cost of his prison cell,[6] prisons more than pay for themselves. Incapacitation can be compatible with other utilitarian purposes, such as deterrence and restitution, and with simple retribution.

However, there is an argument over how best to employ incapacitation. Rather than spend more money on additional prison cells, many argue, we should instead try to save money by allocating existing prison space more rationally.

"... [A]ll the evidence we have implies that, for crime-reduction purposes, the most rational way to use the incapacitation powers of our prisons would be to do so selectively," scholar James Q. Wilson writes. "Instead of longer sentences for everyone, or for persons who have prior records, or for persons whose present crime is especially grave, longer sentences would be given primarily to those who, when free, commit the most crimes."[7]

Arguing that we cannot afford to lock up all felons, advocates of selective incapacitation suggest focusing on certain categories of "high-risk" or "high-rate" offenders—usually chronic criminals in their late teens and early twenties. These so-called "serious habitual offenders" would receive longer sentences than other offenders, who may be committing exactly the same kinds of crimes, but at lower rates. While the low-rate offenders would get off easy, the most chronic would be locked up for the duration of their youthful, high-crime years. Then, after age 45 or 50, they could be "safely" released, because of the declining statistical likelihood of their continuing to offend at high rates.

In short, rather than making "the punishment fit the crime," as Gilbert and Sullivan put it, we should try to make "the punishment fit the criminal."

Selective incapacitation has several serious problems, not the least of which is our dismal ability to predict criminal dangerousness. Our current capacity to forecast long-term violent behavior is no better than one accurate prediction out of three.[8] Moreover, anti-prison advocates have found "selective incapacitation" to be a wonderfully elastic concept. In the name of incarcerating only the most serious offenders, they have narrowly redefined what a "serious" offender is. Today, virtually all property criminals, child molesters, and even many violent offenders are being described as "minor" or "low-risk" offenders. These, advocates assert, should not be in prison at all, but instead be allowed "alternatives to incarceration" that would keep them out in the community.

However, we are already using such "community alternatives" to the hilt. Today, three-quarters of all convicted criminals are free either on probation or parole.[9] And notwithstanding deceptive claims to the contrary, the overwhelming majority of state prison inmates deserve to be there. Ninety-four percent of state inmates have been *convicted* either of a violent crime, or have past criminal convictions. Only six percent have been convicted for the first time, and for a non-violent offense. Of these, little more than half—just 3.5 percent of the entire prison population—are first-time drug offenders.[10]

Even if we were to release from prison the entire six percent of first-time, non-violent convicts, we could easily refill their cells from the ranks of the 3.5 million parolees and probationers currently on our streets—nearly two-thirds of whom are rearrested for other crimes within three years.

In addition, there are other problems which selective incapacitation shares with *all* utilitarian strategies.

What About Justice?

In *The Killing of Bonnie Garland*—a brilliant, harrowing, and provocative dissection of the collapse of our modern criminal justice system—Dr. Willard Gaylin points out that "The utilitarian argument is purely future-oriented. It is not concerned with the crime that has been done but the crimes that might be done. Punishment of the individual is justified only in terms of its relationship to other crimes." He adds: "A worthy concept of justice would demand that we look backward as well as forward. . . . "[11]

By looking backward, Gaylin means: remembering the past victim. Justice requires proportionality between the harm done to the victim, and the consequences to be imposed upon his victimizer. But utilitarianism disconnects the past victim from his victimizer. It holds that only the *future* counts—and not even the victim's future: only the future of the criminal, and of victims yet to be.

Consider the various utilitarian strategies. Prevention focuses only on improving general social conditions, in the hope that anonymous citizens of tomorrow will not turn to crime. Rehabilitation focuses only on the criminal, and *his* future status. Deterrence focuses only on the future status of society as a whole. And while incapacitation can be lengthened in proportion to the harm done to the victim, in its "selective" form, even that linkage is broken: punishments no longer have any relationship to the severity of past crimes, only to official predictions of future dangerousness.

By tying the degree of punishment to the degree of harm done, justice imposes *proportionality* on criminal sentences: it fits the punishment to the crime. But because utilitarian strategies ignore the victim, they thereby render proportionality, hence *justice*, impossible.

Not only can criminals get less punishment than they deserve, they can also get more. If reducing crime rates generally is the only goal, why not deter crime by executing every criminal we catch, regardless of the seriousness of his crime? Or, if public safety is the only objective, why not incapacitate all criminals forever?

Crime victims constantly express outrage about how they are ignored and abused by the criminal justice system. But given the utilitarian goals of those who have designed it and run it, how could it be otherwise? In utilitarian social calculations, there is no place for the anguished human face of an individual crime victim. He or she is homogenized and obliterated in faceless statistical tables—reduced to just one more digit amid the annual household victimization rates, parolee recidivism rates, and prison furlough failure rates.

Traditional Retributivism

In contrast to utilitarianism, theories of *retribution*—often incorporating concepts of "retaliation" and "revenge"—hold that a criminal ought to be punished simply because he has done wrong, and therefore deserves it.

According to this view, ultimately it is unimportant whether punishment accomplishes anything practical, such as deterring crime or reforming the criminal. The main purpose of punishment is to assert a moral standard for social behavior—and, perhaps, to satisfy our personal craving for revenge.

An eloquent case for traditional retribution is presented by Willard Gaylin. "I would hope that deterrence works," he writes, "but even if it does not—particularly when it does not—I am prepared to say, 'I don't care what good it may or may not serve. You deserve to be punished.' "[12]

What, he asks, would have been the justification for punishing Adolf Hitler, had he survived the war? Incapacitation? Deterrence? Hitler was an aging, disintegrating man who would no longer have posed a threat, and whose humiliation would have been sufficient deterrent to would-be followers. Rehabilitation? "There was nothing to rehabilitate," says Gaylin.

So why punish him? Because "the concept of Hitler in retirement on a ranch in Argentina painting landscapes is simply intolerable. Even if it cannot be justified on purely utilitarian grounds, that man deserved to be punished with all the righteous wrath of an outraged community sensitivity. . . . We must not mobilize utilitarian justifying excuses. He must be punished because the moral order of things demands it, because it would be unbearable to see a man like that rewarded and allowed to go unpunished. Righteousness demands it."

But what is the source of this moral mandate? Gaylin ties it to the innate dignity of human life. In the case of a murder victim, "A life was lost, an innocent life, and society must indicate the precious nature of that loss."[13] This inherent dignity is attributed even to the criminal: "Human dignity is based on that freedom and autonomy that elevates us above the animal host. In recognition for that autonomy, we must punish the transgressor. As a tribute and testament to his freedom, we must dignify him by making him pay for the evil actions he commits. We show our respect by making him accountable."[14]

One can certainly sympathize with this approach. Unlike utilitarianism, retributivism does not lose sight of the fundamental *moral* purposes of a criminal justice system. Yet there is a troubling emphasis here, one that subtly introduces a serious logical contradiction into the theory.

While Gaylin expresses deep concern for the harm done to the life of the crime victim, that does not appear to be his *primary* concern. The chief focus seems to be not that the criminal violated an *individual*, but that the criminal violated *an abstract moral principle*. The highest value is not justice for individuals, but what Gaylin calls "social justice":

> In one sense, the law always serves the purposes of the state, not the individual.

And:

> Everything is upside down when we insist on approaching justice from the standpoint of the individual. . . . Each individual must conform his behavior to expected models, and if he does not he must be held responsible for his violation of the code.

And:

> Each gain for the individual must be weighed for its impact on the common good. . . .[15]

Under traditional retributivism, justice as an abstraction—and not the individual human life—is held to be an end in itself. This stands the moral and logical hierarchy on its head, and ironically, leads in practice to *injustice:*

> We must not attempt to purchase an elegant and individual justice for each person at the expense of the concept called social justice. . . . We must always balance individual good against the need for social justice. . . . A just society traditionally does some disservice to its individual members.[16]

And it also leads to *collectivism:*

> The common good demands sacrifice of the individual. . . . We are reaching the limits of individualism. . . . We must conserve the sense of the rightness of our social order, even to the point of sacrificing some of that very respect for the

individual which makes our order one that is worth preserving. . . .[17]

Gaylin concludes:

> [T]he chief purpose of law is order, and the justice system is designed to serve the ends of the society at large. . . . An individual human being is only a useful social myth. . . . We cherish the community not merely because it protects us but because it defines the nature of our species. And it is with our species that righteousness resides.[18]

Thus what begins as a rousing defense of justice for individual crime victims collapses, incredibly, into an apology for explicit injustice and outright collectivism.

Gaylin's error rests in treating an abstraction—in this case, justice—as an end in itself. Placing justice at the top of the moral hierarchy logically implies that individual human life lies somewhere beneath it—and that individuals exist to serve "justice," rather than the other way around.

But if individual life and well-being is not the *standard* for distinguishing just from unjust acts, then the principle loses all meaning and purpose. For Gaylin, logic demands that justice finally be abandoned; and in its absence, the only remaining social organizing principle is: collective caprice.

Traditional retributionism offers a compelling critique of the moral bankruptcy of utilitarianism. But because it begins by asserting that justice—not individual life—is an end in itself, it must at last demand the unjust sacrifice of innocent individuals for collective ends.

Justice and Causality

Thus we see the incoherence and failure of both utilitarianism and traditional retributivism. Utilitarianism posits arbitrary, subjective social ends while dismissing the need for any moral standard. Retributivism asserts a standard of justice while dismissing any concern for practical consequences. These two views have left us a so-called criminal justice system which ignores both individuals and justice—*on principle.*

Our nation's Founders made it clear in the Preamble to the U. S. Constitution that they saw no clash between the promotion of justice, and the practical goal of insuring "domestic tranquility." A valid conception of retribution—of "just deserts"—can incorporate many of the practical aims advanced by utilitarian thinkers, as well as providing them a moral grounding.

What, then, is this "justice" we are seeking, and why should we do so? What is "crime"—and what are we entitled to expect of our criminal justice system?

I would define justice as: *a moral principle recognizing causality and attributing individual responsibility in social relationships.* The principle of justice holds that because individuals are thinking causal agents, they are morally responsible for the social consequences of their actions, and must be treated accordingly.

The need for such a principle arises from the objective requirements of individual human life in society.

Causality is a fundamental principle of existence. If there were no links between cause and effect in nature—if events occurred without cause, or if actions had no effects—physical reality itself would be chaotic, irrational, and thus impossible.

So it is in society. If people chose not to recognize the links between human actions and their social consequences, and to respond accordingly, human life in society would become chaotic, irrational, and impossible. *Justice is the recognition of causality in human affairs.*

Contrary to traditional retributivism, justice is not an end-in-itself: it is a virtue, a means to a higher value. And contrary to collectivistic utilitarianism, the ultimate end which justice serves is *individual human life.*

To live, individuals must act in support of their lives. But before they take action, they must have reasonable assurance that their actions will bring about the results they seek. If their actions are *inconsequential,* they will not bother to act. Hence the need for a social principle of ethics whose application guarantees to individuals full recognition of and respect for the material and spiritual fruits of their actions. That principle is justice.

Genetically and logically, then, the concept of justice is dependent upon the ultimate value of individual human life. If individual well-being did not matter, there would be no need to seek justice. Thus justice is inextricably tied to a social philosophy of *individualism*.

Collectivist theories of justice—so-called "social justice," which would sacrifice the individual to the group—are self-contradictory. Collectivism severs the link between cause and effect in human action. It holds that individuals who act should not be the primary beneficiaries of their actions—but that individuals who did not act *should* be the beneficiaries of the actions of others. It forces some to act to no personal effect, while others reap effects without acting. Moreover, by demanding the sacrifice of the individual to the group, collectivism negates the very *purpose* of justice: the furtherance of individual human life.

If this, then, is justice, then what is crime?

Crime and Force

Alone on a desert island, an individual unavoidably would be the sole beneficiary or victim of his own actions. Experience would teach him the concept of cause and effect. But since there would be no one else to interfere with him, no concept of "justice" or "injustice" would arise. We do not speak of the "injustices" committed by forest fires, predatory animals, or robots, because in none of these cases are the destructive consequences the products of free, conscious deliberation and intent. Only in society can the natural causal relationship between one's actions and their personal consequences be *intentionally* short-circuited.

Since justice is the recognition of causality in social affairs, it is intimately bound up with the concept of "the deserved." The dictionary says that to deserve is "to be worthy of recompense" and "to merit (reward, punishment, esteem, etc.) in return for actions, qualities, etc."[19] Because one's qualities and actions have consequences for good or ill, the concept of "just deserts" holds that society ought to reward or punish one accordingly. An injustice, then, occurs when someone denies another what he has deserved or earned.

However, not all injustice is or should be "criminal." Injustice may take the form of simple "unfairness." A boorish diner insults a waitress; an indifferent husband ignores his wife; a boss does not praise his hard-working staff or grant them raises. These may be injustices meriting moral criticism; but they are not proper concerns for the law. Why? Because in a society based upon free, voluntary association, we can simply *avoid* people who are unfair to us. We need not clutter up the courts with personal affronts and petty injustices that we can ourselves remedy without governmental intervention.

No, the law should be more narrowly focused, dealing exclusively with those injustices which are *imposed* upon a victim—i. e., situations in which free, voluntary association has broken down or been abrogated, making it impossible for the victim to avoid an injustice against him.[20]

In such cases, cause and effect are breached *by force*, initiated non-consensually against innocent victims. The natural causal relationship between actor and consequence is in each case forcibly obliterated, so that the victims do not *deserve* the consequences imposed upon them. For such injustices, the only remedy is forcible intervention by an outside agency (government) whose purpose is to define and promote justice.[21]

In an ideal society, based upon consistent recognition of individual rights and autonomy, a "crime" would be defined as: *any intentional, non-consensual act entailing the initiation of force, fraud, or coercion against another person or persons.* These are deliberate, willful acts which abrogate the moral autonomy of other individuals in a voluntary society, and which thereby undermine or destroy their well-being or lives.

Contrary to contemporary thinking, "crimes" are not offenses against an abstraction, such as "the state": they are offenses against *individuals*. Today, the crime victim is typically ignored in court; he or she is a mere "witness" to an offense allegedly committed against the state, whose "interests" are represented by the prosecutor. A justice system based on individualism would grant the individual victim primary standing in court as the offended party, with his interests represented by the prosecutor.

These considerations of justice and crime enable us to define the system that deals with them.

A criminal justice system is a legal framework whose purpose is to insure individual autonomy and responsibility (justice), by defining, proscribing, and punishing intentional, non-consensual initiations of force, fraud, or coercion (crimes) against individuals and their property.

This definition, of course, is based upon the ideal of a *limited* government, such as that defined by America's Founders. Regrettably, today's criminal law has expanded its reach far beyond these boundaries, defining as "crimes" many acts having little or nothing to do with the initiation of force. However, such excesses do not negate the core purpose of the criminal law: to provide a free, peaceful, and just social framework for the voluntary, life-enhancing actions of individuals.

The strategies employed by a rational criminal justice system ought to be logically related to its individualist philosophical premises and ends. This means institutions devised to protect innocent individual life and well-being from forcible or coercive interference. It also means laws, policies, and strategies consonant with the premises of volition, individual responsibility, and just deserts.

Specific reforms of the system are suggested later in this volume. Here, let me touch on just basic strategic questions.

Retribution or Revenge?

I would begin by asserting *moral retribution* as the core strategy of the criminal justice system. Such a strategy would entail the administering of punishment to a criminal, proportionate to the degree of harm inflicted upon his victims. Moral retributivism, however, would be defined and justified in a manner quite different from traditional retributivism.

Moral retribution is grounded in the premises of individual life, individual responsibility, and individual justice. Individual life, as the ultimate purpose of the system—individual responsibility, as the premise underlying its treatment of criminals—and individual justice, as the policy to be implemented in each case.

I use the term "retribution" in the sense of "reflection." The criminal's basic aim is to forcibly gain some value at the expense of someone else. His actions impose undeserved negative consequences—harm and injury—upon the innocent victim. The fundamental goal of a strategy of moral retribution, then, is *to reflect those negative consequences of harm and injury back onto the criminal*.

This policy is both moral and practical. Moral, because it upholds both the ultimate moral value, which is individual human life, and the just social framework upon which individual survival and well-being depend. Practical, because a policy of reflecting proportionate harm back upon the criminal frustrates and negates his goal, which is to profit at someone else's expense. Retribution means that the criminal *will not get away with it*.

An effective system of moral retribution would satisfy the concerns of the traditional retributivist, who wants society to set a clear moral standard, and who understandably wants the criminal "to pay for his crimes." Such a system would also incorporate many of the practical crime-fighting goals of the utilitarian. For example, long terms of confinement under subsistence conditions, with inmates forced to work and to pay restitution to victims and taxpayers, would surely deter far more criminals and would-be criminals than a brief vacation at a country club such as Mercer. Such punishments would also incapacitate, and—who knows?—possibly foster the desire in the occasional inmate to rehabilitate himself.

Because retribution entails punishment, it is often criticized as being motivated by a crude thirst for vengeance. For example, in a tract published by the National Council on Crime and Delinquency, a prominent anti-incarceration group, James Austin and John Irwin (himself a former inmate) warn, "We will severely damage some of our more cherished humanitarian values . . . by our excessive focus on vindictiveness."[22]

Traditional retributivists often play into the hands of these liberal critics of punishment, by equating the concept "retribution" with concepts such as "revenge" and "vengeance." However, these latter concepts have negative connotations and inappropriate implications. My dictionary[23] tells me that "revenge" means "the carrying out of a bitter desire to injure another for a wrong done to oneself or to those who seem a part of oneself." Similarly, "vengeance" is "usually wrathful, vindictive, furious revenge." By contrast, though, "retribution" suggests "just or deserved punishment, often without personal motives, for some evil done."

Revenge-based punishment need not be just. The injured party may vent his rage quite disproportionately to the harm done. How much punishment is "enough"—and should it be the victims who decide such matters, through personal revenge? If we are to have a just and peaceful society, it is clear that the use of after-the-fact, retaliatory force cannot be left to the arbitrary whims of private victims, each employing his own subjective criteria of personal injury. It is precisely to *minimize and avoid* vengeance, vindictiveness, and vendettas, and the disproportionate punishments to which they would lead, that a rational criminal justice system must be based upon *retribution*, and not revenge.

For minor crimes, fines and payments of restitution may be sufficient. But for more serious offenses, prisons are an unavoidable punitive measure. Unlike prevention, rehabilitation, or deterrence, incapacitation is the only *certain* crime-reduction method: while locked up, a felon can't commit more crimes. But since we cannot predict the future dangerousness of a convicted criminal, moral retribution would abandon such utilitarian fads as selective incapacitation. A term of confinement would be gauged solely to the seriousness of the criminal's current offense, and of his criminal history.

Retribution and Career Criminals

This suggests a possible problem. A first-time, minor offender may cause little harm, and merit only minor punishment. Yet suppose he is arrested over and over for petty offenses. Should we continue to punish each offense as an isolated, discrete act, meriting only a wrist slap? Or is it fair to take an extensive or serious criminal history into account in setting the criminal's punishment?

At first glance, retributive justice might seem to require that we punish *only* the current offense, and *only* to the degree of harm that offense caused. We might reason that the criminal has already "paid for" his past crimes, that to punish him for anything more than the instant offense would be unjust. However, the tacit assumption here is that the direct victim of the crime is its *only* victim. That may not be the case.

Take, for instance, a "Peeping Tom." His presence in the community can create a climate of worry and fear, with women changing their locks, schedules, and habits, buying burglar alarms, refusing their daughters permission to go out at night, forcing police to increase neighborhood patrols, etc. Likewise the chronic shoplifter. A few chronic thieves in a community can create such fears that shopkeepers are forced to hire store detectives, buy expensive anti-theft devices, even move to a safer area. Shouldn't these sorts of damages be considered when setting punishment the next time he is caught?

A career criminal does not only initiate force against isolated individuals; his activities and presence in a community create a general *coercive atmosphere*—a climate that imposes costs upon many besides his specific targets. The criminal justice system addresses not only the initiation of force and fraud, but also of *coercion:* the *threat* of force. By his habitual criminality, the chronic offender demonstrates that he poses an ongoing threat of force.

Though a system of retribution must *base* punishments on the amount of harm done to individual victims, there is no reason that such punishments cannot be *enhanced,* commensurate with the seriousness or repetitiveness of the criminal's activities, and their consequent impact upon the climate of public safety.

To this end, I have recommended what I call "progressive sentencing." A first-time felon gets a jail term of X. Upon his second conviction—even if for a less serious felony—he gets a mandatory minimum term of at least 2X. For felony number three, he would get 4X. The multiple increases in prison terms would insure that chronic criminals would soon take themselves out of circulation for good.

Similar considerations might apply to traditional "crimes against the state"—assassination attempts on public officials, interference with government authorities in the execution of their responsibilities, etc. Though penalties for crimes against public officials and property must be rooted in the damage caused identifiable individuals, the fact that such crimes create broader harm to everyone who depends on the government can serve as a rationale for enhanced punishments.

Retribution constitutes the premise that the level of punishment must fit the severity of the crime. This does not mean we need to punish *in kind:* the law need not literally demand "an eye for an eye," sinking to the specific tactics of the criminal. But it does mean that society should punish *in proportion:* that the law ought to recognize gradations of evil and harm, and respond accordingly.

Retribution and Capital Punishment

And this brings us to the controversial subject of the death penalty.

In a society whose ultimate premise is that the individual life is an end in itself, premeditated murder is a crime in a class by itself. Murder negates the highest moral end: the irreplaceable human life. What possible penalty could be proportionate to the crime, except the forfeiture of the murderer's own life?

Moral retributivism would hold that, in the case of premeditated murder, in which there is no question of guilt and no extenuating circumstances, capital punishment should be the *standard* penalty.

Utilitarian arguments are often raised against capital punishment. It costs too much to keep someone on death row for years; it doesn't deter; we could just as well protect society by giving a killer a life sentence.

In reply: It costs too much only because we have not placed rational time limits on the appeals process. Further, the issue is not deterring future killers, but justice for the past murder victim. As for a life sentence: first, the issue is not public protection, but again, justice. Second, "life" rarely means "life," or anything approaching it. Third, even if it did, a life prison term still allows the murderer a multitude of values, options, and experiences his victim will never know (especially if he spends it in a place such as Mercer). Finally, it also prevents the victim's survivors—who are every bit as much victimized by the killer—from ever burying their pain, achieving emotional closure, and resuming their lives.

To deny the death penalty for premeditated murder, then, is to deny the very principle of fitting punishments to offenses. On what grounds can we uphold that principle for lesser offenses, if we dismiss it for this, the most serious of crimes?

The Forgotten Individual

All of these principles, theories and arguments, however, can too easily cause us to lose sight of what these abstractions are all about. My concern is for the names behind all the statistics, the faces behind all the theories. Crime victims are *individuals*, not abstractions. In fact, they have been the *victims* of abstractions: of ideas and doctrines which have taken the safety from our streets, the morality from our laws, and the life from their bodies.

Today, millions of criminals are waging war against decent people. These predators have been unleashed, protected, and pampered by an Excuse-Making Industry of corrupt intellectuals, who have captured the halls of justice, and subverted the laws and institutions which are supposed to protect us.

Those of us who understand what is at stake have a choice. We can ignore the war raging around us; we can hide in our homes and books, retreat into a world of pure abstraction. Or we can take up the cause of real individuals, by bringing *individualist* principles to the war being raged on our streets.

Either way we choose, we shall face unavoidable retribution. But that, too, is justice.

---

1. James Q. Wilson and Richard J. Herrnstein, *Crime and Human Nature* (New York: Simon & Schuster, 1985), Chapter 15. See also Stanton E. Samenow, *Inside the Criminal Mind* (New York: Times Books, 1984), Chapter 12.

2. Morgan O. Reynolds, *Crime By Choice: An Economic Analysis* (Dallas: The Fisher Institute, 1985), pp. xi, 6–7.

3. Wilson and Herrnstein, Chapter 7, esp. pp. 207–208. See also the work of Stanton Samenow.

4. Robert D. Hare, *Without Conscience* (New York: Pocket Books, 1993), pp. 59, 76, and 88.

5. See this volume, Part II, "Ten Deadly Myths," pp. 168–169.

6. *Ibid.*

7. James Q. Wilson, *Thinking About Crime* (New York: Vintage Books, revised edition, 1983), pp. 153–54.

8. Norval Morris and Marc Miller, "Predictions of Dangerousness in the Criminal Law," *Research in Brief*, National Institute of Justice, March 1987, p. 3.

9. "Correctional Populations in the United States, 1990," U. S. Bureau of Justice Statistics, cover; see also 1991 edition.

10. "Survey of State Prison Inmates, 1991," U. S. Bureau of Justice Statistics, p. 11.

11. Willard Gaylin, *The Killing of Bonnie Garland* (New York: Simon & Schuster, 1982), pp. 327–329.

12. *Ibid.*, p. 329.

13. *Ibid.*, p. 325.

14. *Ibid.*, p. 336. Charles Logan and John DiIulio offer a similar rationale elsewhere in this volume; see Part II, "Ten Deadly Myths About Crime and Punishment in the U. S."

15. Gaylin, pp. 245, 270–271, 319.

16. *Ibid.*, p. 341.

17. *Ibid.*, pp. 341–342.

18. *Ibid.*, pp. 343, 348.

19. *The American College Dictionary* (New York: Random House, 1966).

20. There are several basic forms these injustices can take: (1) someone *forces* another to relinquish the rewards of the latter's actions (e.g., via robbery, theft, fraud); (2) someone *forcibly prevents* another from taking actions (e.g., via kidnapping, unlaw-

ful confinement or restraint); (3) someone *forces* another to take actions harmful to himself (e.g., via coercion, extortion, enslavement); or (4) someone *initiates physical force* against another, or *forces* harmful consequences upon him (e.g., via assault, murder, pollution, vandalism, libel, etc.).

21. There is a broad category of injustices covered by *civil law*, which deals with such matters as the resolution of private disputes (e. g., contractual conflicts), and harm caused by accidents and negligence. *Criminal law* deals with a narrower category of more serious injustices: those involving deliberate imposition of force and coercion.

22. John Irwin and James Austin, "It's About Time: Solving America's Prison Crowding Crisis" (San Francisco: National Council On Crime and Delinquency, 1987), p. 20.

23. *American College Dictionary, op. cit.*

How to Reduce Crime

by Morgan O. Reynolds

Crime remains a silent contender for the number one domestic ill. It won't go away. Criminal experts are prone to explain this by saying that crime is "intractable," that there is little we can do. This claim is false. Crime is complex, to be sure, because it involves factors beyond law enforcement such as the strength of the family, neighborhoods, schools, and churches. But crime is simple in the sense that government officials can reduce crime by doing their job, namely, by making crime too unprofitable to practice.

No added resources are needed by the criminal justice system in order to accomplish this. Government finds it easy enough to spend money, but difficult to spend it productively. Between 1960 and 1982, for example, the number of serious crimes known to the police jumped from 3.3 million to 12.8 million, while government spending on police, courts, and corrections was doubling as a share of GNP, rising to one percent of total output. Furthermore, victimization surveys show that only about one third of crimes are reported to the police.

The key to making our cities less dangerous is to change the rules of the game. We must reduce the enormous daily waste of time and effort that makes it so expensive to arrest, convict, and punish the guilty.[1] While the machinery of government and its bureaucrats is always plagued by weak accountability and inefficiency, the law enforcement problem has increased dramatically over the last twenty years. Since 1961 the criminal justice system has been transformed from a law enforcement system into a thicket of criminal rights and make-work projects for nearly 2 million lawyers, judges, social workers, psychologists, criminologists, prison officials, and other bureaucrats. More people now produce less justice.

The quadrupling of crime over the past twenty years is due to a top-down revolution, as all revolutions in public policy are. Friedrich von Hayek points out that political opinion over the long run is determined by the active intellectuals. That is why in every country that has moved toward socialism, there was a long preceding phase during which socialist ideas governed the thinking of most intellectuals. Expanded rights for criminal defendants, sociological theories of crime, theories of rehabilitation, and dubious legal processes have followed the same path.

The Short Run: Rebuilding External Constraints

Suppose that we had a *carte blanche* on crime policy and a mandate to reduce crime. What changes would be prudent and effective? I do not claim that my recommendations are feasible in short-run political terms, only that they are sound ways to reduce crime. The basic short-run strategy is to raise the criminal's chances of arrest and conviction and increase the effectiveness of punishment, all without added burden on the taxpayer. This is far from impossible, provided these five recommendations were followed:

1. Avoid worsening the problem through increased community "rehabilitation" and other "therapeutic" treatments instead of prison terms.
2. Repeal the laws which make the crime problem worse than necessary, such as drug laws, gun control laws, rules restricting the use of prison labor, and those granting coercive privileges to organized labor.
3. Revise the exclusionary rules, suppression of evidence, inordinate delays, technical reversals, instability in criminal procedures, bias in favor of criminal defendants, and disregard for the rule of law by Supreme Court majorities.
4. Make greater use of private incentives and private contractors for police, prosecution, and corrections work, so that the taxpayers get more for their money.
5. Make sentencing fit the crime, not the criminal: Punishment should be usual, even-handed, determinate, prompt, shorter, more severe (though not cruel), and served in full.

The cardinal rule for any physician is "First, do no harm," and recommendations one and two reflect this philosophy. The likely prospect is that things will get worse before they get better because criminal policies are still dominated by unsound ideas and unsound advisers. Legislatures are losing their earlier resolve and bowing to public pressure over the last few years. The people selling therapy for criminals are succeeding once again based on the argument that prisons are crowded and there is no sense in spending more money on failed policies. The legislature in Texas recently accepted this idea, pulling up short just as more plentiful and longer prison terms were beginning to make a dent in crime rates. So the first order of business is to fend off more of the same policies which caused the crime epidemic in the first place.

Perhaps the most controversial recommendation is to repeal the criminal drug laws (and laws against other victimless crime), cases in which the cure is worse than the disease. Over 20 percent of criminal arrests are for drug violations and these clog up the courts, preoccupy police resources, sustain the infrastructure of organized crime, raise the price of opiates so that as much as 30 percent more street crime occurs, promote corruption, and have failed miserably in every respect. Similarly, gun laws are misguided attempts to control crime "on the cheap" which never have worked and cannot work in America. They are counterproductive and reduce citizen protection.[2] The numerous restrictions on the use of prison labor have reduced the output of the economy, raised the prison bill for taxpayers, and denied prisoners wider employment opportunities.[3] Even the prospects of rehabilitation have been harmed by these protectionist measures. Another labor policy adding to the crime problem is the tacit right of labor unions to use "the weapons of labor" in order to create artificial scarcities of labor via violence and threat of violence. The special privileges of labor unions, both by statute and common law, should be revoked. Not only would this directly reduce violence, it would also reduce the close association between organized crime and organized labor.[4]

In addition to discontinuing some things, the public sector should do some things that presently are not being done. The most important step is to rebalance our biased criminal procedures. It is no exaggeration to say that the Warren Court has the blood of thousands of crime victims on its hands. Without the ability to convict the guilty promptly and *conclusively* in fair if less-than-ideal procedures, nothing can substantially reduce crime. With all of the privileges granted to the accused in today's courts, we are fortunate to have as little crime as we have.[5]

The techniques of the marketplace can improve the productivity of the public sector. Police departments, for example, should be at least partially rewarded on the basis of *gains* in reducing crime rates. The crime data should be checked by independent auditors. Private security agencies should be allowed to bid for contracts to supply police services where it is legally feasible. Based on experience, these measures can emerge on a piecemeal basis around the country, learning as we go.[6] Similarly, private incentives and contractors can be more widely used in prosecution and corrections. When the duty of protecting a citizen from criminal harm is left solely to government, there are times due to neglect, malice, or political intrigue that prosecutors fail to act on behalf of the victim. If criminal law were amended to allow wider private rights of enforcement in the courts, then the citizen can protect himself if the government does not, and enforcement will be much more energetic. Prisoners should have more productive opportunities, with the profit motive allowed wider scope on both the demand and supply sides of the highly restricted market for prison labor services and in prison-made products. The ingenuity of the marketplace and competition should be harnessed to serve the cause of crime reduction.

Recommendation five is to change sentencing policies. We should eliminate false advertising: make sentences shorter but served in full. Sentences should fit the crime, not the criminal. The present philosophy about the appropriate procedures for determination of guilt and assignment of punishment basically should be reversed. Evidence about the accused's criminal background, for example, should be allowed in weighing the probability of guilt or innocence, but should be ignored for sentencing. We do it for traffic fines or tax evasion and should do it for criminal offenses as well. Perhaps juveniles should receive special consideration but punishment basically should fit the act, not the age nor the criminal record of the guilty party. One of the tragedies of the current arrangement is that juveniles initially receive tender loving care at the hands of the criminal justice system and are almost seduced into a criminal life. Not taking the system seriously, some of them end up serving long sentences as habitual criminals for crimes so old that nobody can remember them.

Severity of punishment can be humanely increased through greater use of solitary confinement. This serves the cause of justice because anti-social individuals and criminal bands destroy social co-operation, so let them bear the logical consequences of their actions. The English penal system used this technique with great success in days gone by, and their abandonment of the procedure has been a factor in the British crime epidemic. Solitary confinement also has the virtue of decreasing schooling in criminal skills and criminal contacts. Prisoners also should work, but I favor the carrot of productive, re-munerative employment opportunities rather than the stick of break-ing rocks all day.

And what about the death penalty? I personally favor its reinsti-tution to administer just deserts for the absolutely worst crimes. Life imprisonment in an era of color TV and coed prisons cannot do jus-tice for the acts of a Richard Speck. We terminate vicious animals, and if we believe that society is worth protecting we should be willing to execute the vicious killers that spring up among humans. Our present unwillingness to execute the most grotesque evildoers speaks loudly to criminals about our society and its ideological climate.[7] As Friedrich Nietzsche said, "There is a point in the history of society when it becomes so pathologically soft and tender that among other things it sides even with those who harm it, criminals, and does this quite seriously and honestly."[8]

The Long Run: Rebuilding Internal Constraints

The rise of crime has not been an isolated social phenomenon. For instance, there is a striking parallel with the demise of discipline in schools. Why? The basic reason is that a large, influential segment of public opinion came to believe that students should not be pun-ished—made unhappy, reprimanded, scorned—for doing things that are wrong. As a substitute we ended up with "special counseling programs" and other non-answers. Those opposed to punishment share Rousseau's view of man, feeling that social constraints inhibit healthy human development, that people are born friendly and con-siderate. Pro-punishers believe that man is a mixture of good and bad, but that our basic instinct is to look out for number one and trample anyone who gets in the way of what we want. Under the weight of painful experience, our schools may be shifting away from Rousseau's views, but it can only be effective if adults are willing to face up to things, to show some backbone. Without serious steps to restrain the law-breaking minority, of course, the reversion to savagery is never far away.

The breakdown of personal qualities of self-restraint, honesty, integrity, self-reliance, and consideration for others is indissolubly linked with the welfare state. For what is the redistributive state but the glorification of envy? There is an irreconcilable conflict between the rule of law, which depends on limited government, and the welfare state, which depends on limitless government. As government has passed more and more laws and regulations, individual liberty has shrunk and disorder has grown. The rule of man has been substituted for the rule of law.

Crime and the Welfare State

The welfare state does not respect private property. It takes from the politically uninfluential and gives to the politically influential. Redistribution by government is not called stealing, though the same act is if performed by a private individual rather than a government official. Neither shoplifters nor more serious criminals think of themselves as stealing; they say that they just "take" things. In a way, they are right because crime and most of what takes place under the heading of politics amount to the same thing.

Changing the incentives faced by criminals is relatively easy from a technical point of view. Just make punishment swift, sure, and severe. It requires a firm but limited government. But if government is to restore the rule of law and protect private property, government itself must abide by the law. And this is not consistent with the welfare state.

Collectivists like to say that a war on poverty is also a war on crime. I agree with this statement but not in the sense that collectivists mean it. Collectivists mean more coerced redistribution, generous welfare benefits, more social workers and bureaucrats. The consequences of these programs have been family dissolution, illegitimacy, mass unemployment, demoralization, and non-existent work skills. Redistribution perpetuates poverty, intensifies it, and therefore increases crime. The real war on poverty occurs daily in the marketplace. Capitalism, entrepreneurship, commerce, and the creation of new wealth is the real war on poverty. Capitalism encourages independence, self-reliance, honest dealing, expanded employment opportunities, and therefore less crime.[9]

New job opportunities in the private sector reduce the relative attractiveness of crime and do not call for more government training and welfare programs. They demand less welfarism. Government should get out of the way and allow the marketplace to create more opportunities and wealth. Many factors influence the labor market conditions that potential criminals confront. For example, federal minimum wage laws and union wage rates prevent many young people, whose services are not worth the minimum, from finding legitimate work. Stealing then is more attractive because they cannot find occasional jobs to pick up spending money. They also fail to acquire the skills, like basic reliability, that would allow them to raise their value in the marketplace. Many other policies adversely affect crime rates, including monetary and fiscal policies. The graduated tax rates, for example, used to finance destructive social programs retard economic growth and employment opportunities.

Robbery and tyranny by the state is a reflection of the general breakdown of moral law, as it was in ancient Rome, when people had lost all respect for the sanctity of private property. If the lights go out in any major American city, many thousands of people will go on a crime spree, as they did in New York City in the blackout of 1977. The intellectuals have spent decades telling people that they are underdogs in an unjust and decaying society, and that violating the laws against theft or rape is a form of social protest, a form of higher morality.

The long-run problem of producing more considerate people means greater reliance on the private market and less on government. It is no surprise that a decline in criminal behavior occurred with the growth of capitalism, and that greater criminality has been associated with the rise of the welfare state and socialism. Reviving internal constraints means gradually reversing the growth of Leviathan. If we are to solve the problem of crime, as with other ills of the welfare state, we must work toward a society where economic and social policies are determined by free markets, not centralized coercion.

The underlying problem is to change the intellectual climate in this country toward liberty and justice and away from collectivism and injustice. No one can avoid this intellectual battle in our politicized era. The purpose of the criminal justice system must become the pursuit of justice once again.

---

1. Also see Ernest van den Haag, "Making Crime Cost and Lawfulness Pay," *Society*, vol. 19 (July/August 1982), p. 22.

2. For evidence, see David T. Hardy, "Gun Control: Arm Yourself with Evidence," *Reason* (November 1982), pp. 37–41.

3. For a dramatic example, see Jeffrey Shedd, "Making Goods Behind Bars," *Reason* (March 1982), pp. 23–34.

4. See Morgan O. Reynolds, "Unions and Violence," *The Freeman* (February 1983), pp. 98–106, and "Contradictions of Unionism," *Journal of Political, Social, and Economic Studies* (Winter 1982), pp. 387–409.

5. For the arguments, see Steven R. Schlesinger, "Criminal Procedures in the Courtroom," especially pp. 192–200 on the exclusionary rule in *Crime and Public Policy*, edited by James Q. Wilson (San Francisco, Calif.: Institute for Contemporary Studies, 1983).

6. Theodore Gage, "Cops, Inc.," *Reason* (November 1982), pp. 23–28.

7. Walter Berns, *For Capital Punishment* (New York: Basic Books, 1979).

8. Friedrich Nietzsche, *Beyond Good and Evil*, trans. Walter Kaufman (New York: Vintage, 1966), sec. 201., p. 114.

9. For corroborating views, see Christie Davies, "Crime, Bureaucracy, and Inequality," *Policy Review*, 23 (Winter 1983), pp. 89–105; James Q. Wilson, "Crime and American Culture," *The Public Interest*, 70 (Winter 1983), pp. 22–48.

The Case for More Incarceration

U.S. Department of Justice

Ask many politicians, newspaper editors, or criminal justice "experts" about our prisons, and you will hear that our problem is that we put too many people in prison. The truth, however, is to the contrary; we are incarcerating too few criminals, and the public is suffering as a result.

Every violent criminal who is in prison is a criminal who is not committing other violent crimes. Too many violent criminals are sentenced to probation with minimal supervision. Too many violent criminals are sentenced to prison but are released early on parole or simply to relieve the pressure of prison crowding. None of us is naive enough to think that these criminals will suddenly become upstanding, law-abiding citizens upon release. And indeed they do not. Much violent crime is directly attributable to our failure to sentence violent criminals to prison and our failure to keep them in prison beyond a fraction of their sentence.

Yes, we would have to build more prisons to implement a policy of more incarceration. Yes, this would cost money. But it would plainly reduce crime and help to protect the public—which is the first responsibility of any government. State and local governments are spending a growing but still modest portion of their budgets on corrections, and it is time to consider our priorities. How much does our failure to incarcerate cost our communities when released offenders commit new crimes? How much does it cost in victims' medical expenses and lost wages, in lost opportunities in inner cities, in lost jobs for the community? How much do government treasuries suffer from the resulting lost tax revenues?

The argument for more incarceration makes three basic points. First, prisons work. Second, we need more of them. Third, inadequate prison space *costs* money. Correspondingly, the most common objections to incarceration do not hold up under scrutiny. Prisons do not create criminals. We are not over-incarcerating. In fact, we could reduce crime by simply limiting probation and parole—by putting criminals in prison for a greater portion of their sentences.

Finally, amid all the concern we hear about high incarceration rates for young black men, one critical fact has been neglected: The benefits of increased incarceration would be enjoyed disproportionately by black Americans living in inner cities, who are victims of violent crime at far higher rates than whites and persons who live outside the inner cities.

Prisons Work

How do we know that prisons work? To begin with, historical figures show that after incarceration rates have increased, crime rates have moderated. In addition, when convicted offenders have been placed on probation or released early from prison, many of them have committed new crimes. One can legitimately debate whether prisons rehabilitate offenders; one can even debate whether, and how much, prisons deter offenders from committing crimes. But there is no debate that prisons incapacitate offenders. Unlike probation and parole, incarceration makes it physically impossible for offenders to victimize the public with new crimes for as long as they are locked up.

Incarceration rates and crime rates

In the 1960s violent crimes reported to police more than doubled, but the nation's prison population declined by almost 8 percent from about 213,000 to under 197,000 in 1970.[1] If the prison population had simply kept pace with the crime rate during this period, the population would have been over 495,000 by 1970—about 2+ times the actual figure.[2] How can it be that so few persons were in prison during a period of soaring crime rates? The answer is that the chances of imprisonment for serious crimes fell dramatically. At the beginning of the decade, for every 1,000 adults arrested for a violent crime or burglary, criminal courts committed 299 offenders to a state prison; by 1970, the rate had dropped to 170.[3]

This drop in the incarceration rate was no accident. The prevailing attitude among policy-makers at the time was that social spending and not imprisonment was the answer to crime. By the 1970s, it had become painfully apparent that the anti-punishment policies of the 1960s had failed. There was a change of direction in criminal

Table 1
Prisoners sentenced to more than one year

Year	Total Prisoners (State and Federal)	Imprisonment Rate (per 100,000)
1960	212,953	117
1970	196,441 (- 8%)	96 (- 18%)
1980	304,692 (+ 55%)	134 (+ 38%)
1990	713,216 (+134%)	282 (+110%)

Source: Bureau of Justice Statistics

justice toward tough law enforcement—arrest, prosecution, *and incarceration*—a change that continued through the 1980s and continues today.

This change was reflected in two different ways. First, there were more inmates sentenced to prison (traditionally measured by the rate per 100,000 population). In 1960, the rate of imprisonment (state *and* federal) per 100,000 was 117. This rate fell during the 1960s, and by 1970 was 96 per 100,000. As a result of the new direction in criminal justice during the 1970s and 1980s, the imprisonment rate rose to 134 per 100,000 in 1980 and to 282 per 100,000 in 1990.[4]

Second, the changed attitude toward incarceration was reflected in an increase in the chance of incarceration after arrest. In an article in *Science* magazine, a scholarly journal published by the American Association for the Advancement of Science, Patrick A. Langan, Bureau of Justice Statistics statistician, has shown that the most important factor in the increased prison population between 1974 and 1986 was the greater likelihood that an arrest would result in a conviction and a sentence to prison. This factor was far more important than any increases in crime-prone populations, increases in reported crime and arrest rates, or increases in drug arrest and imprisonment rates.[5]

The increase in incarceration has been accompanied by a significant slowing of reported crime and by a decrease in estimates of total crime (reported and unreported crime combined). Using rates of crime *reported to police*, measured by the Federal Bureau of Investigation's Uniform Crime Reports, we see that from 1960 to 1970, the murder rate per 100,000 Americans rose by 55 percent, and from 1970 to 1980, it rose by 29 percent. From 1980 to 1990, however, it dropped by 8 percent. From 1960 to 1970, the number of rapes reported to police per 100,000 Americans increased by 96 percent, and by 97 percent from 1970 to 1980. From 1980 to 1990, the increase was only 12 percent. The same pattern can be shown for rates of reported robbery, which increased by 186 percent from 1960 to 1970 and increased by only 2 percent from 1980 to 1990. The FBI's "crime index" offense rate, which includes not only violent crimes but also burglary, larceny-theft, and motor vehicle theft, has seen an even more pronounced trend. From 1960 to 1970, the crime index rate more than doubled, increasing by 111 percent; from 1970 to 1980, it rose by 49 percent; but from 1980 to 1990, it actually *declined* by 2 percent.[6]

The National Criminal Victimization Survey, sponsored by the Bureau of Justice Statistics, estimates total crime against persons age 12 and above—both reported and unreported—based on interviews with a representative sampling of households. In 1973, the first year in which the survey was taken, there were an estimated 94.7 rapes per 100,000 population. This rate remained virtually unchanged in 1980 but had dropped by 32 percent by 1990. Similarly, there were an estimated 674 robberies per 100,000 population in 1973. By 1980, that rate had dropped by 3 percent and by 1990, it had dropped by another 14 percent. Aggravated assaults, which occurred with an estimated frequency of 1006.8 per 100,000 population in 1973, occurred at an 8 percent lower rate in 1980. By 1990, the rate had decreased by another 15 percent.[7]

Imprisonment and prison-construction policies have had a demonstrable effect in individual states. In the early 1980s, the Texas legislature adopted an approach that reduced the time that prisoners served, in an effort to open up space for the next class of felons. Between 1980 and 1989, the average prison term served fell from about 55 percent of the sentence to about 15 percent of the sentence, and by 1989 the parole population grew to more than 5 times its 1980 level. The "expected punishment"—average time served, reduced by the probabilities of arrest, prosecution, conviction, and sentence to prison—for serious crimes (murder, rape, robbery, aggravated assault, burglary, theft) fell 43 percent in Texas during the 1980s while it was increasing by about 35 percent in the nation as a whole, and the rate of these serious crimes reported in Texas rose by about 29 percent, while national rates fell by almost 4 percent.[8]

Table 2
Uniform Crime Reports
(crime rates per 100,000 population)

	1960	1970	1980	1990
Murder	5.1	7.9 (+ 55%)	10.2 (+29%)	9.4 (− 8%)
Rape	9.6	18.7 (+ 95%)	36.8 (+97%)	41.2 (+12%)
Robbery	60.1	172.1 (+186%)	251.1 (+46%)	257.0 (+ 2%)
Aggravated assault	86.1	164.8 (+ 91%)	298.5 (+81%)	424.1 (+42%)
All Violent	160.9	363.5 (+126%)	596.6 (+64%)	731.8 (+23%)
All Index	1887.2	3984.5 (+111%)	5950.0 (+49%)	5820.3 (− 2%)

Note: Figures do not include unreported crimes.

Table 3
National Crime Victimization Survey
Crime Victimization Rates
(per 100,000 persons age 12 or older)

	1973	1980	1990
Rape	94.7	94.3 (−0.5%)	64.0 (−32%)
Robbery	674.0	656.0 (−3%)	565.7 (−14%)
Aggravated assault	1006.8	926.0 (−8%)	787.6 (−15%)
Totals	1775.5	1676.3 (−6%)	1417.3 (−15%)

Note: Figures include estimates of reported—and unreported—crimes, based upon interviews of a sampling of households nationwide. In 1990, approximately 95,000 people in 47,000 households were interviewed. Murders are not included. Survey began in 1973.

In Michigan, when funding for prison construction dried up in the early 1980s, the state instituted an early-release program and became one of only two states whose prison population declined from 1981 to 1984.[9] Between 1981 and 1986, the rate of violent crimes reported to police in Michigan rose by 25 percent at the same time national crime rates were declining. In 1986, however, when Michigan embarked on a major prison-building effort, the state's violent-crime rate began to fall and by 1989 had dropped by 12 percent.[10]

It strains credulity to believe that the lowered crime rates have been unrelated to the unprecedented increases in the nation's incarceration rates, even if there may have been other causes as well. As Langan put it in his *Science* article:

> Whatever the causes, in 1989 there were an estimated 66,000 fewer rapes, 323,000 fewer robberies, 380,000 fewer assaults, and 3.3 million fewer burglaries attributable to the difference between the crime rates of 1973 versus those of 1989 [*i.e.*, applying 1973 crime rates to 1989 population]. If only one-half or even one-fourth of the reductions were the result of rising incarceration rates, that would still leave prisons responsible for sizable reductions in crime.[11]

A Failure to Incarcerate Leads to Increased Crime

One proposition is abundantly clear: *Failure* to incarcerate convicted criminals will lead to additional crimes. There are two sources of direct evidence of this proposition. First, offenders placed on probation commit new crimes while on probation. Second, offenders who are released early commit new crimes during the period when they would otherwise have been confined in prison.

Crimes by probationers. In theory, probation is a sentence meted out to an otherwise law-abiding person who has gone astray. The idea is that such a person deserves a stern warning, with the threat of more serious punishment if the person offends again. There are two main problems when this theory is put into practice. First, considerable evidence indicates that many "first-offenders" have committed crimes in the past for which they have not been caught and convicted, or for which they were treated as juveniles with the adult criminal justice system prohibited by law from seeing their records. Second, about one-fourth of probationers have prior adult felony convictions and are not "first-offenders" under any definition. Nevertheless, some states have determined that probation is a suitable, cost-effective alternative to incarceration. Let us consider what happens to the population of felons on probation.

A recent Bureau of Justice Statistics (BJS) study found over half of the estimated 583,000 state felony convictions in 1986—or 306,000—resulted in a sentence of probation. Of these, about three-fifths received straight probation, and about two-fifths received probation combined with a period in jail or prison (a so-called "split sentence"). Based on a survey of 79,000 felons sentenced to probation in 17 states—over one-fourth of the nation's total—BJS estimated that 12 percent of all probationers had been sentenced to probation after being convicted of a violent offense (one out of every 40 probationers among this 12 percent had been convicted of murder); 34 percent of a drug offense; 29 percent of burglary or larceny; and 3 percent of a weapons offense.[12]

BJS estimated that 43 percent of the 79,000 probationers studied were arrested at least once on a felony charge within 3 years after being placed on probation, and that 62 percent had either a felony arrest or a disciplinary hearing during that period. The 34,000 arrestees counted for a total of 64,000 arrests, with about 8,000 having 2 felony arrests in the 3-year period, and about 7,500 having 3 or more felony arrests. About 8.5 percent of probationers were arrested for violent crimes; those arrests represented 20 percent of felony arrests of probationers.[13] Extrapolating the 43 percent arrest rate and the proportions of multiple arrests and violent crime arrests in the sample to the group of all 306,000 felons sentenced to probation in 1986, this means almost 132,000 probationers were arrested on felony charges about 248,000 times (including nearly 50,000 times for violent felonies) over the following 3 years.

Although these figures sound high, the number of crimes actually committed by felony probationers is almost certainly higher. The most important reason for this is that the survey tallied only *arrests* of probationers, not the total crimes they committed. Arrests on multiple charges were listed only under the most serious charge. Considering that arrests account for only a portion of all crimes, it is likely that the probationers committed other unreported or unsolved crimes as well. In addition, the survey did not include either out-of-state arrests or arrests after 3 years from the start of probation. Also, some probationers were deported, had absconded, or had died.

Even after a person on probation for a felony conviction is convicted after a new felony arrest, there has been a lukewarm reaction by the courts. Of probationers who were convicted after a first new felony arrest while on probation, 42 percent were sentenced to prison, 10 percent to jail, 36 percent to probation with some jail (split sentence), and 9 percent to straight probation (3 percent were "other"). Thus, a full 45 percent of these repeat offenders received a new sentence of probation.[14]

Crime by prisoners released early. Quite a few states have parole systems that release prisoners before they have served their full sentences. Others have implemented early-release programs—either on their own or pursuant to a court order—that are specifically designed to keep down their prison populations. As a result of all these arrangements, crimes are committed by prisoners released early that would not have been committed if the prisoners had remained in prison for the duration of their sentences. These are avertable crimes.

In 1989, the Orlando *Sentinel* conducted a survey of almost 4,000 prisoners released early in Florida because of prison crowding and found that nearly one-fourth were rearrested for a new crime at a time when they would otherwise have been in prison. (In a follow-up survey, the number rose to about 31 percent.) The 950 prisoners rearrested were charged with 2,180 new crimes, including 11 murders or attempted murders, 63 armed robberies, 6 sexual assaults, 7 kidnappings, 104 aggravated assaults, 199 burglaries, and 451 drug offenses. Some were rearrested more than once; 33 were released early, rearrested, convicted, incarcerated, released early again, and rearrested again, all within a two-year period.[15]

This experience in Florida should not be surprising. In a study of the effects of incapacitation on crime, sponsored by the National Academy of Sciences and published in 1986, a research panel concluded that incarceration has a definite incapacitative effect on crime:

> Under 1970 incarceration policies, incapacitation was estimated to have reduced the number of FBI index crimes by 10 to 20 percent. For robberies and burglaries, incapacitation is estimated to have reduced their number by 25–35 percent in 1973; in 1982, after the national inmate population had almost doubled, the incapacitative effect for these offenses is estimated to have increased to about 35–45 percent.[16]

This general conclusion is bolstered by other evidence. The Bureau of Justice Statistics surveyed a sampling among the approximately 108,000 persons released from prison in 11 states in 1983, and found that 62.5 percent were arrested for a new felony or serious misdemeanor within 3 years. The estimated 68,000 prisoners who were rearrested in these 11 states were charged with over 326,000 new offenses, including about 50,000 violent offenses, 141,000 property offenses, and 46,000 drug offenses. Of those who were re-arrested, 40 percent (representing one-fourth of all prisoners released in those states) were rearrested within the first 6 months of release.[17]

Another BJS study looked at male prisoners entering state prisons in 1979 and found that approximately 28 percent of all males admitted to prison that year (or 46 percent of the male recidivists admitted to prison) would still have been in prison at the time of their new admission if they had served the maximum of the sentence range imposed by the court instead of being paroled.[18] The figure we have cited—28 percent of all persons admitted to prison in 1979, or over 43,000 offenders out of a total of about 153,500—represents persons who had committed crimes, had been arrested, prosecuted, and convicted, and had been recommitted to prison, all within the time they would have served on their original sentences.

Further evidence comes from a BJS study of recidivism among young-adult parolees. Based on a sampling of 17- to 22-year-olds paroled from prison in 22 states in 1978, the study estimated that about 69 percent of all such persons were rearrested and charged with a felony or serious misdemeanor within 6 years of release from prison, and that about 29 percent of new arrests occurred before the parolees were first eligible for discharge from parole on the original conviction.[19] In other words, had these offenders remained in prison pursuant to their original sentences instead of being paroled, they would not have been able to commit the new crimes.

A different way of estimating the extent of crime prevention through incapacitation is based on self-reporting of offenders in prison. In 1982, the RAND Corporation conducted a sophisticated survey of a sampling of inmates incarcerated in California and Michigan prisons and jails, as well as in Texas prisons. The survey contained a variety of internal and external checks in an effort to validate inmates' responses. According to the inmates' self-reports, inmates on average committed between 187 and 278 crimes per year, *excluding drug deals.* But the distribution was skewed; about half the population claimed to have committed fewer than 15 crimes per year, while about 25 percent claimed more than 135 crimes and about 10 percent claimed more than 600 crimes per year.[20] A more recent study by the Treasury Department's Bureau of Alcohol, Tobacco and Firearms showed, similarly, that a group of career criminals had committed an average of about 160 crimes a year.[21] These individual crime rates represent the incapacitative effect of prison on the particular offender. Even if we reduce these numbers by one-half or two-thirds on the theory that the inmates were simply boasting of their criminality, incapacitation of such offenders would, by their own admission, prevent them from committing numerous crimes. If released early, however, they would become free to return to wholesale criminality.

This "avertable recidivism"—crime that could have been avoided simply by following through on a sentence of imprisonment on an earlier conviction—proves that prisons work.

Prisons Do Not Create Criminals

We hear all the time that prisons create crime—that imprisonment turns first-time offenders into hardened criminals. If this argument were true, then two other propositions would have to be true as well: first, that many offenders sentenced to prison are not already hardened criminals; and second, that the rate of recidivism increases with the length of time served in prison. Both of these propositions are false.

First, so-called "first-offenders" are often nothing of the sort. In some cases, "first-offenders" have lengthy juvenile records that are unavailable by law to the adult criminal justice system. These "first-offenders" are already hardened criminals. In other cases, offenders get probation for their first adult offense, and sometimes, as we have seen, even for subsequent offenses committed while on probation. In a report on inmates in state prisons in 1986, the Bureau of Justice Statistics found that only about 5 percent of all state prisoners were non-violent first-offenders.[22] This figure would have to be adjusted downward to take into account those who had simply been *caught* for the first time. Former Attorney General Hal Stratton of New Mexico has summed it up: "I don't know anyone that goes to prison on their first crime. By the time you go to prison, you are a pretty bad guy."[23]

Second, as a BJS study of prisoners released in 1983 has shown, the rate of recidivism has little to do with the length of time served in prison before release. In fact, those who had served over 5 years before release had *lower* recidivism rates than those who had served less than 5 years.[24]

Table 4

Time served (in months)	% Rearrested within 3 years
0–6	61.2%
7–12	64.6%
13–18	63.0%
19–24	64.6%
25–30	60.7%
31–36	61.3%
37–60	59.0%
61 +	48.3%

Source: Bureau of Justice Statistics

In the BJS study, the recidivism rate was linked most closely with the offender's age when released and the number of prior arrests. For example, in the 18- to 24-year-old age-of-release group, 48.6 percent of prisoners with one prior arrest were rearrested within 3 years. Among inmates with the same number of prior arrests, the rearrest rate declined as the age of the releasee increased. For example, among prisoners with 4–6 prior arrests, 72.8 percent of 18- to 24-year-olds were rearrested within 3 years, whereas 57.9 percent of 25- to 29-year-olds, 51.0 percent of 30- to 34-year-olds, 41.6 percent of 35-to 39-year-olds, and 30.1 percent of those 40 or older were re-arrested.[25]

Prisons simply aren't responsible for turning unsophisticated young wrongdoers into hardened criminals. To put it differently, prisons don't commit crimes; criminals do.

More Prisons are Needed

It is not news to anyone familiar with prisons that many state prison systems are seriously overcrowded. Nor is it news that many other systems that are *not* overcrowded have kept their inmate populations low by letting criminals go free—either by not incarcerating them in the first place or by releasing them early from prison to make room for the next group of criminals. It is also not news that there is a solution to this problem: Build more prisons.

As we have seen, prison population has increased enormously

in recent years. Although this increase has been accompanied by a considerable amount of construction of new prison space, the building has not kept pace with the expanding inmate population. As of the end of 1991, state prisons in the aggregate were at about 123 percent of average capacity.[26]

In a real sense, this figure understates the problem. Some of the states with populations at or below capacity have reached that position only after being put under court order. Instead of building new prisons to house their prisoners, these states have chosen (or been ordered) to create a revolving door by releasing enough prisoners to meet a cap on population. The "real" inmate population of these states would have to be computed by including in the total those inmates who are released early to make room for others.

When crime rates are intolerably high, the public and many elected officials say that more police are needed. And indeed more police usually *are* needed. Yet this common response focuses on only one part of the solution, at the front end of the criminal justice system, and ignores the need for prison space, which is a critical link in the system at the back end. Even if we have more police, and therefore more arrests, and even if we have more prosecutors and courts, and therefore more prosecutions, trials, and convictions, we will ultimately make no dent in crime if we have so little prison space that we have to send convicted offenders back out on the street well before they have completed their sentences.

Table 5 is based on maximum sentence lengths and actual time served by persons released from state prison in 1988. One can see that the length of time served in prison was a mere fraction of the length of sentence imposed. The median offender received a maximum sentence of 4 years but the median time served was only 1 year and 1 month, slightly over one-quarter. (The *average* maximum sentence length is 5 years and 9 months, while the average time served in prison is 1 year and 10 months, or 32 percent.)[27] Parole decisions are, in theory, based on an evaluation that the offender has been adequately rehabilitated, but these figures show that such decisions are also driven by prison crowding. If prisons are already above capacity, it would be impossible to hold offenders for much longer without placing a severe strain on the prison system.

Given these circumstances, a state that fights crime by increasing arrests, prosecutions, and convictions, but refuses to build more

Table 5
Time served: 1st Release from State Prison

Most serious offense	Max. sentence (median)	Time served (median)
All crimes	4 yrs.	1 yr. 1 mo. (27%)
Violent	5 yrs.	2 yrs. 2 mos. (42%)
Murder	15 yrs.	5 yrs. 6 mos. (37%)
Rape	8 yrs.	3 yrs. 0 mos. (38%)
Robbery	6 yrs.	2 yrs. 3 mos. (38%)
Drugs		
Trafficking	3 yrs.	1 yr. 0 mos. (33%)
Weapons	3 yrs.	1 yr. 1 mo. (36%)

Note: A sentence length is the median if half the sentences are longer and half are shorter.

Source: Bureau of Justice Statistics

prison space, will see one or more of three possible outcomes: first, judges who are forced to grant probation to felons who deserve hard time; second, an increase in prison crowding that is difficult to manage; and third, earlier release of more prisoners. The choice, then, is simple: more prisons or more crime.

We Are Not Over-Incarcerating

Opponents of incarceration often release studies purporting to show that we have too many people in prison or that our incarceration rate is too high. Typically, American incarceration rates are shown to be higher than those of most, if not all, other nations surveyed. These studies, however, take little notice of the high crime rates that plague our country, almost as if imprisonment were unrelated to crime. If differences in national crime rates were taken into account, much of the difference in incarceration rates among nations might disappear.

For example, *arrest*-based imprisonment rates yield results far different from those trumpeted by the opponents' studies. The rate of imprisonment among those who have been arrested for certain

crimes does not vary greatly between the United States and comparable Western democracies. The Bureau of Justice Statistics estimated
that arrest-based imprisonment rates for robbery were 49 percent in
the United States, 52 percent in Canada, and 48 percent in England.[28]
To the extent arrests are proportionate to crime, these data would
suggest that we are not over-incarcerating, at least not in comparison
with England or Canada.

In fact, as high as American incarceration rates appear to be, only
a fraction of all criminals under supervision are in prison at any time.
In 1990, an estimated 4.35 million Americans were under correctional
supervision, of whom about 745,000 were in prison, 403,000 in jail,
531,000 on parole, and 2.67 million on probation. In other words,
nearly three-quarters of those under correctional supervision were
being supervised in the community.[29]

Moreover, if we were actually over-incarcerating, surely we could
find numerous prisoners who do not deserve to be in prison. When
the Bureau of Justice Statistics examined profiles of inmates who
were incarcerated in state prisons in 1986, it found that almost 55
percent were serving time for a violent offense and that another 11
percent had a prior conviction for a violent offense. Still another 29
percent were non-violent recidivists, having a prior sentence to probation or incarceration as an adult or juvenile. In sum, 95 percent of
all state inmates were either violent or repeat offenders. Over half of
the remaining 5 percent had been convicted of drug trafficking or
burglary.[30] (Preliminary results for state inmates in 1991 are similar.[31]) Which of these offenders should we not incarcerate?

What is more, the word recidivist does not tell the whole story.
Nearly 62 percent of state inmates had two or more prior sentences
to probation or incarceration; about 45 percent had 3 or more; over
19 percent had 6 or more; and 6.6 percent had 11 or more.[32] (Table
6) Which of these offenders should we not incarcerate?

The problem, then, is not too much incarceration; the problem is
too much crime, and the simple fact is that the best way to stop crime
is to put criminals in prison.

Failure to Incarcerate Costs Money

Much of the opposition to prison construction is based on cost.
But this concern about cost ignores the costs that are imposed on
society by our failure to incapacitate convicted criminals.

Table 6
Prior Sentences of
State Inmates 1986

Probation and/or incarceration	percent of inmates
None	18.5%
Juvenile	10.6%
Adult	35.9%
Both	34.9%
Number of times	
0	18.5%
1	19.8%
2	16.5%
3–5	26.0%
6–10	12.6%
11 or more	6.6%

Source: Bureau of Justice Statistics

State and local expenditures on prisons, while increasing, are modest portions of the budget. In fiscal year 1990, per capita state and local direct spending on corrections—including not just construction but all aspects of running prisons and jails—was only $94.50.[33] This represented only 2.4 percent of state and local direct spending. (States alone spent only 3.9 percent on corrections.)[34]

Construction costs per bed vary tremendously, from about $11,000 to close to $100,000. But whatever the cost, we must remember that prisons have a useful life of decades. On an annualized basis, construction costs are relatively small; they are a fraction of operating costs, which in fiscal year 1990 averaged $15,513 per inmate.[35]

More important, figures on expenditures for corrections inherently overstate the costs of building and operating prisons. The monetary benefits of prisons—the expenditures that are saved and the revenues that are retained or increased—are left out of the calculus. A proper evaluation of the cost of increasing prison space must include an analysis of the cost of *not* increasing prison space. This requires us to examine the cost of crime, and the cost of crime that could be averted.

It is not easy to give a precise figure for the true cost of crime, but we will suggest a few ways of putting together some estimates. The point to remember when reading this discussion is that even if our estimates are *twice* as high as the true figures, the cost of crime— and in particular the cost of *avertable* crime—is intolerably high. While prisons may be costly to build and operate, those who say they cost *too* much have the burden of showing that the cost of avertable crime is a price we should be willing to pay.

Let us begin with an estimate compiled by the Bureau of Justice Statistics of the direct economic costs to crime victims. In 1990, according to these estimates, victims had total out-of-pocket losses of $19.2 billion.[36] This sounds large, but it represents a modest cost per crime on average. What, after all, are the direct costs to the victim of a mugging (robbery) at gun-point? Perhaps some cash, maybe a watch or a ring. Suppose the victim loses one day of wages in working with police and prosecutors; this amounts to $120 for a person earning $30,000 a year. Let us make a crude estimate of $500 direct economic costs per mugging at gun-point. Does anyone seriously believe that $500 is the true value of such a crime—that if the cost of averting the crime is over $500 we should affirmatively choose to let it happen?

Suppose the mugger flees before taking the cash and goods. Is there *no* cost to this crime? Suppose the mugger takes no cash, but puts his gun to the victim's head, pulls the trigger, and the gun backfires. Should we spend *no* money to avert crime? Plainly, there are other costs to crime.

One analyst, Mark Cohen, has tried to compute the costs of pain, suffering, and fear that the victims endure, based in part upon how juries have apportioned damages between direct economic losses and pain and suffering. While criminal justice professionals may never agree about methodology, we present some of Cohen's findings because his analysis includes some factors that are ordinarily left out of the estimation of costs of crime.

Cohen estimates the average per-crime cost to victims in 1984 (using 1985 dollars) as follows: rape, $51,058; robbery, $12,594; assault, $12,028; personal larceny, $181; motor vehicle theft, $3,127; burglary, $939; and household larceny, $173. In the aggregate, he writes, the estimated total cost of these crimes to the victims in 1984 was $92.6 billion in 1985 dollars.[37] (Table 8) This figure would obvi-

Table 7
Total direct economic loss to
victims of crime, 1990

Type of crime	Gross loss (in millions)
All crimes	$19,216
Personal crimes	4,575
Crimes of violence	1,338
Rape	63
Robbery	618
Assault	657
Crimes of theft	3,237
Personal larceny	
With contact	141
Without contact	3,096
Household crimes	14,641
Burglary	4,340
Household larceny	1,752
Motor vehicle theft	8,550

Source: Bureau of Justice Statistics
Note: Figures do not include justice system costs, pain and suffering, personal anti-crime expenditures, or "macro" costs, such as lost sales, lost jobs, or lost tax revenues.

ously be far higher if computed today. Between 1984 and 1990, the direct economic costs of crime to victims, as estimated by BJS, rose by 54 percent;[38] if intangible losses simply kept pace with victims' direct, out-of-pocket losses, the total cost of crime as computed by Cohen's method would have been over $140 billion by 1990.

Consider what these figures mean. If it costs about $15,500 in operating costs plus a few thousand dollars in annualized construction costs to keep one rapist in prison for only one year, and we thereby prevent him from committing only one rape, we have prevented a crime at bargain-basement prices. This would remain true even if Cohen's figures were twice the "true" costs of the crime. And we are working on the assumption that one year of incarceration prevents only one rape; indeed, as noted earlier, studies indicate that most offenders, when out of prison, commit *numerous* crimes for which they are not caught.

The same kind of reasoning applies to crimes other than rape and to criminals other than rapists, although the precise cost savings of incarceration will differ. Incarceration of certain offenders will result in massive savings, whereas incarceration of others will simply reduce the *net* cost of incarceration. The fundamental point is that one cannot analyze the cost of incarceration without also considering the cost of *non*-incarceration.

Cohen's study shows that we tend to underestimate the cost of crime, but even Cohen leaves out some of the important, though indirect, costs of crime. These indirect costs are the larger societal costs, and they include:

- lost sales, when people are afraid to go out to do their shopping;
- lost jobs, when businesses move out of high-crime areas;
- lost opportunities, when schools become the playgrounds of gangs and drug dealers, rather than places where inner-city kids can learn their way out of poverty; and
- lost tax revenues, when sales, businesses, and jobs evaporate.[39]

David Cavanagh and Mark Kleiman of BOTEC Analysis Corporation, a Cambridge, Massachusetts consulting firm, performed a complex cost-benefit analysis of incarceration that tried to include as many indirect, societal costs and benefits as possible. Cavanagh and Kleiman estimated the most plausible range of costs for incarceration of one inmate per year at $34,000 to $38,000 and the benefits of incarcerating that *one inmate* for a year at between $172,000 and $2,364,000. They did not even include homicide (except where committed in the course of a felony), rape, or drug crimes when evaluating the benefits of incarceration.[40]

Decisions about the cost of building prisons must necessarily take both intangible costs and the broader societal costs into account. Those who think that building prisons is too expensive have the profound moral burden of justifying the additional crimes—and the costs of the additional crimes—that will certainly result from a failure to build.

A Failure to Incarcerate Hurts Black Americans Most

Many well-intentioned people argue that we are incarcerating too many blacks, particularly young black men. Some argue that reduc-

Table 8
Per-Crime Cost of Crime to Victims
(1985 dollars)

Crime	Direct Losses	Pain and Suffering	Risk of Death	Total Cost
Personal				
Rape	$4,617	$43,561	$2,880	$51,058
Robbery	1,114	7,459	4,021	12,594
Assault	422	4,921	6,685	12,028
Larceny	179	——	2	181
Household				
Motor vehicle	3,069	——	58	3,127
Burglary	939	*	*	939*
Larceny	173	——	——	173

Aggregate cost of crime to victims in 1984: **$92.6 billion**

*For burglary Cohen values pain and suffering at $317 and risk of death at $116, but he excludes these because burglary with personal contact becomes a more serious crime, accounted for elsewhere in the table.

Source: Mark Cohen, "Pain, Suffering, and Jury Awards: A Study of the Cost of Crime to Victims," 22 *Law and Society Review* 537 (1988).

ing the numbers of blacks in prison is more important than pushing tough law enforcement policies—indeed, that tough law enforcement has the effect, and perhaps the intent, of putting more blacks in prison. But a failure to incarcerate criminals would result in disproportionate harm to law-abiding black citizens.

Blacks are victims of crime at rates far in excess of their proportions in the general population. The FBI reported that in 1990 more blacks were murdered than whites.[41] This does not mean murder *rates;* it means actual murder victims. Blacks constitute only about 12 percent of the American population. In 1985, the lifetime risk of being a homicide victim was 1 in 179 for white men, but 1 in 30 for black men; it was 1 in 495 for white women, but 1 in 132 for black women.[42]

In 1987, murder was the 12th leading cause of death in the United States but was the leading cause of death among young black men aged 15 to 24, accounting for 42 percent of all deaths in that group. Among persons aged 15 to 24, the 1987 murder rate for black men

Table 9
Summary of Costs and Benefits of Incarceration

	Low	High
Costs (Most Plausible Range)		
Annualized construction costs	$4,094	$5,333
Annual operating costs	18,826	20,912
Inmate's lost legitimate income	8,653	8,653
Annual avg. welfare costs	2,715	2,715
	$34,288	$37,613
Benefits		
Avg. annual costs to victims from crimes committed by a currently imprisoned felon	$49,019	$525,326
Est. social costs (250%–350% of direct costs to victims)	122,547	1,838,641
	$171,566	$2,363,967

Source: David P. Cavanagh & Mark A. R. Kleiman, *A Cost Benefit Analysis of Prison Cell Construction and Alternative Sanctions*, May 1990.

was 4.8 times the rate for black women, 7.7 times the rate for white men, and 21.9 times the rate for white women.[43]

Although the murder figures are the most striking, blacks for many years have been victims of almost all crimes at greater rates than whites. From 1979 to 1986, the rate of violent crime victimization was 44 per 1,000 blacks, and 34 per 1,000 whites.[44] In 1990, the rate of violent crime victimization was 40 per 1,000 blacks, and 28 per 1,000 whites.[45] Robbery victimization rates from 1979 to 1986 were 7 per 1,000 white men, but 18 per 1,000 black men; they were 4 per 1,000 white women, but 9 per 1,000 black women.[46] In fact, black crime victimization rates were higher for each crime other than simple assault and personal larceny without contact.[47] In central cities, blacks suffered higher rates of robbery and burglary than whites regardless of age group or income group, and higher rates of aggravated assault in most age and income groups.[48]

The vast majority of violent crimes against blacks were committed by other blacks. For murders in 1990 in which there was a single offender and a single victim (about 53 percent of murders known to police), 93 percent of the black murder victims were murdered by a black offender.[49] In 1990, 83.9 percent of black violent crime victims reported that the offender was also black.[50] From 1979 to 1986, blacks were victims of about 13 percent of all single-offender violent crimes other than murder nationwide, but in about 11 percent of all cases (that is, in over 80 percent of black-victim cases) the offenders were also black. During that same period, blacks were victims of about 17 percent of all multiple-offender violent crimes other than murder, but in about 13 percent of all cases (over three-quarters of black-victim cases) all the offenders were black, and in another 1 percent (roughly 5 percent of black-victim cases) more than one race was represented in the offender group.[51] White offenders accounted for only 8.9 percent of violent crimes against blacks in 1990.[52]

Color-blind incarceration of violent offenders does not portend a disproportionate increase in black incarceration rates. These rates have changed little during the massive increase in incarceration during the 1980s. In 1980, 46.6 percent of state prisoners and 34.3 percent of federal prisoners were black. In 1990, 48.9 percent of state prisoners and 31.4 percent of federal prisoners were black.[53]

In short, while increasing incarceration might result in higher *numbers* of black men in prison (just as it would with white men), it would disproportionately benefit innocent black victims of their crimes. It is time that those who are concerned for the welfare of black Americans pay more attention to their right to be free from crime.

---

1. Figures are based on comparisons of 1960 and 1970 statistics from U.S. Department of Justice, Federal Bureau of Investigation, *Crime in the United States, 1975*, August 1976, at 49; U.S. Department of Justice, Federal Bureau of Investigation, *Crime in the United States, 1979*, September 1980, at 41; and U.S. Department of Justice, Bureau of Justice Statistics, *Historical Statistics on Prisoners in State and Federal Institutions, Yearend 1925–86*, May 1988, at 10–11 (NCJ-111098).

2. The FBI's Uniform Crime Reports show that the rate of "crime index" crimes (murder, rape, robbery, aggravated assault, burglary, larceny-theft, and motor vehicle theft) rose by 111% from 1960 to 1970. To take account of the increase in population during this period, the 495,000 figure in the text is based on a hypothetical 111% increase in the incarceration rate.

3. U.S. Department of Justice, Bureau of Justice Statistics, *Prisoners in 1990*, May 1991, at 7 (NCJ-129198).

4. *Historical Statistics on Prisoners in State and Federal Institutions, Yearend 1925–86*, *supra* note 1, at 10, 11, 13 (figures for 1960, 1970, and 1980); U.S. Department of Justice, Bureau of Justice Statistics, *Correctional Populations in the United States, 1990*, July 1992,

at 81 (NCJ-134946) (1990 figures). All figures are based on prisoners in custody of the jurisdictions.

5. Patrick A. Langan, "America's Soaring Prison Population," *Science*, March 29, 1991, at 1568.

6. *Crime in the United States, 1975, supra* note 1, at 49 (1960 rates); *Crime in the United States, 1979, supra* note 1, at 41 (1970 rates); U.S. Department of Justice, Federal Bureau of Investigation, *Crime in the United States, 1989*, August 1990, at 48 (1980 rates); U.S. Department of Justice, Federal Bureau of Investigation, *Crime in the United States, 1990*, August 1991, at 50 (1990 rates).

7. U.S. Department of Justice, Bureau of Justice Statistics, *Criminal Victimization in the United States: 1973–88 Trends*, July 1991, at 15, 20, 31 (NCJ-129392); U.S. Department of Justice, Bureau of Justice Statistics, *Criminal Victimization in the United States, 1990*, February 1992, at 16 (NCJ-134126).

8. See generally Eugene H. Methvin, "An Anti-Crime Solution: Lock Up More Criminals," *Washington Post*, October 27, 1991, at C1. Figures for parole population are from U.S. Department of Justice, Bureau of Justice Statistics, *Probation and Parole 1981*, August 1982, at 2–3, and U.S. Department of Justice, Bureau of Justice Statistics, *Probation and Parole 1990*, November 1991, at 3. Figures for "expected punishment" are taken from Morgan O. Reynolds, *Crime in Texas*, National Center for Policy Analysis Report No. 102, at 4 (1991), and Morgan O. Reynolds, *Why Does Crime Pay?*, National Center for Policy Analysis *Policy Backgrounder* No. 110, at 5 (1990). Figures for reported crime rates are taken from U.S. Department of Justice, Federal Bureau of Investigation, *Crime in the United States, 1980*, September 1981, at 57 (1980 Texas rates), and *Crime in the United States, 1989, supra* note 6, at 48, 54 (1989 Texas rates and 1980 and 1989 national rates).

9. *Historical Statistics on Prisoners in State and Federal Institutions, Yearend 1925–86, supra* note 1, at 13.

10. U.S. Department of Justice, Federal Bureau of Investigation, *Crime in the United States, 1981*, August 1982, at 50 (1981 figures); U.S. Department of Justice, Federal Bureau of Investigation, *Crime in the United States, 1986*, July 1987, at 56 (1986 figures); *Crime in the United States, 1989, supra* note 6, at 62 (1989 figures).

11. Patrick A. Langan, *supra* note 5, at 1573.

12. U.S. Department of Justice, Bureau of Justice Statistics, *Recidivism of Felons on Probation, 1986–89*, February 1992, at 2 (NCJ-134177).

13. *Id.* at 5–6.

14. *Id.* at 8.

15. Mark Vosburgh & Sean Holton, "Florida Prison Failure Churns Out Crime Before Its Time," *Orlando Sentinel*, August 13, 1989, at A-12; Mark Vosburgh, "Florida's Early Releases: Flood of Rearrests May Sink Crowded Prisons," *Orlando Sentinel*, December 17, 1989, at A-1.

16. *Criminal Careers and "Career Criminals"* (Alfred Blumstein, Jacqueline Cohen, Jeffrey A. Roth & Christy A. Visher, eds., 1986).

17. U.S. Department of Justice, Bureau of Justice Statistics, *Recidivism of Prisoners Released in 1983*, April 1989, at 3 (NCJ-116261).

18. U.S. Department of Justice, Bureau of Justice Statistics, *Examining Recidivism*, February 1985, at 4 (NCJ-96501).

19. U.S. Department of Justice, Bureau of Justice Statistics, *Recidivism of Young Parolees*, May 1987, at 3 (NCJ-104916).

20. Jan M. Chaiken & Marcia R. Chaiken, *Varieties of Criminal Behavior* 215 (1982).

21. U.S. Department of the Treasury, Bureau of Alcohol, Tobacco and Firearms, *Protecting America: The Effectiveness of Federal Armed Career Criminal Statutes*, May 1991, at 27.

22. U.S. Department of Justice, Bureau of Justice Statistics, *Profile of State Prison Inmates, 1986*, January 1988, at 2 (NCJ-109926).

23. Panel discussion during Attorney General's Summit on Law Enforcement Responses to Violent Crime: Public Safety in the Nineties, March 5, 1991.

24. *Recidivism of Prisoners Released in 1983, supra* note 17, at 9.

25. *Id.* at 8.

26. U.S. Department of Justice, Bureau of Justice Statistics, *Prisoners in 1991*, May 1992, at 7 (NCJ-134729). Capacity can be measured in several different ways. Average capacity refers to the average of the highest and lowest capacity figures reported by the jurisdictions.

27. U.S. Department of Justice, Bureau of Justice Statistics, *National Corrections Reporting Program, 1988*, May 1992, at 28 (NCJ-134929).

28. U.S. Department of Justice, Bureau of Justice Statistics, *Imprisonment in Four Countries*, February 1987, at 2 (NCJ-103967). The report lists a range for West Germany (23%-58%) because that country does not have a practice exactly equivalent to an arrest. *Id.*

29. U.S. Department of Justice, Bureau of Justice Statistics, *Probation and Parole 1990*, November 1991, at 4–5 (NCJ-125833).

30. *Profile of State Prison Inmates, 1986, supra* note 22, at 2–5.

31. Of inmates in state prison in 1991, 20.6% had no prior conviction; 8.1% had at least one prior conviction as a juvenile; 41.1% had at least one prior conviction as an adult; and 30.3% had prior convictions both as a juvenile and as an adult. About 20% had one prior sentence to probation or incarceration; about 16% had two prior sentences; and about 44% had three or more prior sentences. About 45% had a current conviction for a violent offense (note that drug crimes are considered non-violent), and about another 14% had at least one prior conviction for a violent offense. Still another 33% were non-violent recidivists. Thus, about 93% of state inmates in 1991 were either violent or repeat offenders. (Figures do not add up because of rounding.) U.S. Department of Justice, Bureau of Justice Statistics, *Prisons and Prisoners in the United States*, April 1992, at 15–16 (NCJ-137002).

32. *Profile of State Prison Inmates, 1986, supra* note 22, at 4.

33. U.S. Department of Justice, Bureau of Justice Statistics, *Justice Expenditure and Employment 1990* (forthcoming).

34. *Id.*

35. U.S. Department of Justice, Bureau of Justice Statistics, *Census of State and Federal Correctional Facilities, 1990*, May 1992, at 17 (NCJ-137003).

36. *Criminal Victimization in the United States, 1990, supra* note 7, at 148.

37. Mark A. Cohen, "Pain, Suffering, and Jury Awards: A Study of the Cost of Crime to Victims," 22, *Law & Society Review* at 537, 539 (1988).

38. BJS estimated that the direct economic costs of crime to victims in 1984 were $12.473 billion. U.S. Department of Justice, Bureau of Justice Statistics, *Criminal Victimization in the United States, 1984*, May 1986, at 123 (NCJ-100435).

39. *See, e.g.*, James K. Stewart, "The Urban Strangler: How Crime Causes Poverty in the Inner City," *Policy Review*, Summer 1986, at 6.

40. *See generally* David P. Cavanagh & Mark A.R. Kleiman, *A Cost Benefit Analysis of Prison Cell Construction and Alternative Sanctions*, May 1990 (prepared under contract with the National Institute of Justice).

41. *Crime in the United States, 1990, supra* note 6, at 11.

42. U.S. Department of Justice, Bureau of Justice Statistics, *Report to the Nation on Crime and Justice* 28 (2d ed. 1988) (NCJ-105506).

43. Centers for Disease Control, "Homicide Among Young Black Males—United States, 1978–1987," 39 *Morbidity and Mortality Weekly Report* at 869–73 (December 7, 1990).

44. U.S. Department of Justice, Bureau of Justice Statistics, *Black Victims*, April 1990, at 2 (NCJ-122562).

45. *Criminal Victimization in the United States, 1990, supra* note 7, at 24.

46. *Black Victims, supra* note 44, at 4.

47. *Id.* at 2.

48. *Id.* at 6.

49. *Crime in the United States, 1990, supra* note 6, at 11.

50. *Criminal Victimization in the United States, 1990, supra* note 7, at 61.

51. *Black Victims, supra* note 44, at 9. Figures showing percentages of black-victim cases with black offenders were derived from these same data.

52. *Criminal Victimization in the United States, 1990, supra* note 7, at 61. According to victim reports, white offenders account for 71.5% of violent crimes against whites. *Id.*

53. *Prisoners in State and Federal Institutions on December 31, 1981,* March 1983, at 35 (NCJ-86485) figures); *Correctional Populations in the United States 1990, supra* note 4, at 83 (1990 figures).

Truth in Sentencing: Why States Should Make Violent Criminals Do Their Time

by James Wootton

Introduction

More and more state legislators are coming to realize that America's criminal justice system is failing, and that too many Americans literally are dying from a severe case of bad public policy.

ITEM: Consider a heinous crime that has shocked the nation. Twelve-year-old Polly Klaas of Petaluma, California, was abducted from her home during a sleepover with two friends on October 1, 1993, and subsequently murdered. During the abduction, both of Polly's friends were gagged and bound by the assailant, while little Polly was forcibly taken into the night. Richard Allen Davis, the alleged assailant, already had been sentenced to sixteen years in prison for kidnapping, but was released on June 27, 1993, after serving only eight years of that sentence.[1]

ITEM: James Jordan, the 56-year-old father of basketball star Michael Jordan, was fatally shot in the chest on Interstate 95 in North Carolina on July 23, 1993. Charged in the murder of James Jordan were Larry Martin Demery and Daniel Andre Green. Demery had been charged in three previous cases involving theft, robbery, and forgery. Green had been paroled after serving two years of a six-year sentence for an assault in which he hit a man in the head with an axe, leaving his victim in a coma.[2]

ITEM: Sister MaryAnn Glinka, aged 50 and a member of the Franciscan Sisters of Baltimore Motherhouse in Baltimore, Maryland, was strangled to death at the convent. Baltimore police concluded that Sister MaryAnn was murdered during

233

a robbery at the convent. On March 21, 1993, Melvin L. Jones was arrested and subsequently charged with robbery and the murder of Sister MaryAnn. The alleged assailant had been sentenced in North Carolina in 1979 to eighteen to twenty years in prison for voluntary manslaughter, but had escaped on November 27, 1986. In 1989, Jones was arrested again in Baltimore for three burglaries, but let out on parole in 1990. In 1991, the North Carolina judiciary sentenced Jones to a year in jail on the escape charge, and contacted Maryland officials in December 1991 to arrange for Jones to be paroled in Maryland.[3]

Not surprisingly, Americans are increasingly alarmed at news stories of violent crimes committed by individuals who had received long sentences for other crimes and yet were released after serving only a small fraction of their time. This alarm is legitimate, for a high proportion of such early-release prisoners commit serious crimes after being released. If crime is to be reduced in America, this trend needs to be reversed. Experience shows clearly that the first step in fighting crime is to keep violent criminals off the street. Keeping violent criminals incarcerated for at least 85 percent of their sentences would be the quickest, surest route to safer streets, schools, and homes.[4]

Comparing Sentences and Time Served

Offense	Median Sentence	Median Time Served
Murder	15 years	5.5 years
Rape	8 years	3 years
Robbery	6 years	2.25 years
Assault	4 years	1.25 years

Government statistics on release practices in 36 states and the District of Columbia in 1988 show that although violent offenders received an average sentence of seven years and eleven months imprisonment, they actually served an average of only two years and eleven months in prison—or only 37 percent of their imposed sentences.[5] The statistics also show that, typically, 51 percent of violent criminals were discharged from prison in two years or less, and 76 percent were back on the streets in four years or less.[6]

When these prisoners are released early, a high percentage commit more violent crimes. As a result, Americans are suffering a fearful epidemic of violent crime. Studies indicate that over 25 percent of all males admitted to prison were being reincarcerated after a new trial for a new offense before the prison term for the first offense had expired. Since 1960, the compounding effect of these crimes by prisoners or early-release prisoners has driven the violent crime rate up by over 500 percent. Now eight out of ten Americans are likely to be victims of violent crime at least once in their lives,[7] at a total cost of $140 billion.[8]

Not surprisingly, the fear of violent crime is intensifying. Polls indicate a growing loss of public confidence in their personal safety and the safety of their streets and neighborhoods. Some 90 percent of Americans think the crime problem is growing, and 43 percent say there is more crime in their neighborhood than there was a year ago.[9] The reason: despite rising arrest rates and prison overcrowding, 3.2 million convicted felons are out on parole or probation rather than in prison. Studies show that within three years, 62 percent of all prisoners released from prison are rearrested,[10] and 43 percent of felons on probation are rearrested for a felony.[11]

The public understandably wants individuals who have committed serious crimes to be off the streets, serving full prison terms. A recent survey for *Parade* magazine finds that 92 percent of Americans want repeat serious offenders to serve all of their sentences without being paroled.[12] This finding is consistent with an earlier Gallup poll showing that 82 percent of Americans favor making it more difficult for those convicted of violent crimes like murder and rape to be paroled.[13]

The federal government and the states have begun in recent years to address the problem. Toward the end of the Bush Administration, for example, then-Attorney General William Barr issued a report making 24 specific recommendations to the states to help to reduce violent crime.[14] The second recommendation was to institute truth-in-sentencing laws that restrict the ability of parole boards and prison officials to release a prisoner before a specified percentage of his sentence has been served. As of 1987, the federal system requires prisoners to serve 85 percent of their sentences before they can be released. In 1993, Arizona passed a similar restriction on early release.

In November 1993, Governors-elect George Allen of Virginia and Christine Whitman of New Jersey promised full support for enactment of truth-in-sentencing laws in their respective states. The time is right for the introduction of truth-in-sentencing legislation in the states where violent criminals are being released before serving the bulk of their sentences.

At the same time, state legislators should get substantial help from Congress. Representative Jim Chapman, the Texas Democrat, and Representative Don Young, the Alaska Republican, have sponsored "The Truth in Sentencing Act of 1993," which would encourage states to adopt truth-in-sentencing legislation and would help fund truth-in-sentencing programs. Instead of tax increases to finance the enforcement of truth-in-sentencing initiatives, including prison construction, funding would come from reduction of the size of the federal bureaucracy and cuts in federal spending.

High Recidivism: The Failure of Parole

Releasing violent criminals from prison before they have completed their sentences is justified by proponents for one of three reasons: first, prisons are overcrowded and it is too costly to build more prisons; second, "good time" credits, which have the effect of reducing sentences, are and should be given to well-behaved prisoners; and third, prisoners sometimes can be rehabilitated, and so should be paroled.

The problem is that the evidence seriously questions the second and third rationales, and shows the first to be very shortsighted.

Recidivism among violent criminals is high. Consider a three-year follow-up of 108,850 state prisoners released in 1983 from institutions in eleven states, conducted by the Bureau of Justice Statistics.[15] The study, the conclusions of which are consistent with those of other such studies, found that within three years some 60 percent of violent offenders were rearrested for a felony or serious misdemeanor, and 42 percent of all violent offenders released were reincarcerated. Of all the violent offenders released, 36 percent were rearrested for a violent crime. Among nonviolent prisoners released, 19 percent were rearrested within three years for a violent crime.

The prisoners in the study accounted for over 1.6 million arrest charges for the time before they had entered prison and for the three years afterwards. These included nearly 215,000 arrests for violent crimes before going to prison and 50,000 violent crimes within three years after release. Altogether they were arrested for:

- 14,467 homicides
- 7,073 kidnappings
- 23,174 rapes or sexual assaults
- 101,226 robberies
- 107,130 assaults

The Problems of Determining Parole

The U.S. Parole Board uses a sophisticated Salient Factor Score (SFS) to guide it in deciding who will be paroled. Unfortunately for law-abiding Americans, the Parole Board turns out to be over-optimistic. Of those classified by the Parole Board staff as "good risks" for parole, the Parole Board assumes that 18 percent will be re-arrested and again sentenced to prison for over one year within five years of release. In addition, the Parole Board expects that 29 percent of "fair risks" who are paroled will be resentenced to over a year in prison within five years of release.[16]

Considering the government's—and the American people's—anxiety about risk, this parole policy is remarkable. Where else would such a high failure rate be tolerated when it results in the death, rape, or injury of ordinary Americans? The Federal Aviation Administration certainly does not allow airplanes to fly with critical parts that fail 29 percent of the time. And the Food and Drug Administration does not allow drugs on the market that have dangerous side effects 18 percent of the time.

Twenty years ago, James Q. Wilson, then a professor of government at Harvard University, asked a basic question about rehabilitation:

> If rehabilitation is the object, and if there is little or no evidence that available correctional systems will produce much rehabilitation, why should any offender be sent to any institution? But to turn them free on the grounds that society does not know how to make them better is to fail to protect

society from those crimes they may commit again and to violate society's moral concern for criminality and thus to undermine society's conception of what constitutes proper conduct. [Because the correctional system had not reduced recidivism], we would view the correctional system as having a very different function—namely, to isolate and to punish. It is a measure of our confusion that such a statement will strike many enlightened readers today as cruel, even barbaric. It is not. It is merely a recognition that society at a minimum must be able to protect itself from dangerous offenders and to impose some costs (other than the stigma and inconvenience of an arrest and court appearance) on criminal acts; it is also frank admission that society really does not know how to do much else.[17]

Until there are dramatic improvements in the techniques of rehabilitation and identifying those who can safely be paroled, state legislators would be wise to follow Professor Wilson's admonition: society must protect itself from dangerous offenders and impose real costs on criminal acts. Or, as Douglas Jeffrey, executive vice president of the Claremont Institute says, "We need to put justice back into the criminal justice system by putting convicted criminals behind bars and keeping them there for appropriate periods of time."[18] If state legislators were to adopt that simple mission, today's unacceptable risks to law-abiding Americans would be reduced.

Incarceration Saves Money

While full sentences may mean more spending on prison, lawmakers and taxpayers need to understand that early-release programs cost dollars rather than save them. A 1982 RAND Corporation study of prison inmates found that the average inmate had committed 187 crimes the year before being incarcerated.[19] When criminals are released early, many commit a similar volume of crimes when back on the streets.

The cost of crime committed by these early-release criminals is both direct and indirect. Taxpayers must finance the criminal justice system. Householders and businesses must buy private protection such as lighting, locks, dogs, fences, and alarm systems. They must

Crimes Committed by Felons
Not Incarcerated

One Criminal	Crimes Per Year
Burglar	76–118 burglaries
Robber	41–61 robberies
Thief	135–202 thefts
Auto Thief	76–100 auto thefts
Forger	62–98 frauds
Conman	127–283 frauds
Drug Dealer	880–1,299 drug deals

buy insurance. The victims lose property and wages, and often incur heavy hospitalization costs. In addition to the direct costs, there is the hidden cost of crime. Businesses, for instance, pass on to customers some of their costs for security and stolen merchandise. Households also must "pay" for crime by altering their behavior and life-styles.[20] It has been estimated that the crime increases in the early 1980s caused "150,000 more New Yorkers to take taxis instead of public transportation; some 140,000 more New York City households sacrificed trips rather than leave their apartments unprotected. 50,000 put bars on their windows and 40,000 bought weapons. Even more difficult to assess are the costs of 'urban blight,' such as abandoned buildings, unsafe schools, and inner-city unemployment. Quite possibly the costs we can't count exceed the ones we can."[21]

It is easy for policy-makers to underestimate the tremendous costs of crime, particularly the cost of injuries and deaths of victims. Mark Cohen, a researcher at the U.S. Sentencing Commission, broke new ground in this area in 1988 by using jury verdicts in personal injury cases to estimate the value of injuries to victims. As the table on the next page indicates, the cost to society of each rape is $51,058, each robbery $12,594, each assault $12,028. These costs are invisible to all but the victims, who are randomly burdened by society's failure to keep repeat offenders in prison.[22]

David Cavanagh and Mark Kleiman of the BOTEC Analysis Corporation, a Cambridge, Massachusetts, consulting firm, performed an even more ambitious and complex cost-benefit analysis of incarceration. The analysis includes as many indirect, societal costs and

Per-Crime Cost of Crime to Victims
(1985 Dollars)

Crime	Direct Losses	Pain and Suffering	Risk of Death	Total Cost
Rape	$4,617	$43,561	$2,880	$51,058
Robbery	$1,114	$7,459	$4,021	$12,594
Assault	$442	$4,921	$6,685	$12,028
Larceny	$179		$2	$181

benefits as possible. Cavanagh and Kleiman estimate the most plausible range of the cost of incarceration of one inmate per year at $34,000 to $38,000. But the total benefits occurring from incarcerating that one inmate for a year, eliminating the cost of the individual's probable crimes, could run between $172,000 and $2,364,000.[23] In a recent paper Cavanagh and Kleiman computed a range of ratios from 3-to-1 to as high as 17-to-1 of benefits over costs.[24] Edwin W. Zedlewski, of the National Institute of Justice, estimated a benefit/cost ratio for incarcerating prisoners of 17-to-1.

The 1982 RAND Corporation study finds that the average robber commits between 41 and 61 robberies a year. Mark Cohen estimates that the actual cost to society of each robbery is $12,569.[25] Assuming the cost to society of keeping a robber in prison is Cavanagh and Kleiman's high estimate of $37,614 a year, from a strictly financial point of view, it makes sense to incarcerate a robber if that individual commits three or more robberies each year.

Investing in Safety

The imprisonment rate is higher in the United States than it is in other Western democracies mainly because Americans commit crime at a higher rate. The homicide rate in the United States is five times as high as in Europe; the rape rate is more than six times as high; and the robbery rate is four times as high.[26]

Given the higher crime rates in the United States, and the benefits to society of incarcerating criminals, state and federal officials have underinvested in public safety. According to one estimate, more than 120,000 additional prison beds were needed across the nation at the close of 1990.[27] Some might argue that some inmates do not belong in prison, and should be replaced with hardened criminals. But 95 percent of Americans in prison are repeat or violent offenders.[28] Despite this enormous need for additional prison space, spending on corrections remains a very small percentage of state and local budgets. In fiscal year 1990, only 2.5 percent of the $975.9 billion in total expenditures by state and local governments went for corrections (about $24.7 billion). Investment in new prison construction is only a small fraction of that figure.[29]

The experience of these states shows the folly of trying to save money by reducing prison budgets, and the benefits of increased prison construction.

Michigan: In the late 1970s, Michigan's state legislators and voters refused to build new prisons. The state soon was forced to deal with severe overcrowding. Governor William G. Milliken granted emergency releases to 20,000 inmates over four years, some more than two years early. The violent crime rate for Michigan, as reported by the FBI, soared 25 percent from 1978 to 1986 amid mounting public outrage.

Starting in 1986, a crash prison-building program doubled the inmate population in five years. Michigan's crime rate dropped. By 1990, robbery and burglary rates each fell more than 20 percent. In Detroit, burglaries went down 32 percent, robberies 37 percent.

California: Since 1982, Californians have approved $3.7 billion in bonds to build prisons. From 1980 to January 1991, the inmate population quadrupled from 22,600 to 87,300. By 1990, murder rates fell almost 24 percent from their 1980–1982 peaks, rape fell nearly 28 percent, burglary rates were down 38 percent. This translates as an annual reduction of nearly a thousand murders, 16,000 robberies, and a quarter of a million burglaries.[30]

Illinois: In 1980, the state released 21,000 prisoners three months before completion of their sentences, in an effort to reduce the cost of detention. But while the state saved $60 million, those prisoners committed 23 murders, 32 rapes, 262 acts of arson, 681 robberies, 2,472 burglaries, 2,571 assaults, and 8,000 other crimes in the three months following their release.[31]

Why Truth in Sentencing Helps

Truth in sentencing will increase the length of time convicted violent criminals are incarcerated. Currently, violent criminals are serving 37 percent of the sentence that has been imposed. If required to serve at least 85 percent of their sentences, violent criminals would serve 2.3 times longer than they do now.

If the 55 percent of the estimated 800,000 current state and federal prisoners who are violent offenders were subject to serving 85 percent of their sentence, and assuming that those violent offenders would have committed ten violent crimes a year while on the street, then the number of crimes prevented each year by truth in sentencing would be 4,400,000.[32] That would be over two-thirds of the 6,000,000 violent crimes reported in the National Criminal Victimization Survey for 1990.[33]

Targeting Hardened Criminals

Truth-in-sentencing laws would require state prison officials to retain more prisoners, at a higher cost to the state. But research shows that these prisoners are generally society's most dangerous predators.[34] In a landmark study, University of Pennsylvania criminologist Marvin Wolfgang compiled arrest records up to their 30th birthday for every male born and raised in Philadelphia in 1945 and 1958. He found that just 7 percent of each age group committed two-thirds of all violent crime, including three-fourths of the rapes and robberies and virtually all of the murders. Moreover, this 7 percent not only had five or more arrests by age 18 but went on committing felonies. Wolfgang and his colleagues estimate these criminals got away with about a dozen crimes each.[35] Their studies suggest that about 75,000 new, young, persistent criminal predators are added to the population every year. They hit their peak rate of offenses at about age 16.[36]

In response to these findings, Alfred Regnery, who was Administrator of the Office of Juvenile Justice and Delinquency Prevention at the Justice Department from 1982 to 1986, funded projects in cities in which police, prosecutors, schools, and welfare and probation workers pooled information to focus on the "serious habitual offender." The program had a significant effect in many cities. Thanks to this Justice Department program, for example, Oxnard, California, was able to place the city's thirty most active serious habitual offenders behind bars, and violent crimes dropped 38 percent in 1987, more than double the drop in any other California city. By 1989, when all thirty of the active serious habitual offenders were behind bars, murders declined 60 percent compared with 1980, robberies 41 percent, and burglaries 29 percent.[37]

Thus in conjunction with a criminal justice system that convicts and incarcerates hardened criminals, a truth-in-sentencing policy will reduce crimes by keeping these serious and habitual offenders in prison longer.

Deterring Criminals

Incarceration incapacitates violent criminals, and directly benefits law-abiding Americans, by protecting families and also by yielding greater financial savings from reduced crime than the cost of incarceration itself. But stepped-up imprisonment also deters crime. Criminologist Isaac Ehrlich, of the University of Chicago, estimated that a one-percent increase in arrest rates produces a one-point decrease in crime rates, and a one-percent increase in sentence length produces a one-percent decrease in crime rates, for a combined deterrent and incapacitation effect of 1.1 percent.[38] Observed trends seem to support Ehrlich's broad conclusion and hence the claim of deterrence. When the rate of imprisonment per 100 crimes began dropping in the early 1960s, for instance, the rate of crime per 100 population began to climb steeply.

A recent report by the Dallas-based National Center for Policy Analysis, written by Texas A&M economist Morgan Reynolds, makes a strong case for the deterrence value of longer sentences. According to Reynolds:

> Crime has increased as the expected costs of committing crimes has fallen. Today, for a burglary, for example, the chance of arrest is 7 percent. If you are unlucky enough to be one of the 7 percent arrested, relax; only 87 percent of arrestees are prosecuted. Of those, only 79 percent are convicted. Then only 25 percent of those convicted actually go

to prison. Multiplying out all these probabilities gives your would-be burglar a 1.2 percent chance of going to jail.[39]

So, too many criminals do not go to jail for the crimes they commit. Reynolds points out that "once in prison, a burglar will stay there for about 13 months, but since more than 98 percent of burglaries never result in a prison sentence, the average expected sentence for each act of burglary is only 4.8 days. Similar calculations yield an expected punishment in 1990 of 1.8 years for murder, 60.5 days for rape, and 6.7 days for arson. Thus, for every crime, the expected punishment has declined over the decades. The decline continues between 1988 and 1990. When punishments rise, crime falls."[40] In short, Reynolds's argument is that raising expected punishment deters crime. Expected punishment is a function of the risk of being caught and convicted multiplied by the median time served. Therefore, everything being equal, increasing the length of sentence increases expected punishment, and hence a criminal is more likely to be deterred when the sentence is longer.

Reynolds also finds that since 1960, the expected punishment for committing a serious crime in Texas has dropped by more than two-thirds, while the number of serious crimes per 100,000 population in Texas has increased more than sixfold.[41]

While these data do not separate out the deterrent effect of longer sentences from the incapacitation effect, it is clear that longer sentences can generally be expected to reduce crime rates.

Objections to Truth-In-Sentencing Laws

State truth-in-sentencing laws have great potential to combat violent crime. While academics and legislators in Washington and the states often focus on long-term solutions to the crime problem, such as social or economic conditions or the "root causes" of crime, the special merit of the truth-in-sentencing approach is simply that it keeps violent criminals off the streets while citizens, legislators, and professionals debate the merits of differing approaches in relative safety.

In spite of its appeal to common sense, opponents of truth-in-sentencing legislation often make invalid objections. Some argue that truth in sentencing simply costs too much. But such an objection overlooks the opportunity cost of not keeping dangerous offenders in prison. For example, the cost of incarcerating a criminal is approximately $23,000 per year, but the cost of that criminal on the street is $452,000 per year. Some financial estimates are much higher. And, of course, for the families and victims of violent crime, such as James Jordan's and Polly Klaas's, the human cost is beyond calculation.

Others argue that the already large numbers of persons in American jails is an international scandal. While there are indeed more criminals in America who serve more time than criminals in other countries, the fact remains that the violent crime rate in America is proportionately higher than in virtually all other countries. And if there is any scandal, it is the perpetuation of a failing criminal justice system that allows convicted rapists, kidnappers, and armed robbers back on the streets, ignoring the concerns of an American public that desperately needs security from predatory, violent criminals.

Beyond the questions of cost and the higher percentage of individuals being incarcerated, another objection to the enactment of truth-in-sentencing laws is that they ignore the "root causes" of crime. These root causes are often discussed in terms of persistent poverty, poor education, and deteriorating families. Liberal academics, of course, are not alone in addressing these maladies; and conservative social criticism, including recent analyses by scholars from the Heritage Foundation, have enriched the growing national debate on America's failing criminal justice system.[42] But an academic focus on "root causes," whatever its long-term impact on public policy, should not ignore the fact that violent crime itself immediately aggravates these social problems.

Beyond these general reservations, there are other objections to truth-in-sentencing laws:

Objection #1: Truth in sentencing interferes with other policies.

Truth in sentencing does not. For instance, it does not affect *habeas corpus*, mandatory minimum sentences, the exclusionary rule, the death penalty, or gun control. Moreover, truth in sentencing is no threat to existing programs designed to divert criminals from jail or prison, such as community-based corrections, intensive probation, house arrest, restitution, or boot camps for first-time offenders. A judge or jury sentencing a convicted criminal to any of these alternatives would not be in conflict with truth in sentencing. But if a judge or jury imposes a prison sentence on a criminal with such a law on the books, another government official cannot later amend the sentence and send that person to an alternative program not involving incarceration. If a judge or jury feels comfortable permitting alternatives to prison for a criminal after listening to the evidence, learning the criminal's background, and hearing from the victim, then truth-in-sentencing requirements would be satisfied.

Objection #2: Truth in sentencing discriminates against minorities.

Some critics argue that the criminal justice system discriminates against black Americans, and so truth-in-sentencing rules will unfairly hit those inmates. On their face, the raw statistics are indeed disturbing. Blacks comprise only 12 percent of the population, but constitute 48.9 percent of state prisoners and 31.4 percent of federal prisoners. The impact of truth-in-sentencing laws would depend on whether blacks or whites are disproportionately convicted of the crimes covered by the laws, and whether parole currently favors blacks or whites. However, these laws would be evenhanded. All convicted offenders, regardless of race, would have to serve 85 percent of their sentences before being eligible for parole.

A more significant question is whether the higher percentages of blacks in prison are the result of racial bias or of higher rates of crime. A number of studies have been conducted to answer that question and appear to demonstrate that it is higher rates of crime among blacks, and not bias, that accounts for their disproportionate representation in America's prisons.

Alfred Blumstein, Professor of Urban and Public Affairs at Carnegie-Mellon University, in a 1982 study, concluded that about 80 percent of the observed racial disparity in prison population was the result of differential involvement in crime. He acknowledged, however, that the decision to arrest could be affected by bias.[43]

Patrick A. Langan, a statistician at the Bureau of Justice Statistics, attempted to test whether bias in arrests might be a factor in the rates of imprisonment. He analyzed the racial composition of lawbreakers from victims' reports to derive an estimate of what the prison composition should be, and then compared that with the actual percentage

**Estimate of Prison Admissions
From Victims' Reports,
Compared with the Actual Admissions**

Year	Estimated Black %	Actual Black %
1973	48.1	48.9
1979	43.8	48.1
1982	44.9	48.9

of prison admissions. As the above table shows, the estimated percentage was only a few points below the actual percentage.[44]

Furthermore, a 1990 RAND Corporation study concludes that it is possible to predict with 80 percent accuracy whether an offender will be sentenced to probation or prison.[45] Adding the offender's race to the equation does not improve the accuracy of the prediction. Race also is unrelated to the length of prison term imposed.

Conclusion

The time has come for states to enact truth-in-sentencing laws. There are few viable alternatives that protect citizens from the immediate threat of violent crime. Parole, for example, is a failed experiment. The American people deserve better.

The task before America's state legislators and governors is to pass truth-in-sentencing legislation that would require violent criminals to serve the bulk of their sentences—85 percent is a good benchmark—and to provide the resources it will take to implement such laws. The federal government can encourage this common-sense approach. One such initiative is the Truth in Sentencing Act of 1993, H.R. 3584, introduced by Representatives Jim Chapman and Don Young. This bill would encourage each state to adopt truth-in-sentencing laws and would fund assistance to the states, amounting to $10.5 billion over five years, to help them implement such laws, including the building and operating of prisons. Trimming the federal bureaucracy, not tax increases, is the financing mechanism for these efforts.

The cost of doing nothing is unacceptably high. Crime is a leading concern for Americans. Political leaders and state legislators who can focus the public's attention on a common sense reform like truth in sentencing will be setting the terms of the national debate.

1. Representative Jim Chapman (D-TX), Press Release, December 6, 1993.

2. Michael Tackett and Bob Sakamoto, "Suspects in Jordan Slaying Have Previous Records, The Two Teenagers Charged in the Killing of Michael Jordan's Father Were Arraigned on Monday," *The Chicago Tribune*, August 17, 1993, p. D1.

3. Jason Grant, "Parolee Charged in Slaying of Baltimore Nun," *The Washington Times*, March 22, 1993, p. B1.

4. Bureau of Justice Statistics, U.S. Department of Justice, *National Corrections Reporting Program, 1988*, table 2–7.

5. *Ibid.*, table 2–4.

6. *Ibid.*, table 2–7.

7. Bureau of Justice Statistics, U.S. Department of Justice, *Lifetime Likelihood of Victimization*, technical report, March 1987.

8. U.S. Department of Justice, "The Case for More Incarceration," 1992, p. 16. [Reprinted as the previous chapter in this volume.]

9. See CNN/Gallup Poll, cited in *USA Today*, October 28, 1993, p. 1A.

10. Bureau of Justice Statistics, U.S. Department of Justice, Special Report, *Recidivism of Prisoners Released in 1983*, April 1989.

11. Bureau of Justice Statistics, U.S. Department of Justice, Special Report, *Recidivism of Felons on Probation*, February 1992.

12. Mark Clements, "Findings from *Parade's* national survey on law and order," *Parade*, April 18, 1993, pp. 4–7.

13. George Gallup, Jr., *The Gallup Report*, Report No. 285 (Princeton, N.J.: The Gallup Poll, June 1989), pp. 29, 30.

14. U.S. Department of Justice, *Combatting Violent Crime: 24 Recommendations to Strengthen Criminal Justice*, July 1992. For an excellent discussion of these recommendations, see Mary Kate Cary, "How States Can Fight Violent Crime: Two Dozen Steps to a Safer America," Heritage Foundation *State Backgrounder*, No. 944/S, June 7, 1993. [See the next chapter in this volume.]

15. Bureau of Justice Statistics, *Recidivism of Prisoners Released in 1983*. See also, Bureau of Justice Statistics, U.S. Department of Justice, Special Report, *Examining Recidivism*, February 1985.

16. Peter B. Hoffman and James L. Beck, "Recidivism Among Released Federal Prisoners: Salient Factor Score and Five Year Follow-Up," *Criminal Justice and Behavior*, vol. 12, no. 4 (December 1985), pp. 501–507.

17. James Q. Wilson, "If Every Criminal Knew He Would Be Punished If Caught," *The New York Times Magazine*, January 28, 1973, pp. 52–56.

18. Editor's note in Joseph M. and Anne Nutter Bissette, *Ten Myths About Crime and Justice* (Claremont, Cal.: The Claremont Institute, March 1992).

19. See generally Peter Greenwood *et al.*, *Selective Incapacitation*, Report R-2815-NIJ, The Rand Corporation, Santa Monica, Cal., 1982.

20. Edwin Zedlewski, *Costs and Benefits of Sanction: A Synthesis of Recent Research*, unpublished paper, National Institute of Justice, June 1992.

21. William W. Greer, "What Is The Cost of Rising Crime?" *New York Affairs*, January 1984, pp. 6–16.

22. Mark Cohen, "Pain, Suffering, and Jury Awards: A Study of the Cost of Crime to Victims," *Law and Society Review*, Vol. 22, No. 537 (1988).

23. See generally David P. Cavanagh and Mark A. R. Kleiman, *A Cost Benefit Analysis of Prison Cell Construction and Alternative Sanctions*, May 1990 (prepared under contract with the National Institute of Justice).

24. *Ibid.*

25. Cohen, *op. cit.*

26. "International Crime Rates," May 1988, NCJ-110776.

27. Bureau of Justice Statistics, U.S. Department of Justice, *Prisoners in 1990*, table 9 (1991).

28. Bureau of Justice Statistics, U.S. Department of Justice, *Prisons and Prisoners in the United States* (1992), p. 16.

29. Bureau of the Census, U.S. Department of Commerce, *Government Finances: 1989–90* (1991), p. 2.

30. Eugene H. Methvin, "An Anti-Crime Solution: Lock Up More Criminals," *The Washington Post*, October 27, 1991, p. C1. Methvin is a Senior Editor of *Reader's Digest* and served on the President's Commission on Organized Crime from 1983 to 1986.

31. James Austin, "Using Early Release to Relieve Prison Crowding: A Dilemma in Public Policy," *Crime & Delinquency*, vol. 32, no. 4 (October 1986), pp. 480–481.

32. The median number of crimes reported in RAND Study was 15. See Greenwood *et al.*, *op. cit.*

33. See U.S. Department of Justice, *Criminal Victimization in the United States, 1990*, p. 4.

34. Methvin, *op. cit.*

35. P.E. Tracy, M.E. Wolfgang, and R.M. Figlio, *Delinquency Careers in Two Birth Cohorts* (New York: Plenum Press, 1990), pp. 279–280.

36. *Ibid.*

37. Methvin, *op. cit.*

38. Isaac Ehrlich, "Participation in Illegitimate Activities: A Theoretical and Empirical Investigation," *Journal of Political Economy*, May/June 1973, pp. 521–564.

39. Morgan O. Reynolds, "Why Does Crime Pay?" National Center for Policy Analysis *Backgrounder*, No. 110 (1990), p. 5.

40. *Ibid.*

41. Morgan O. Reynolds, *Crime in Texas*, National Center for Policy Analysis Report No. 102 (1991), p. 4.

42. For an excellent summary of the relationship between crime and the deterioration of family life, particularly in urban areas, see Robert Rector, "A Comprehensive Urban Policy: How to Fix Welfare and Revitalize America's Inner Cities," Heritage Foundation *Memo to President-Elect Clinton*, No. 12, January 18, 1993; see also, Carl F. Horowitz, "An Empowerment Strategy For Eliminating Neighborhood Crime," Heritage Foundation *Backgrounder*, No. 814, March 5, 1991.

43. Alfred Blumstein, "On the Racial Disproportionality of United States' Prison Populations," *Journal of Criminal Law and Criminology*, vol. 73 (1982), p. 1259; U.S. Department of Justice, "The Case for More Incarceration," 1992, p. B4.

44. Patrick A. Langan, "Racism on Trial: New Evidence to Explain the Racial Composition of Prisons in the United States," *Journal of Criminal Law and Criminology*, vol. 76 (1985), p. 666.

45. *Race and Imprisonment Decisions In California* (1990).

How States Can Fight Violent Crime

by Mary Kate Cary

[Editor's note: the following article is condensed from a report for the Heritage Foundation by Mary Kate Cary, and is based on a list of 24 recommendations originally proposed by former U.S. Attorney General William Barr.]

Introduction

Violent crime remains at intolerably high levels. Gang violence is spreading across the country. And juveniles are committing more and more serious crimes. At the same time, crime is becoming more ruthless and wanton. Too many Americans—especially residents of the inner cities—have become prisoners in their homes, behind bars and chains. It is not surprising, therefore, that the strongest support for tougher law enforcement is found among inner-city, largely minority residents.[1]

Despite this plague, a powerful bloc of liberal lawmakers in Congress prevented the passage of tough anti-crime measures proposed by the Bush Administration. If President Clinton is to launch a war on crime, he will have to overcome this resistance on Capitol Hill.

Nevertheless, the impact of federal policy necessarily is limited, since 95 percent of crimes fall within the jurisdiction of state and local government. State and local law enforcement agencies, with limited resources, are under great strain to deal effectively with the increase of violence in this country.

The Tide of Violent Crime in America

State officials must address a simple fact: the United States is in the grip of a violent crime wave.

As the graphs show, the number of violent crimes has jumped dramatically in the last thirty years, over three times the rate in the 1990s than in 1960. Measuring the increase in terms of population

Crime Numbers and Rates

Year	Violent Crimes	Violent Crime Rate (per 10,000)	Total Crimes	Total Crime Rate (per 10,000)	Total Population (in millions)
1960	288,460	16.1	3,384,200	188.7	179.3
1965	387,390	20.0	4,739,400	249.9	193.5
1970	738,820	36.4	8,098,000	398.5	203.2
1975	1,039,710	48.8	11,292,400	529.9	213.1
1980	1,344,520	59.7	13,408,300	595.0	225.3
1985	1,273,280	53.3	12,431,400	520.5	238.7
1990	1,820,130	73.2	14,475,600	582.0	248.7
1991	1,911,770	75.8	14,872,900	589.8	252.2

Source: FBI

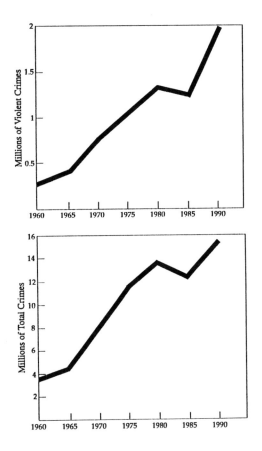

over the same time period, the U.S. population has increased by 41 percent, while the violent crime rate has increased by more than 500 percent. As Heritage Foundation Distinguished Fellow William J. Bennett, former National Drug Control Policy Director, observes, "The rate of violent crime in the U.S. is worse than in any other industrialized country."[2]

As noted, the victims of violent crime tend to be disproportionately poor and members of racial and ethnic minorities, particularly blacks. "Given current crime rates," observes Bennett, "eight out of every ten Americans can expect to be a victim of violent crime at least once in their lives."[3]

Protecting America's Communities from Dangerous Criminals

Most of the criminal violence in American society is committed by a very small group of chronic, violent offenders—hardened criminals who commit many violent crimes whenever they are out on the streets. They begin committing crimes as juveniles, and they go right on committing crimes as adults, even when on bail, probation, or parole.

Recommendation: Give judges legal authority for pretrial detention of dangerous defendants.

Every state should grant statutory, and if necessary, state constitutional authority to its trial judges to hold, without bail, those defendants who are a danger to witnesses, victims, or the community at large—both before trial and pending appeal.

A study by the Department of Justice's Bureau of Justice Statistics (BJS) of individuals on pretrial release in 75 of the nation's most populous counties found that 18 percent of released defendants were known to have been rearrested for the commission of a felony while on pretrial release. Two-thirds of those rearrested while on release were again released.[4]

This revolving door justice adds significantly to crime and destroys public confidence in the criminal justice system. Law-abiding citizens understandably are reluctant to inform police of criminal activities when they know that those arrested will be back on the street in a few days, or even in a few hours. Citizens fear retaliation, intimidation, and harassment by returning criminals if they help police.

At the federal level, the Bail Reform Act of 1984 grants federal judges the authority to deny bail or pretrial release to defendants who pose a danger to specific individuals or the community in general.[5]

Despite the proven effectiveness of the federal statute, and its soundness as federal constitutional law,[6] only a few states have effective pretrial detention provisions. In many states, pretrial detention is not currently possible because of an absolute right to bail in the state constitution. Thus where state constitutional reform is necessary to remedy this, it should be enacted.

States also should consider other key provisions of the Bail Reform Act of 1984, such as the serious penalties for jumping bail and enhanced penalties for crimes committed while on release.

In Philadelphia in 1986, for example, a judge placed a limit on the number of criminals that could be housed in the Philadelphia jail, in order to prevent overcrowding. Released because of this order were dangerous arrestees who otherwise would be held without bail or on very high bond. The result was an increase in violent crimes committed by the releasees. In the face of this crisis, the federal government stepped in to use federal pretrial detention in cooperation with state authorities. Over 600 gang members, who would have been turned loose by state judges because there was no room to hold them, were placed in federal facilities under federal law while awaiting trial. The homicide rate in Philadelphia declined as a result.[7]

Punishing and Deterring Violent Criminals

Imprisoning the hard-core population of chronic, violent offenders will reduce the level of violent crime in America. The reason: When these criminals are on the streets, they are victimizing citizens; when they are in prison, they are not committing crimes against the public. While liberals may question the deterrent and rehabilitative aspects of imprisonment, one thing is beyond debate: Prison incapacitates chronic, repeat offenders.

Consider the American experience of the last three decades. In the 1960s and early 1970s, incarceration rates dropped and violent crime rates skyrocketed. Conversely, when incarceration rates jumped in the 1980s, the rate of increase of crime was substantially reduced.[8]

The best way to reduce crime is to identify, prosecute, and incarcerate hard-core criminals. Study after study shows that a relatively small portion of the population is responsible for the lion's share of criminal violence in this country. For example, one California study found that 3.8 percent of a group of more than 236,000 men born in 1956 were responsible for 55.5 percent of all serious felonies committed by the study group.[9]

Putting chronic offenders in prison for long periods, especially upon second and third convictions, is the most effective way to reduce violent crime.

Recommendation: Restrict parole and increase the time actually served by violent offenders.

An axiom of effective law enforcement is that punishment should be swift, certain, and severe. Yet in too many jurisdictions, it is none of these. In fact, most violent offenders who are sent to state prison serve only a small fraction of their sentences. According to the Bureau of Justice Statistics, analysis of release practices in 36 states and the District of Columbia in 1988 shows that although violent offenders received an average sentence of seven years and eleven months imprisonment, they served an average of only two years and eleven months in prison—or 37 percent of their imposed sentence. Overall, 51 percent of the violent offenders in the survey were discharged from prison in two years or less, and 76 percent were out in four years or less.[10]

This huge gap between the nominal sentence given and the real time served is dishonest, and it is bad policy. It is dishonest because the public—especially victims of crime—is often under the impression that the sentence will be served in full, when in fact no such thing happens. It is bad policy because it puts the public at risk.

There are several reasons why states should restrict parole practices. First, parole is based on the mistaken idea that the primary reason for incarceration is rehabilitation (prisoners can be released as soon as they are rehabilitated, so the argument goes), and ignores the deterrent, incapacitative, and retributive reasons for imprisonment. A clear and truthful sentence increases the certainty of punishment, and both its deterrent and incapacitative effects.

Second, in too many cases parole simply does not work. Studies of the continuing failure of parole obscure the terrible human cost to law-abiding citizens.[11] For example, Suzanne Harrison, an eighteen-year-old honor student, three weeks from graduation, left her home in Texas with two friends, nineteen and twenty years old, on May 4, 1986. Her body was found the next day. She had been raped, beaten, and strangled. Her two companions were shot to death, and their bodies were found ten days later in a ditch.

Their killer, Jerry Walter McFadden (who calls himself "Animal"), had been convicted previously of two 1973 rapes, and sentenced to two fifteen-year sentences in the Texas Penitentiary. Paroled in 1978, he was again sentenced to fifteen years in 1981 for a crime spree in which he kidnapped, raped, and sodomized a Texas woman. Despite the fact that his record now contained three sex-related convictions and two prison terms, he was released again on parole in July 1985. McFadden's crime spree finally came to an end when he was convicted of the capital murder of Suzanne Harrison and sentenced to death in 1987. McFadden raped and killed Harrison and killed her two friends less than a year after being released on parole. This tragic example is all too common, and the cost of failed parole practices to the public safety is all too high.

Parole sometimes is used as an answer to prison overcrowding. This is hardly a reasonable justification for the premature release of violent criminals into the community. The answer to a lack of prison space is to build more prisons, not to release dangerous criminals.

Until recently, the Texas prison system was not expanding rapidly enough to house that state's criminals. Under federal court order to remain at a maximum of 95 percent of capacity, the Texas prison system responded by increasing the number of inmates released on parole. The number of felons on parole increased by 430 percent during the 1980s,[12] and inmates served an average of only 62 days for each year of their sentence.[13] As a result, reported crime rates in Texas increased 29 percent in the 1980s, according to the FBI, while they fell for the nation as a whole.[14]

States should enact "truth in sentencing." Parole should be restricted so that the sentence served more closely matches the sentence imposed. While "good behavior" incentives may be used to control prisoners, the mechanism should not exceed federal standards requiring 85 percent of a sentence to be served.

Recommendation: Enact mandatory-minimum sentences for gun offenders, armed career criminals, and repeat violent offenders.

In many states, sentences for violent crimes are too short. To many criminals, jail time is little more than a brief cost of doing business. For example, in 1988, of an estimated 100,000 persons convicted in state courts of murder, rape, robbery, and aggravated assault, some 17 percent—or about 17,000 violent criminals—received sentences that included no prison time at all.[15]

State legislators should enact mandatory minimum sentences for aggravated crimes of violence, and for such crimes committed by repeat offenders. Every state should follow the example of federal law, which mandates imprisonment where a firearm is used or possessed in the commission of certain serious felonies.[16] Every state should also enact laws similar to the federal armed career criminal statute, which targets repeat violent criminals who possess a gun.[17]

Recommendation: Build more prisons.

As former Attorney General William Barr says: "The choice is clear: More prisons or more crime." Building more prisons is not only morally the right thing to do, it is also economically the right thing to do. As Heritage Foundation scholar Robert Rector argues, crime is a high tax on the economic life of America's cities.[18] The cost to society of releasing violent criminals prematurely is far higher than the cost of building and operating prisons. When a violent offender is released after conviction because of insufficient prison space, all the money used to apprehend, try, and convict the criminal is wasted. And although incarcerating criminals is not cheap, the cost of not incarcerating criminals is far more expensive.

The overall cost of crime to victims—including direct losses, pain and suffering, and risk of death—has been estimated in the billions of dollars.[19] And this does not include larger costs of crime to society, such as lost sales, because people are afraid to go out shopping; lost jobs, when businesses leave crime-ridden neighborhoods; and lost tax revenues, when sales, businesses, and jobs no longer exist.

Despite the huge costs of not incarcerating criminals, states are reluctant to invest in prison space. In fiscal year 1990, only 2.5 percent of total expenditures by state and local governments went for corrections. And investment in new prison construction was only a small fraction of that figure, according to 1989–1990 figures on government finances from the Bureau of the Census.[20]

In the face of the overwhelming need for more prison space, spending on corrections remains a tiny percentage of state and local budgets. States need to commit sufficient resources to building and operating prisons, or risk the continuing collapse of the criminal justice system.

Recommendation: Impose an effective death penalty for the most heinous crimes.

The death penalty has an important role to play in deterring and punishing the most heinous violent crimes.[21] But it must be a real and certain penalty to be effective. In addition to its deterrent value, capital punishment permanently removes extremely violent offenders from society. And the death penalty upholds society's goal of just retribution. It affirms the moral outrage of the community at the ruthless taking of human life and assures the victim's loved ones that society takes their loss seriously.

At the very least, states should make the death penalty an option for juries to consider in three situations:

First, it is appropriate for the killing of a law enforcement officer. This sends a clear message to violent criminals: Murdering a police officer to avoid identification or later arrest is not worth it, no matter how long a prison term the criminal faces.

Second, it is appropriate for those who kill while also committing serious felonies. In the California case of *People v. Love,*[22] a collection of convicts' statements from police files and other sources indicates that their decisions to use toy guns during felonies, not to use firearms to resist arrest, and not to kill hostages were motivated by fear of the death penalty. The death penalty raises the stakes for these criminals, and therefore helps protect the victims of their crimes.

Third, it is appropriate for killing while in prison. Many criminals already serving life sentences in jail feel they have little to lose by killing a correctional officer or fellow inmate. The death penalty introduces a new level of punishment.

Recommendation: Require prisoners to work or perform community service to defray the costs of their imprisonment.

Taxpayers pay for a prisoner's room and board, health care, and all other expenses. In return, able-bodied prisoners should be required to do something useful for the taxpayers, such as maintaining prison property. Restrictions on this practice should be applied only where there is a significant risk of taking jobs away from law-abiding American workers.

There are many benefits associated with prison work. The Federal Bureau of Prisons recently published preliminary findings from its Post Release Employment Project (PREP), which compared federal convicts who received training and work in prison with a control group which did not. The study's preliminary findings offer strong support for prison labor programs. Inmates who worked in prison were less likely to engage in prison misconduct, less likely to commit crimes after release, and significantly more likely to be gainfully employed one year after release.[23]

States should enact laws or promulgate regulations requiring all able-bodied felons in prison to perform some labor useful to the public. State legislators also should enact laws making a certain percentage of the cost of each prisoner's incarceration part of a mandatory fine imposed as part of the sentence. Proceeds from both of these should be used to defray correctional costs.

Punishing and Deterring Young Criminals

Juvenile crime has risen rapidly over the last two decades, especially violent offenses. The real answer to this problem lies outside the criminal justice system. As Heritage Foundation scholar Robert Rector demonstrates, it is the basic institutions of society—family, schools, churches, and neighborhood groups—that instill values and mold children into good citizens.[24] Only when these institutions once again intervene effectively in shaping the lives of young Americans will juvenile crime be cut substantially.

Still, law enforcement has a key role. State legislators and officials need to distinguish between categories of juvenile offenders. The vast majority of juvenile offenders have only one or two brushes with the law and straighten out as they mature. But there is a smaller group of chronic hardened juvenile offenders, who commit most of the violent juvenile crime. Unfortunately, juveniles are the fastest growing group of violent offenders. As the following graph shows, the arrest rates of juveniles for violent crime have increased significantly in recent years, particularly since 1985.[25] And the increase in juvenile crimes is responsible for a large share of the general increase in violent crime.[26]

Recommendation: Toughen juvenile sanctions to deter nonviolent first-time offenders from a life of crime.

In the case of the first, larger group of juvenile offenders, the goal of policy-makers and law enforcement officials is to prevent these youths from becoming chronic offenders. The best way to do this is to impose tough sanctions that are carefully tailored to the offender and are meant to instill the values of discipline and responsibility. Excessive leniency, on the other hand, wastes the opportunity to turn the young person around, and instead puts him or her on the conveyor belt to becoming a career criminal. The juvenile does not get the message that crime does not pay when he or she is not penalized for committing a crime. Tough but fair sanctions can stop the all-too-common pipeline from juvenile offender to adult criminal.

One of the worst statistics from the 1980s is the sharp increase in the number of juveniles arrested for murder: It rose by 60 percent between 1981 and 1990, according to the FBI. The corresponding adult increase was 5.2 percent. In 1990, more than a third of all murders in America were committed by people under the age of 21.[27]

For example, in 1988 a fourteen-year-old drug runner in the District of Columbia shot and killed three people on the same day. The drug dealer for whom the juvenile worked was convicted of felony murder, but the juvenile served only 26 months in juvenile detention for the killings. He was back out on the streets taunting local police before his seventeenth birthday.[28]

State criminal justice officers must realize that some youthful offenders are simply hardened criminals who happen to be young. State legislators should ensure that their legal systems permit the

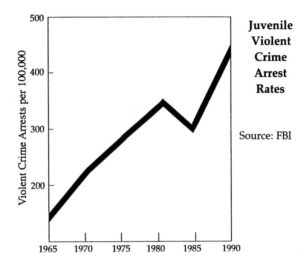

Juvenile Violent Crime Arrest Rates

Source: FBI

discretionary waiver or certification of juveniles into adult court in appropriate circumstances. One approach would be to create a legislative presumption that any juvenile age fourteen or older who commits certain crimes of violence (murder, rape, kidnapping, armed robbery, for example) will be tried as an adult. The presumption could be rebutted by showing mitigating factors that argue otherwise.

But where violence is involved, a firearm is used, or multiple offenses have occurred, the youth has already—through his own willful criminal conduct—left the intended focus of the juvenile justice system.

Recommendation: Allow judges to use juvenile offense records in adult sentencing.

Many seemingly first-time adult offenders in this country were chronic offenders as juveniles, yet evidence of their crimes may not be available or may be considered legally irrelevant to sentencing for adult crimes. The Bureau of Justice Statistics estimates that 38 percent of convicted murderers in state prison in 1986 had a prior juvenile conviction; and 13 percent of those had no adult record, only juvenile ones.[29] While it is commendable to forgive a youthful indiscretion and not penalize an otherwise law-abiding adult with a criminal record, that is hardly reasonable when a juvenile offender continues a life of crime into adulthood.

To address this problem, the FBI now includes juvenile criminal history information from the states in the national criminal records system, and states are urged to forward records of serious offenses to the FBI. So that this is possible, state officials should review their expungement and confidentiality statutes affecting juvenile offenses. State laws, moreover, should allow for the fingerprinting of juveniles convicted of serious crimes, and career criminal statutes should provide that juvenile convictions for serious drug and violent crimes be considered relevant factors in the sentencing of adults.

Promoting Fair and Speedy Trials and Streamlining the Appeals Process.

While it is essential for state officials to increase the certainty and severity of punishment, it is equally important to ensure its swiftness and finality. The key to this is the ability of the criminal justice system to seek and find the truth. Several steps would help achieve this, substantially enhancing the efficiency of state criminal justice systems and the deterrent effect of their punishments.

Recommendation: Enforce speedy trial laws.

Victims of crime and members of society at large want to see justice done and criminals removed quickly from society. Defendants have an interest in clearing their good names if innocent, or in beginning to serve their sentences if guilty. All sides have an interest in determining the facts while evidence and the recollections of witnesses are still fresh.

Despite the clear common interest in speedy trials, and despite the fact that some form of speedy trial law exists in 45 states,[30] delays in prosecution still pervade many state systems. In fact, a 1988 study of felony convictions in 300 counties across America found that the average time between arrest and sentencing was 208 days.[31]

These delays benefit no one but the guilty—and cause particular anguish and even danger to the victims of violent crime awaiting the trial proceedings. Many docket-management techniques are available to clerks and other state officials to help states ensure criminal trials take place at the earliest possible date. They should be used more aggressively.

Recommendation: Reform the rules of evidence to secure the truth in criminal trials.

The cost of keeping probative evidence away from juries in criminal cases is very high, and can result in the release of guilty criminals to further victimize the innocent. State officials should review their evidentiary rules to ensure that they promote the search for truth.

State laws also should allow for admission of evidence seized by officers acting with an objectively reasonable belief that they are complying with the law. State legislators can, for example, ensure by statute that whenever police officers act in good-faith, but make a technical error of law or fact, the evidence should nevertheless be admitted in court.[32] Colorado, for example, has enacted a good faith exception to the exclusionary rule for both warrant and warrantless cases. In some states, however, this may require a constitutional amendment.

State officials also should review evidence rules governing the use of prior convictions or acts. There are two settings in which this is particularly important. The first is in the impeachment of a defendant who takes the stand. Traditionally, any past conviction for a felony or a crime involving dishonesty was admissible to impeach the credibility of the witness. Now, Federal Rule of Evidence 609 imposes a general ten-year time limit on admissible convictions and requires a special determination by the judge that the probative value of a defendant's prior felonies outweighs any prejudicial effect.

At a minimum, state evidence codes should be no more restrictive than Rule 609. Allowing the admission of all convictions involving felonies and crimes involving dishonesty against all witnesses (including a defendant) would be even better.

Second, many state evidence rules limit the use of past criminal conduct of the defendant as evidence of guilt. Evidence that the defendant has committed the same type of crime in the past is particularly probative in sex crime cases, such as rape and child molesting, where it shows common *modus operandi* or other relevant factors. Studies suggest that recidivism runs high among a substantial percentage of sex offenders,[33] and such information may be key to an informed evaluation of the credibility of the defendant's denial and the victim's allegations. In such cases, often the only eyewitness is the victim, who carries the burden of proof in the trial. State legislators should provide clear statutory authority for the admission of evidence of past sex offenses whenever the charge is sexual assault or child molestation.

Recommendation: Reform state *habeas corpus* procedures and end repetitive challenges by convicted criminals.

In recent years, the writ of *habeas corpus* has been transformed from a monument of individual liberty, protecting individuals from imprisonment without trial, into a device used by prisoners to reexamine endlessly the issues decided by a full trial, and often even after unsuccessful appeals. The result: a sapping of judicial resources, a diminishing of punishment, and a continuing torment of victims of violent crime.

State officials should thoroughly review their *habeas corpus* laws to deter frivolous litigation and to close loopholes that can be abused. Four specific reforms would help improve many state laws:

- **States should allow only truly collateral claims to be raised in state *habeas corpus* cases.** Any claim that was or could have been brought forward in a prisoner's direct appeals should be barred explicitly from *habeas* proceedings.
- **States should adopt explicit time limits for the filing of *habeas corpus* petitions** (as there are for other categories of cases, from tort suits to contract claims), beginning from the time the petitioner has concluded his direct appeals.
- **States should bar successive *habeas corpus* petitions,** except where sufficient cause is shown for previous failure to raise the claim and the claim, if proved, would address the prisoner's factual guilt.
- **States should adopt the retroactivity standard of the 1988 Supreme Court case** *Teague v. Lane*,[34] which provides that changes in the law after trial and appeal will not apply retroactively unless they prohibit a particular crime or sentence, or greatly improve the truth-seeking function of the trial.

Assuring Victims' Rights

Criminal justice serves a twofold purpose: to bring criminals to justice, and to bring justice to victims. One way to make sure that appropriate weight is given to victims' rights is to codify and enforce a "Victims' Bill of Rights." Congress did just this in the Victims' Rights and Restitution Act of 1990 and urged the states to follow suit. Victims of a crime have the right to be protected from further violence, to expect restitution from financial loss, and to participate in the criminal justice process. And the criminal justice system should do all it can to lessen the pain of victims and victim-witnesses.

Potential victims of crime also have the right to protection. Victims of stalkers, for instance, should not have to wait until they are attacked to have effective recourse. State legislators should enact stalking laws that make it a crime to harass or follow a person if it puts the victim in fear of death or serious injury. If a restraining order is in effect at the time of an attack, an enhanced penalty should be considered.

Recommendation: Give victims a hearing and consideration of sentencing.

In most states, defendants have the right to address the court after conviction and before sentencing—to tell their story and to ask for mercy. State officials should provide the victim with a similar right to inform the court about the impact of the crime on his or her life before a sentence is given. The right should be extended to victims' families in capital cases. Likewise, parole statutes should provide that the impact of early release on victims or their survivors be a consideration bearing on early release decisions or other discretionary actions of the parole authority.

The victim also should have a right to be present at all public court proceedings related to the crime, which is often the most traumatic thing that has ever happened to that person. Victims deserve the right to watch the criminal justice system address the wrong done to them.

Recommendation: Help victim-witnesses with case coordinators.

Victim-witness coordinators are an important link between victims of crime and the criminal justice system, keeping victims apprised of developments in the case, informing them of possibilities of restitution, and notifying them of the release status of the offender.

Victim-witness coordinators should be made more aware of the state programs funded through the Victims of Crime Act, and such services offered by programs for victim compensation and assistance, counseling, and even shelter for battered women.

Recommendation: Assure restitution, adequate compensation, and assistance for victims of crime.

While every state has some type of victim restitution law, not all are well enforced. Effective mechanisms for collecting fines and restitution payments must exist, so that victims are relieved of the humiliating task of having to chase down the offender personally to obtain recompense for their injuries.

State officials should also make sure that any profits a criminal makes directly or indirectly from his crimes—including from book and movie deals—are made available to the victim for restitution. Where possible, states also should provide for reasonable compensation for victim-witnesses, including payment for travel and loss of work time, and assistance with day care and similar costs of giving testimony.

Recommendation: Adopt rules to protect victim-witnesses from courtroom intimidation and harassment.

Every state should enact two evidentiary protections for complaining witnesses. The first is the rape-shield law. A good model is Federal Rule of Evidence 412, which makes reputation or opinion evidence concerning the past sexual behavior of the alleged victim inadmissible in the trial for sex crimes. Admission of such evidence violates the victim's privacy, increases the trauma of the trial, and discourages victims from coming forward in the first place.

Second, every state should protect child witnesses from traumatic confrontations with their alleged abusers. In the 1990 case of *Craig v. Maryland*, the Supreme Court noted that placing a child witness in proximity to an alleged abuser or molester may do serious psychological damage, and may overwhelm the child so much that he cannot accurately testify to events.

The Maryland statute, upheld by the Supreme Court in *Craig*, provides a useful model. If the trial judge deems it necessary, the child's testimony is taken by closed-circuit television with only the attorneys and, if necessary, a guardian present.

Recommendation: Require HIV testing of sex offenders before trial.

Because of the AIDS epidemic, sex crimes have become even more terrifying and traumatic for victims. At the request of the victim, states should provide for mandatory HIV testing of defendants in sexual offense cases before trial, in order to reduce the uncertainty victims must endure. Test results should be available to the victim and to the court in a way that safeguards the victim's confidentiality. Also, at the request of the victim, defendants should be tested again periodically, consistent with the latency period of the virus. Most important of all, states should provide enhanced penalties for HIV-positive offenders who commit sexual offenses in the knowledge that they may transmit the virus to the victim.

Recommendation: Notify victims of all criminal justice proceedings and the release status of the offender.

Many victims of crime understandably fear that they will be victimized again by the same offender after his release. Victims should be told of any change in a convicted criminal's status, such as enrollment in work-release programs, weekend furlough, or community incarceration. States should also ensure that adequate protective measures be taken before release, where there is a legitimate fear of more victimization.

Conclusion

State legislators and judicial officials can and should take concrete steps to make America safer. Concerned citizens, victims of crime, and law enforcement leaders are working to strengthen the criminal justice system. Law-abiding citizens, however, are asking if their state and local public safety laws are as effective as those of the federal government and the more rigorous states. They want states to ensure that dangerous criminals are in prison, not in their neighborhood. And they want victims of crime to have the same say as the criminals do in the system.

These recommendations provide a sound foundation for making the fundamental changes necessary to protect the safety of all Americans.

1. Robert Rector, "A Comprehensive Urban Policy: How to Fix Welfare and Revitalize America's Inner Cities," Heritage Foundation *Memo to President-Elect Clinton* No. 12, January 18, 1993.

2. William J. Bennett, *The Index of Leading Cultural Indicators*, published jointly by Empower America, The Heritage Foundation, and the Free Congress Foundation, Washington, D.C. 1993, p. 2.

3. *Ibid.*

4. Bureau of Justice Statistics, U.S. Department of Justice, *Pretrial Release of Felony Defendants, 1988* (Washington, D.C.: U.S. Government Printing Office, 1991), p. 1. See also Lazar Institute, "Pretrial Release: A National Evaluation of Practices and Outcomes," prepared for the National Institute of Justice, U.S. Department of Justice, by Mary A. Toborg (October 1981), Grant No. 71-NI-AX-0038, p. 48 (reporting similar rates of pretrial rearrest).

5. 18 U.S.C. sec. 3141–56.

6. The Supreme Court rejected a constitutional challenge to the pretrial detention provisions of the Bail Reform Act in *United States v. Salerno*, 481 U.S. 739 (1987).

7. Mike Baylson (U.S. Attorney ED-PA) and Willie Williams (Philadelphia Police Commissioner), "Here's Why Murders are Down in the City," *The Philadelphia Inquirer*, January 15, 1992, p. A13.

8. Federal Bureau of Investigation, U.S. Department of Justice, *Crime in the United States, Uniform Crime Reports 1959-90* (Washington, D.C.: U.S. Government Printing Office, various years); Bureau of Justice Statistics, U.S. Department of Justice, *Historical Statistics on Prisoners in State and Federal Institutions, Yearend 1925–86* (Washington, D.C.: U.S. Government Printing Office, 1988) and *Prisoners in 1989* (Washington, D.C.: U.S. Government Printing Office, 1990).

9. These numbers are derived from Robert Tillman, "Prevalence and Incidence of Arrest among Adult Males in California," prepared for California Department of Justice, Bureau of Criminal Statistics and Special Services, Sacramento, California (1987).

10. Bureau of Justice Statistics, U.S. Department of Justice, *National Corrections Reporting Program, 1988* (Washington, D.C.: U.S. Government Printing Office, 1992), tables 2–7 and 2–4.

11. See, for example, Mark Vosburgh and Sean Holton, "Florida Prison Failure Churns Out Crime Before Its Time," *Orlando Sentinel*, August 13, 1989, p. A-12; Mark Vosburgh, "Florida's Early Releases: Flood of Rearrests May Sink Crowded Prisons," *Orlando Sentinel*, December 17, 1989, p. A-1; U.S. Department of Justice, Bureau of Justice Statistics, *Recidivism of Prisoners Released in 1983*, April 1989 (NCJ-116261); U.S. Department of Justice, Bureau of Justice Statistics, *Examining Recidivism* February 1985 (NCJ-96501); U.S. Department of Justice, Bureau of Justice Statistics, *Recidivism of Young Parolees*, May 1987 (NCJ-104916).

12. Bureau of Justice Statistics, U.S. Department of Justice, *Probation and Parole 1981* (Washington, D.C.: U.S. Government Printing Office, 1982), p. 2; *Probation and Parole 1989* (Washington, D.C.: U.S. Government Printing Office, 1990), table 1.

13. Texas Department of Corrections, *1991 Fiscal Year Statistical Report*, Summary Table 4 (1992).

14. Federal Bureau of Investigation, U.S. Department of Justice, *Crime in the United States, Uniform Crime Reports, 1980,* table 3 (1981) and *1989,* table 5 (1990).

15. Bureau of Justice Statistics, U.S. Department of Justice, *Felony Sentences in State Courts, 1988* (Washington, D.C.: U.S. Government Printing Office, 1990), p. 2.

16. 18 U.S.C. sec. 924(c)(1).

17. 18 U.S.C. sec. 924 (e).

18. Rector, *op. cit.*

19. Mark A. Cohen, "Pain, Suffering and Jury Awards: A Study of the Cost of Crime to Victims," *Law and Society Review,* Vol. 22 (1988), p. 539. Cohen estimated the 1984 aggregate cost of crime to victims at $92.6 billion in 1985 dollars.

20. Bureau of the Census, U.S. Department of Commerce, *Government Finances: 1989–90* (Washington, D.C.: U.S. Government Printing Office, 1991), p. 2.

21. On the deterrent effects of capital punishment see generally Stephen J. Markman and Paul G. Cassell, "Protecting the Innocent: A Response to the Bedau-Radelet Study," *Stanford Law Review,* Vol. 41 (1988), pp. 121, 154–56 (collecting studies that demonstrate deterrent effects of the death penalty); Stephen K. Layson, "Homicide and Deterrence: A Reexamination of the United States Time-Series Evidence," *Southern Economics Journal,* Vol. 52 (1985), pp. 68, 75–80 (estimating that each execution in the U.S. deters approximately eighteen murders). On its retributive effects see, for example, Senate Committee on the Judiciary, *Establishing Constitutional Procedures for the Imposition of Capital Punishment,* S. Rep. No. 251, 98th Cong., 1st Sess. (1983), p. 13 ("Murder does not simply differ in magnitude from extortion or burglary or property destruction offenses; it differs in kind. Its punishment ought to also differ in kind. It must acknowledge the inviolability and dignity of innocent human life. It must, in short, be proportionate.")

22. 366 P.2d 33, 41–42 (Cal. 1961).

23. Federal Bureau of Prisons, U.S. Department of Justice, *Post Release Employment Project, Preliminary Findings* (Washington, D.C.: U.S. Government Printing Office, 1991), pp. 6, 10–11.

24. Rector, *op. cit.*

25. Bennett, *op. cit.,* p. 4.

26. Federal Bureau of Investigation, U.S. Department of Justice, *Age-Specific Arrest Rates and Race-Specific Arrest Rates for Selected Offenses, 1965–89* (Washington, D.C.: U.S. Government Printing Office, 1990), pp. 31, 73, 213.

27. Federal Bureau of Investigation, U.S. Department of Justice, *Crime in the United States, Uniform Crime Reports, 1990* (Washington, D.C.: U.S. Government Printing Office, 1991), tables 27 and 36.

28. "D.J." *Washington Post* editorial, July 31, 1991, p. A20.

29. The figures are similar for other violent crimes. For example, 54 percent of state prisoners convicted of robbery as adults had a juvenile record—15 percent had only prior juvenile convictions. These figures are based on the raw data underlying the BJS Special Report, *Profile of State Prison Inmates, 1986* (Washington, D.C.: U.S. Government Printing Office, 1988).

30. Bureau of Justice Statistics, U.S. Department of Justice, *Prosecution of Felony Arrests, 1981* (Washington, D.C.: U.S. Government Printing Office, 1986), table 30.

31. Bureau of Justice Statistics, U.S. Department of Justice, *Felony Sentences in State Courts, 1988* (Washington, D.C.: U.S. Government Printing Office, 1990), p. 7.

32. In recent years, the Supreme Court has identified a number of situations where it has declined to apply the exclusionary rule to enforce the Fourth Amendment;

primary among these is the 1984 case of *U.S. v. Leon*. [Editor's note: see also "The Paradox of the Exclusionary Rule," in Part II of this volume.]

33. See, for example, Bureau of Justice Statistics, U.S. Department of Justice, Special Report, *Recidivism of Prisoners Released in 1983* (Washington, D.C.: U.S. Government Printing Office, 1989), table 10.

34. 489 U.S. 288 (1989).

Community Supervision That Works

by Edward F. Leddy

The Problem of the Released Offender

People complain endlessly about crimes by ex-convicts. We hear of the spectacular murder, robbery, or rape and demand that criminals be kept off the streets. Most of us feel that the way to prevent crime is to put offenders in prison and throw away the key.

But in reality, we can't lock up every burglar or shoplifter forever. Few crimes merit sentences of more than a few years. One day, almost all convicts are going to come out, ready or not. For the great majority of criminals, eventual release is a certainty, no matter whether state sentencing schemes are determinate or indeterminate, tough or lenient, long or short. And if the offender is simply released, with no one watching him, he is likely to resume his career of crime.

Today, most convicted criminals are outside prison on parole or probation. A criminal on probation is put in the community, under the supervision of an officer trained for the task, instead of going to prison. By contrast, a criminal on parole serves a part of his sentence in prison, then is released under supervision.

In most cases, both systems work. Most criminals can change. Better than 60 percent of parolees don't return to prison; neither do 80 percent of probationers, who tend to be younger offenders, guilty of fewer or less serious crimes.

Parole and probation officers must visit the offenders' homes and jobs, contact police, and make frequent checks on their charges. Meanwhile, they provide advice, family counseling, drug and alcohol treatment. They help the offender find a job, aid, housing, and many other services with the aim of keeping him from returning to crime.

When this works—as it usually does—you rarely hear anything about it. Reformed criminals don't go around bragging about their records. But they also don't commit more crimes.

The cases you do hear about are the ones who don't go straight. Some criminals, perhaps six percent, are hard-core repeaters who

270

can't be reformed by any means known to today's science. They will revert to crime whenever opportunity arises. Among the population released to the community, unfortunately, it is difficult to predict which ones they will be.

However, crime is usually preceded by telltale predictors; and some probation and parole departments—the better ones—look carefully for the first signs of the development of criminal behavior patterns. If officers are alert to such things as drug use, spouse abuse, failing to report or absconding from supervision, false employments, criminal associations, carrying weapons, and other violations of their terms of release, many offenders reverting to their old habits can be returned to custody before they commit new crimes.

The Traditional Role of Parole and Probation

Historically, the job of probation and parole was to protect the community primarily by reforming the offender. The idea, developed in the 1930s, was that this was to be done by counseling and social work. These methods can be helpful. However, they don't work with many criminals.

What *does* work is intensive supervision of conduct. That means visiting homes and jobs, knowing the families, detecting drug and alcohol use, keeping close track of behavior, and acting to avert crime.

The key to making community supervision work is to convince the released offender that he cannot get away with crime. To make this credible, officers must be trained and equipped to arrest violators, and must initiate law enforcement actions against the delinquent. Violations of rules have to be taken seriously, as unmistakable signs of relapse into criminality.

In the past, parole departments such as those in New York, California, and Pennsylvania trained their parole officers as lawful peace officers, armed them, and required them to track down and arrest violators. These states historically had higher rates of return to prison for violations of the rules; but they also had fewer new crimes by parolees.

Unfortunately, many other departments are still ruled by the rehabilitation ideas of decades past. They feel that criminals are victims of society—"clients" who need only their help and sympathy.

They reject the supervision task and concentrate only on social work. Usually, they forbid their officers to carry guns, don't train them as peace officers, and refuse to let them make arrests for "mere technical violations" of the "client's" release conditions, such as for drug abuse or failing to report.

In Texas, a wanted murderer was allowed simply to walk out of the Fort Worth parole office. No effort was made to arrest him, because Texas parole agents are unarmed and are not legal peace officers. The parolee promptly killed again. The last I heard, this department was trying to decide whether to let its officers carry Mace for self-protection.

By contrast, a department that watches, checks up, investigates complaints of suspicious actions, carefully monitors and controls the activities of released offenders, can prevent crime and help keep the community safe. Those violating the terms of their release can be returned to secure custody at the first sign of the behaviors that usually lead to crime.

At the same time, such a department can give the many who want to go straight the help to make it. Some ex-offenders, who can go either way depending on circumstances, can be convinced that crime doesn't pay—at least not while they are under supervision.

No, this approach doesn't always work; what does? But it works a lot better than the alternative of unsupervised release.

Focused Supervision

The question sometimes arises: Why not let the police arrest violators, instead of parole or probation officers? Experience shows that in places where this is the policy, an attitude quickly develops in the parole department that "*we* are not law enforcement officers." Soon, that attitude is reflected in lax supervision and a lack of concern for violations.

Some go even further, asking: Since the police are chiefly responsible for crime intervention, why not leave the community supervision of ex-offenders entirely to them? Why have parole and probation officers at all?

The reason is focus. The main roles of the police are to maintain a general deterrent presence in the community, respond to emergencies, and solve specific crimes. They have little or no time and capability to closely monitor individuals with past crime histories, as well. And legally, they could be accused of harassment if they attempted to do so. Police are restrained by laws on search, confessions, and court procedures which the Supreme Court has held do not bind parole and probation officers.

The supervision of offenders in the community is best done by a department designed exclusively for that purpose. Its agents should have both the full power and the legal responsibility to police their charges.

From Parole and Probation to Offender Supervision

Parole and probation should be abolished in their present form. They should be replaced by Offender Supervision. The name change is essential to get away from the failed "social worker" approach, and to emphasize instead the "control and law enforcement" approach.

The law-enforcement-oriented departments are already on the right track. Experienced agents and police could develop a law enforcement training course tailored to the needs of Offender Supervision Agents/Officers.

Part of the reason that some departments avoid law enforcement is the hazard. Supervising serious offenders can be dangerous. Officers making routine home visits walk in to find drugs, guns, loot, and evidence of other criminal activities. Some officers have been murdered.

Unarmed officers cannot effectively do anything but give counseling and advice in their offices. They place their lives in danger by visiting homes in dangerous neighborhoods or attempting to arrest violators. That's why unarmed departments tend to avoid potentially dangerous tasks such as home visits, and become office-bound. They don't find out what's really going on at the offender's home or job until the police call with the report of his latest crime. Then they can only write a violation report. They can't act effectively to stop crime.

We need to get the agents out on the streets where they can control criminal behavior—not leave them in their offices writing violation reports. They need to have the training and power to stop the criminal *before* the next crime happens, and *before* there is another victim.

At the same time, they should be *allowed* to do their jobs.

When I was a parole officer, I discovered that one prisoner's proposed release program was a fraud. Using a letterhead stolen from a community program, he forged a letter to pretend he had a job offer.

I recommended he be prosecuted for attempted escape. But administrators wanted to release prisoners regardless of their behavior. I was instead ordered to create another release program for the prisoner, so that he could be let out anyway. He got out—and soon committed a new crime.

This sort of thing must stop. Prisons should not be allowed to release people early just to free up beds. We should never grant early freedom to those who show clear signs that they are going to go back to crime. Instead, we must let Offender Supervisors return rule violators to prison at the start of their delinquency, not after a new crime.

How You Can Help

You should look into your local parole and probation departments and ask these questions:

A. Are they legally peace officers?

B. Do they go armed?

C. Do they track down and arrest violators—or just mail a warrant to the police, to be filed after the next arrest for a new crime?

D. Do they visit homes and employers, conduct searches, investigate complaints, contact families, check conduct, and prevent crime? Or do they sit in their offices making calls and writing reports?

E. Do they view their primary responsibility as protection of the people of the community? Or do they talk only of helping the offender, and feel that law enforcement is beneath them?

F. Do they claim that law enforcement and reforming the offender are incompatible? If so, they are wrong. Helping someone go straight protects the community. Arresting someone for "technical rule violations" before he commits a new crime helps keep him out of greater trouble. The law-enforcement-oriented departments have proven this.

G. Finally, are caseloads under fifty per officer? With too many cases, it becomes almost impossible to do effective work on crime prevention. Part of our problem today is that judges and correctional officials are demanding that prisoners be released on parole to avoid overcrowding in prison. As a result, officers' caseloads are climbing into the hundreds in some states.

If the answers to these questions are unsatisfactory, you should lobby for peace officer status and training. The proper goal of Offender Supervision is to control criminal behavior—and the proper role for the Offender Supervision Agent is as an armed peace officer, responsible for enforcing both laws and offender release agreements.

Introduction of this approach will, of course, require both legislative reforms to change the direction of "social work" departments, and practical training programs for Offender Supervision Agents/ Officers.

Public safety demands no less. A community supervision system that passes its law enforcement responsibilities onto the police usually ensures that, in a few years, its failures will return to prison with new convictions—after creating new victims.

Restoring Responsibility

by Robert James Bidinotto

What to do with criminals? Those relatively few criminals netted by the criminal justice system must be dealt with somehow. Over the centuries, society has employed countless methods to accomplish a variety of purposes: punishment and retribution, deterrence, incapacitation, moral education, and rehabilitation.[1]

And yet crime continues to increase. Here again, Aristotle's point about causality applies: the nature of an entity determines what it will do. The fundamental reason for the intractable crime problem is that previous crime-control efforts have failed to consider *the nature of the criminal himself.* To reform the criminal justice and correctional systems—and, we hope, the criminal—we must first understand something about the criminal mind.

"Inside the Criminal Mind"

Numerous empirical studies demonstrate that criminals simply don't *think* like non-criminals.

A representative study in Colorado found that, even at an early age, future delinquents had "less regard for the rights and feelings of their peers; less awareness of the need to accept responsibility for their obligations . . . and poorer attitudes toward authority, including failure to understand the need for rules and regulations in any well-ordered social group. . . . They were significantly less likely than their nondelinquent [peers] to be viewed as dependable, friendly, pleasant, considerate, and fair." Many other studies have echoed these findings.[2] Stanton Samenow describes the criminal mind thusly: "Despite a multitude of differences in their backgrounds and crime patterns, criminals are alike in one way: *how they think.* . . . [All] regard the world as a chessboard over which they have total control, and they perceive people as pawns to be pushed around at will. Trust, love, loyalty, and teamwork are incompatible with their way of life. They scorn and exploit most people who are kind, trusting, working, and honest. Toward a few they are sentimental but rarely considerate. Some of their most altruistic acts have sinister motives. . . . "

Such traits are also typical of what is called the "psychopath" or "sociopath," as Samenow makes clear. "Although diagnosticians may make distinctions between the psychopath and criminal, for all ostensible purposes, one differs hardly at all from the other." Among the common characteristics of the criminal and psychopath: a short-range, self-indulgent outlook on life; a lack of any sense of self-responsibility; the desire to manipulate and dominate others through chronic deception and force; and the ability to shut off his conscience at will.[3]

At one time, the criminal was even described as a "moral imbecile"—one whose shortcomings were primarily *ethical*.[4] Summarizing numerous studies of criminal psychology, Wilson and Herrnstein note that "one of our recurrent themes in these test data is the lack of internalized constraints"—e.g., what used to be called "conscience."[5]

The criminal welcomes anything that would assist him in his predatory behavior. And here, the Excuse-Making Industry is invaluable to him. Its overall ethical thrust has been to excuse malicious behavior and thus deaden the pangs of conscience. By concocting theories, policies, and programs which excuse irresponsibility, Excuse-Makers have fostered a general social climate of moral relativism—thus undermining any guilt feelings which might act as inner constraints on criminal behavior.

If a salient trait of psychopathic criminality is a deadened conscience, then the sudden takeoff of crime during the heyday of moral relativism—the 1960s—makes even more sense. There is even more specific evidence of this: the simultaneous *geometric* increase in the number of so-called "serial killers" on the prowl.

The serial killer is a nihilistic repeat murderer, who often commits ghastly crimes out of pure hatred for society. As FBI experts describe him, he "exhibits complete indifference to the interests and welfare of society and displays an irresponsible and self-centered attitude. While disliking people in general, he does not avoid them. Instead, he is capable of displaying an amiable facade for as long as it takes to manipulate people toward his own personal goal. He is a methodical and cunning individual . . . fully cognizant of the criminality of his act and its impact on society, *and it is for this reason that he commits the crime.*" [Emphasis added.][6]

Ominously, as many of these multiple murderers emerged during the 1960s as during the four preceding decades combined. During the 1970s, their number nearly tripled over that of the 1960s; and that figure, in turn, has been tripling again during the 1980s.[7] If a deadened conscience is a salient feature of the criminal, it is a *defining* trait of the serial killer. The abrupt geometric increase in this most depraved form of antisocial behavior is inexplicable—unless we consider the abrupt erosion of the moral landscape, and moral conscience, since the 1960s, courtesy of the Excuse-Making Industry.

The failure of the Excuse-Makers to understand the criminal mind has crippled their ability to design effective remedies for crime. We've already seen the disastrous consequences of their influence upon the criminal justice system. Now consider, more briefly, their corruption of the so-called "correctional system."

The Correctional System

The Excuse-Makers' revolution in penology was consolidated during the 1960s and 1970s. "The day—if there ever was one—when vengeance could have any moral justification passed centuries ago," declared former Attorney General Ramsey Clark in his influential 1970 book *Crime In America.* "Punishment as an end in itself is itself a crime in our times. . . . The use of prisons to punish only causes crime. . . . Rehabilitation must be the goal of modern corrections. Every other consideration should be subordinated to it."[8]

And it was. Today's "correctional facilities" are designed for the outwardly mobile. Closer relationships between prison staff and inmates are encouraged. Discipline has been relaxed, and punishment largely banished. Inmates are to be enticed from their criminal ways—through counseling and group therapy sessions, vocational and educational opportunities, input into prison policy-making, a host of programs for "self-expression" and entertainment, and participation in various release programs. This atmosphere is primarily a result of indeterminate sentencing provisions, under which an inmate may be released on parole whenever authorities feel he has reformed.

For example, under Massachusetts law, a "state prison" sentence means that only one-third of the inmate's *minimum* sentence must be served; and a six- to twelve-year "reformatory" sentence means he'll be parole-eligible in one year—or, if he's a repeat offender, in 18 months.[9] Likewise, in Oregon, a felon sentenced to five years for a major crime may do as little as *one month;* for a lesser felony, he'll do *one day.* (Outraged Oregonians recently passed a "truth-in-sentencing" referendum to end such practices.)[10]

The most egregious instances of early release are in the case of "life" sentences. Contrary to public impressions, a sentence of "life"—or even "life without possibility of parole"—almost never means that. In states like Massachusetts and Nebraska, "life without parole" sentences "routinely are commuted to parole at some point."[11] In Wyoming, "life" means 20–25 years before parole eligibility; but with "good time" (i.e., good behavior reductions), a "lifer" might spend half that time in prison. "Life" actually means about twelve years before parole eligibility in Virginia[12] and Kentucky; ten years in Mississippi and West Virginia; and seven in Georgia.[13]

The likelihood of speedy release on parole has shaped the entire prison environment. In essence, the "plea bargaining" process, which begins in the courtroom, extends into the prison itself.

The inmate generally behaves himself, participates in rehabilitation programs, and perhaps proclaims a sudden religious conversion. If single, he may place "lonely hearts" classified ads in newspapers, hoping to spark an outside romance that (thanks to furloughs) will lead to marriage and children—and hence, evidence of a "stable family" of dependents who "need" his presence. This all looks good to the parole board.

For their part, prison authorities make deals, extend privileges, tend to inmate grievances, and are rewarded with a relatively quiet prison population. Pragmatic considerations—costs, overcrowding, and the desire to curtail violence—have reduced them to tacit co-conspirators with inmates in an awkward charade: the inmates pretend to reform themselves, while their keepers pretend to believe them.

In short, the carrots of outside release programs, special privileges, and ultimately, early parole, have replaced the disciplinary sticks of punishment in keeping the prison system running smoothly. The only casualties are truth and justice.

From Rehabilitation to "Reintegration"

But while prisons were reshaping themselves according to the new rehabilitation dogma, a distressing thing was happening: rehabilitation efforts were failing, universally and miserably.[14] Yet the collapse of rehabilitation didn't prompt the Excuse-Making Industry to question its deterministic premises. Instead, its members rooted about desperately for still another excuse to continue the rehabilitation approach.

"While numerous theories have been offered to explain the failure of rehabilitation," admitted the Massachusetts Department of Correction (DOC) in a 1988 report, "many have commonly traced this failure to the very nature of the incarceration process itself, as well as counter-productive forces operating within the prison community or, in other terms, 'prisonization.'"

And what is "prisonization"? "According to the prisonization hypothesis, prison incarceration produces damage by interrupting and interfering with the offender's life-cycle—school, work, heterosexual relationships, finances, etc.—at a time when the damage is most harmful, between the ages of 18 and 30. . . . Offenders have traditionally been taken out of our society and placed in another social system, the prison, that in no way constructively resembles the society to which they will eventually return."

The DOC concluded that " . . . rehabilitation per se is not the problem, but rather those 'prisonization' forces which greatly overshadow and diminish rehabilitation efforts."[15] The problem, in short, is that we're trying to rehabilitate inmates *in prison.*

The Excuse-Makers' ingenious "solution" was that inmates should still be rehabilitated—not behind prison walls, but *out in the community.* Hence, the "reintegration model," which "assumes that offenders can better learn to obey the law if they are involved through personal and social ties with the normal institutions of the community—family, church, and the workplace."[16] Observe that the DOC report refers to "prisonization" as a mere "hypothesis," and makes clear that the reintegration model only "assumes" the benefits of what is often called community-based rehabilitation. This is appropriate, for there is no evidence to support them. The Excuse-Makers' deterministic premises prevent them from ever asking how it is that a "normal" outside environment managed to "shape" the inmate into a criminal in the first place—or how returning him to it will keep him out of future trouble. In fact, the criminal, by choice, was never part of normal society.

"It is misleading to claim that the criminal wants what the responsible person wants, that he values the same things that a responsible person values," Samenow argues. Rehabilitation "cannot possibly be effective because it is based on a total misconception. To rehabilitate is to restore to a former constructive capacity or condition. *There is nothing to which to rehabilitate a criminal.* There is no earlier condition of being responsible to which to restore him. . . . [Likewise] the notion of 'reintegrating the criminal into the community.' It is absurd to speak of reintegrating him when he was never integrated in the first place."[17]

The criminal lives within a criminal subculture, where "normal" people and institutions are to be used, victimized, and manipulated. Typically, his family is neglected or exploited; his jobs (if any) serve as mere launch pads for wider criminal activity; and his involvements with respectable institutions are a cover, masking his felonious activities. Without his changing his *thinking*—something the criminal must *want* to do himself—his rehabilitation and reintegration prospects are nil, Samenow concludes.[18]

"Prisonization" is only the latest rationalization to mask the Excuse-Makers' visceral hostility to punishment and prisons as such. As early as 1951, in his widely acclaimed *Break Down the Walls*, John Barlow Martin wrote that "Prisons should be abolished."[19] Writers such as Ramsey Clark, John G. Wilson, Jessica Mitford, Donald Powell Wilson, and Karl Menninger (among many others) sometimes went as far, or nearly so. Their views won a quasi-official status. The National Council on Crime and Delinquency recommended that no new prisons be built until all other options were examined.[20] Likewise, the American Law Institute's influential Model Penal Code recommended that courts not impose a prison sentence except as a last resort for public safety.[21] The idea of imprisonment was even subverted from within. In a revealing instance of the fox guarding the chicken coop, John O. Boone—who pioneered "community-based corrections" as Commissioner of Corrections both in Washington, D. C., and in Massachusetts in the early 1970s—later founded the National Campaign Against Prisons.[22]

But the Excuse-Making Industry would take what it could get, and its last-gasp efforts to salvage rehabilitation paid off. In 1965, the Federal Prisoner Rehabilitation Act gave federal sanction and support to nationwide "community-based corrections" experiments, such as work-release programs, home furloughs, halfway houses, and the like. This seed money, one proponent wrote, "began a new era, with community-based corrections as a major component in the field of criminal justice."[23] Like the phoenix, rehabilitation had risen from the ashes in new garb. But has "community-based corrections" worked any better than traditional rehabilitation?

Prison Furloughs

A "prison furlough" is the temporary release of an inmate back into the community.

Furloughs, usually under armed guard, used to be granted only as rare exceptions, typically to let an inmate attend a family funeral or get emergency medical care. Yet thanks to the Excuse-Making Industry, unescorted prison leaves, in the guise of "community-based corrections," are now a routine part of prison life in most states.

Given that only a tiny percentage of criminals are ever imprisoned, it makes no sense to allow them, once captured, the chance to escape or commit further crimes. Yet every week, across the nation, thousands of society's most vicious robbers, rapists, and killers are allowed to participate in what is supposed to be an "honor system." In 1987 alone, some 200,000 furloughs—ranging in duration from four hours to 210 days (in Oregon)—were granted to more than 53,000 prison inmates.[24] In many states, furloughs are granted, at least occasionally, even to murderers serving nominal "life" sentences, usually when they are nearing parole or after a sentence commutation. Until aroused citizens forced a change in its laws in 1988, Massachusetts routinely furloughed first-degree murderers supposedly *ineligible* for parole.

The Massachusetts example shows just how far the Excuse-Making Industry is willing to go. As a sympathetic writer put it, "Under the Massachusetts concept of repair rather than revenge, no person is believed beyond redemption, not even a rapist or a killer."[25] That's why, despite "the fact that 85 percent of the DOC inmate population has a present or past violent criminal history,"[26] 28 percent of that population had participated in the furlough program as of January 1987. Since the program's inception in 1972, 121,713 furloughs had been granted to 10,835 Massachusetts inmates; 5,554 of those unescorted leaves were taken by *first-degree murderers*, supposedly serving "life without parole" sentences.[27]

The results, predictably, have included chronic escapes, and grisly crimes committed by furloughed inmates—up to and including multiple murders.[28]

If rehabilitation is one excuse for granting furloughs, there are pragmatic ones, too. Former Massachusetts Correction Commissioner Michael Fair testified that furloughs for murderers were "a management tool for [inmate] behavior. . . . [I]t would be more dangerous to run a system without a furlough program."[29] Why? "Once we have removed all hope from someone," he explained, "then we have the difficulty of dealing with someone who has nothing to lose. We would have a very dangerous population in an already dangerous system."[30] But if armed guards can't control "very dangerous" killers inside prison walls, how are unsuspecting, unarmed citizens supposed to deal with them on the streets?

Such release programs, and the tragedies they foster, are inexcusable, and can be defended only by factual misrepresentations. Similar techniques are commonly used to defend *all* release programs, so a brief survey is appropriate.

For instance, Massachusetts officials proclaimed a furlough "escape rate" of only 0.5 percent. This impressive-sounding number was calculated by dividing the 428 escapees by the 121,713 furloughs granted from 1972 through 1987. However, those furloughs were granted repeatedly to only 10,835 *inmates*.[31] Dividing 428 by *that* number reveals an actual escape rate of *one out of every 25 furlough participants*—hardly a record to boast about.

The tale of Peter J. Limone shows another way in which "escape statistics" mislead. Limone is a gangland figure sentenced to "life without parole" for a contract murder. Nonetheless, in 1987 he was in a Boston pre-release center, preparing for "reintegration," when authorities found that he'd been using the center—and some 160 furloughs—to manage a local loan-shark operation. Limone's furloughs, of course, still count as 100 percent successful on DOC records—simply because he always returned.[32]

Another way of claiming the "success" of furlough and other

release programs is by manipulating recidivism statistics. A "recidivism rate" is the percentage of inmates who, once released, return to crime. Depending on how one measures "return to crime," however, such numbers can show glowing success where there is none.

Does one measure "return to crime" over a six-month period, one year, three years, or five years? The shorter the time span, the smaller the recidivism rate. Does one simply count re-arrests? re-convictions and re-commitments to a state prison? The latter numbers also artificially reduce the recidivism rate.

Another trick is to use selected samples. One report claimed that 1984 parolees who had *not* had the "benefit" of a furlough program had a 31 percent recidivism rate. This was much higher than the 12 percent reported by parolees who had furloughs. The conclusion: furloughs reduce recidivism.[33] But unmentioned was the fact that inmates are *pre-screened* for admission into release programs: those with the worst prison disciplinary records are not eligible. This biases the sampling procedure at the outset, by comparing bad apples with the *worst* apples. Program participation itself, therefore, has nothing to do with lowering recidivism.

Statistics aside, the most compelling argument against inmate furlough programs is their fundamental injustice, both to past and prospective crime victims. For victims and their families, the emotional strain of knowing that the perpetrator is allowed to walk the streets freely becomes unbearable. They often dread the day—or night—of the criminal's return, or of a chance encounter on a street or in a restaurant.

It is inexcusably cruel that taxpaying crime victims should have to bear these additional burdens, imposed on them by their paid protectors. It's even more monstrous that, in some states, they aren't even informed when their tormentor is turned loose.

Work Release

Everything said about furloughs applies to "work release"—the (supposedly) supervised release of an inmate to work at a job in the community.

From their earliest days, work-release programs—like all other outside release schemes—have been exploited by criminals bent on remaining criminal. Because of their low-security status, work-release programs are responsible for a huge share of all prison escapes. In Massachusetts, for example, 26 percent of all prison escapes were from work release.[34]

Work programs—inside or outside the walls—don't reduce inmate recidivism. For instance, about 50 percent of work-program graduates in New York are re-arrested *within six months*—roughly the same percentage as those who simply come out of jail.[35] Other programs surveyed have shown similarly dismal results.[36] And those few studies showing lower recidivism for work release inmates invariably suffer from the same "selection bias" sampling errors cited earlier for furlough studies.

In general, vocational training of inmates is based on the idea that unemployment causes a life of crime. Train the inmate in a job, the reasoning goes, and help him find employment on the outside, and he's less likely "to have to steal" for a living.

But a fallacy underlies the assumption. Does unemployment lead to criminality—or vice versa? "Criminals are at heart antiwork," Samenow argues. "For many criminals, work means to sell your soul, to be a slave." When employed, many criminals use their jobs as further opportunities for crime. Indeed, a RAND Corporation survey of 624 California prison inmates found that 27 percent had been regularly employed at the time they were engaged in crime. Being employed and being a criminal, then, are not mutually exclusive.[37]

To assume that a job will reform a criminal is to assume an economic cause for criminality—just another symptom of the "sociological excuse" for crime.

Other Community-Based Correction Programs

There are many other outside release programs to ease the transition of the inmate back into society: for instance, pre-release centers, halfway houses, and drug treatment centers. All suffer from the same fundamental flaws.

There may be some argument for a gradual introduction of a long-term inmate back into the community at the end of his sentence, when there's little incentive for him to escape or commit crimes. But a lengthy stay in a pre-release institution, long before his release date, is simply inviting trouble.

Because its correctional system sports a wide variety of such "alternative" and "diversionary" institutions, Massachusetts again provides interesting evidence of the "success" of such programs. During 1985, 71 percent of the 284 escapes occurring in all Department of Correction facilities were from pre-release centers.[38]

Some might find that acceptable, if there were any evidence that participation in pre-release centers lowers recidivism. But there isn't. It's another example of the Excuse-Maker's wishes being father to his thoughts and plans. The earlier-cited example of the mobster using a pre-release facility as a headquarters for loan-sharking illustrates the rehabilitative powers of such institutions.

There are countless hybrid programs, combining work release with community service, or involving prisoners in the rehabilitation of mental patients. These have been plagued by inmate escapes, abuse of patients and staff, access to drugs and contraband, and the like.[39]

But it's pointless to belabor every variation on the theme of "community-based corrections." Such programs can't work, because "reintegration" is a flawed concept. Reintegration programs are designed by normal people, for normal people. They all assume that criminals think and feel like normal people. But they don't.

The Failure of Rehabilitation and Reintegration

Practical Considerations

The argument is often made that such experiments, even if flawed, are (a) no less successful than imprisonment, and (b) far less costly to society. Both arguments are false.

(a). After thorough research, Wilson and Herrnstein concluded: "However one measures crime, it is less common in places where sanctions are more likely." For instance, one study of boys convicted of serious crimes found that those sent to reformatories showed a *greater* reduction in their re-arrest rates than those put into community-based programs like foster homes, halfway houses, and wilderness camps. In fact, "the more restrictive the supervision in these more benign programs, the greater the reduction in recidivism."[40]

(b). The National Institute of Justice (NIJ) released a 1987 study comparing the social costs of prisons to having prisoners out on parole, probation, or in community-release programs. It found that building more prisons and filling them with criminals cost far less than what society pays for having criminals on the loose.

The NIJ survey of 2,190 inmates in three states found that each committed an average of 187 crimes per year. These cost an estimated $430,000 per criminal in law enforcement expenditures, victim and insurance losses, and private security measures. This compares with about $25,000 a year to build a prison cell and keep a prisoner in it. Putting 1,000 more offenders behind bars during the 1980s would have cost an additional $25 million a year—but would have averted an average of 187,000 crimes each year, costing society about $430 million.[41]

On practical grounds, *incarceration works*, serving the goals of retribution, deterrence, incapacitation, and punishment.

Moral Considerations

But the moral issue is of overriding importance; and here, the "reintegration model" is utterly indefensible. At the core of their defenses of parole, furloughs, and all other release programs, Excuse-Makers believe that occasional innocent victims are "acceptable losses."

"The [low escape rate] numbers cannot excuse the harm suffered by victims of crime committed by furloughed inmates," conceded one Excuse-Maker. "However"—he quickly added, excusing the inexcusable—"public officials making decisions regarding the furlough program . . . must weigh the risk of this harm along with the benefit to the larger community."[42]

This cost-benefit approach—"to balance public protection with the management of our prisons and rehabilitation of inmates"[43]—is ethically appalling. It elevates bureaucrats and politicians to a godlike status, letting them decide who lives and who dies. Worse, it proposes sacrificing innocent human lives merely to appease potentially rowdy inmates, or to let killers and rapists have "another chance."

One magazine's reporters showed how victims are typically reduced to faceless statistics in such calculations. Note the use of the word "only": "Of 457 murderers who were freed on full parole [in Canada] between 1975 and 1986, only two individuals have been convicted of a second homicide. Indeed, convicts on early release committed only 130 of the 7,838 Canadian homicides that occurred during that same 11-year period—less than two percent."[44]

Hugh Haley, executive director of Ontario's John Howard Society—which advocates lenient parole for murderers—summed up the Excuse-Makers' ethical premise even more bluntly. "Are we going to keep hundreds of people in jail," he demanded, "just to save two or three?"[45]

Replied one of Willie Horton's victims, Cliff Barnes, in a similar context: "So we're expendable. Is that what they're saying?"[46]

That, indeed, is what the Excuse-Making Industry is saying. That, in fact, is what the reintegration premise requires.

Reforming the Criminal Justice System

If *justice* is truly to become the central focus of the criminal justice system, then the following reforms—some controversial—must be seriously considered.

Truth in the Courtroom

No facts should *ever* be banished from criminal proceedings. All exclusionary rules concerning evidence and confessions should be eliminated. If police obtain evidence by improper or illegal methods, that should be the subject of *separate* disciplinary or even criminal proceedings against the offending officers. But *evidence is evidence.*

Additionally, it's usually absurd to exclude an individual's past record from court deliberations. Career criminals often operate in unique patterns, which can serve as virtual signatures at certain crime scenes. Yet past records are often excluded as "prejudicial." Admitting these in evidence, to show a pattern consistent with the charged crime, only makes sense. Also, consideration of an individual's past record should be a routine element in all sentencing.

Juvenile offense records are often sealed, allegedly to prevent "early mistakes" from "pursuing the child into adulthood." Today, many teenagers are engaging, not in mistakes, but in serious, sadistic crimes. Sealing or expunging their records when they reach adulthood is another perversion of the fact-finding process. They should be admissible into adult sentencing proceedings, as evidence of career criminality.

Bail, Release on Recognizance, and Probation

Career criminals—and anyone with a history of escapes or failures to show in court—should *never* get bail consideration.

As for probation, every crime, no matter how petty, should merit *some* level of punishment, if only to show that *crime has inescapable consequences.* Probationary "sentences" teach offenders—especially impressionable young offenders—that "the law" is a paper tiger, that they can get away with crime. A young offender's first brush with the law shouldn't be brutal; but it should definitely be something he'd not wish to experience again.

Plea Bargaining

Plea bargaining should be abolished. Neither necessary nor ethical, it corrupts the entire court process and everyone involved. The cooperation of some criminals should not be bought with the bribe of a reduced sentence: the prize never equals the price. Going easy on lower-level crooks in order to buy their testimony against their bosses merely shuffles the underworld hierarchy: the boss is replaced by the lower-level crook who bought his freedom, and crime marches on.

Even if tough, determinate sentencing laws are passed, they will be undermined and bypassed if plea bargaining is permitted: charges will be reduced to evade the harsher penalties. Ending plea bargaining is the key to making tougher sentences stick.

Psychiatry in the Courtroom

The use of psychiatrists and psychologists as "expert" witnesses should be banned. So should the "insanity" and the "diminished capacity" defenses. Criminal intent and the mental state of a defendant should be determined by the same kinds of evidence and testimony as are used in all other criminal proceedings.

Victims in the Courtroom

"Victims are 'legal nonentities' in the justice system," writes William Tucker. "The legal fiction is that 'the state' is the victim of crime.

The victim has no more standing in a criminal trial than any other witness has—and a good deal less than the accused."[47] The defendant, of course, has official standing and defense representation—paid for, in many cases, by the taxes of his victim.

The *individual* is the crime victim, not the state. For that reason, well-meaning "victim compensation" laws should be opposed: it's unjust that every taxpayer should have to compensate a crime victim for a criminal's acts. But there *are* many things that should be done for the victim.

Prosecutors should be required to keep the victim informed of the status of his case; and he should be allowed to attend any proceedings. Victim impact statements should be allowed prior to sentencing, at least whenever the defendant is allowed to introduce "mitigating circumstances." Until release programs are abolished, victims should have the chance to testify prior to any release decisions, before the appropriate agency.

Restitution from the criminal to the victim is good in theory, but tough to enforce. However, it should always be an option, to be added to any sentence.

Sentencing

First, "indeterminate sentencing"—and the parole process which is its offspring—must end. All convicted felons should serve fixed, determinate sentences for their crimes. Early release being out of the question, there's no reason for parole boards (more savings for taxpayers). This will reduce arbitrariness and the unfairness of inmates serving different sentences for the same crime.

Pre-sentencing defense testimony concerning mitigating circumstances should be admissible only in the case of a *guilty plea*. If a defendant pleads innocent, but is later found guilty, he shouldn't be allowed abruptly to concede his guilt after the verdict, then plead mitigating circumstances before sentencing—not after putting everyone through the trouble and expense of a trial. In all cases, mitigating testimony should be balanced by testimony from crime victims. These statements should be gauged on some fixed point system for altering the usual sentence, but only within a very limited range.

Criminal penalties should increase in severity upon subsequent convictions of other felonies. Borrowing terminology from the

Excuse-Makers, I propose "progressive sentencing": the term of imprisonment for repeat offenders should increase in multiples—say, two years for a first burglary conviction; four for a second; eight for a third; and so on. I also propose that this "progressive" feature be transferable among different sorts of crimes, thus preventing criminals from simply varying their crimes in hope of avoiding serious punishment.

Capital punishment never should be applied in cases where a murder conviction depended largely on circumstantial evidence. But in cases of pre-meditated murder in which there is no question of guilt, it should be the *standard* sentence. There also should be a time limit on the appeals process.

The Overcrowding Problem

Our courts and prisons are badly clogged, in large part because of the crime wave fostered by the Excuse-Making Industry, whose only response is to set more criminals free.

The first, obvious solution—as the National Institute of Justice study makes clear—is to build more prisons. Citizens should realize that they're far safer living next door to a prison than having the same criminals free on probation, parole, or release programs because of "overcrowding." And it's far cheaper.

But much of the overcrowding problem is because of laws that shouldn't exist.

Today, we have a terrible drug problem, and an enormous drug-related crime problem. Perhaps 25 percent of prison space is occupied by those who've committed drug-related offenses.[48] Many arrested for burglary, robbery, and larceny are drug addicts, stealing to support expensive habits.

But these habits are expensive precisely *because of the illegality of the drugs.* There are enormous profits in supplying illegal commodities at higher-than-market prices—something criminals are always willing to risk.

Legalizing drugs and other "victimless crimes," many fear, would lower their price, increase their availability, and thus make them even more attractive, particularly to youngsters. But would it? Currently, untold thousands of youngsters see drug-dealing as their best hope for glamor and wealth. This entices them into the subterranean criminal world of drug-peddling and—ironically—drug use. Taking the profits out of drug-dealing, via legalization, would strip away the incentives of wealth and any illusions of glamor. It would end the present widespread seduction of youngsters into the drug world as *suppliers.*

To legalize drugs is *not* to endorse them, and it doesn't mean we approve them. We simply go our own ways, allowing foolish, irresponsible people to be their own victims—because we recognize that laws can't turn fools into sages. More important, we rightly fear granting to government the power to become an armed busybody, intruding into our private lives and most personal decisions.[49]

At root, our drug problem is a self-esteem problem. Happy, fulfilled, self-respecting people don't become drug addicts. But passing laws can't give people self-esteem. The morally confused or emotionally empty will turn to some other palliative: alcohol, cults, or promiscuity.

Legalizing drugs won't cure the drug problem. But it will go a long way toward curtailing drug-related *crime*—and the huge burdens it is imposing on our criminal justice system and on ourselves.

Correcting the Correctional System

Prisons

"Corrections" don't correct. "Correctional facilities" should drop that pretense, and rename themselves "prisons." With the end of indeterminate sentencing and release programs, prisons can focus on their major goal: public safety. The prison exists, first and foremost, to incapacitate the offender from committing further crimes. It need not be brutal or inhumane to accomplish that; but order should be maintained by increasing penalties, not privileges. Prison authorities shouldn't negotiate with criminals for responsibility and calm: they should enforce it.

Opportunities should be afforded to those inmates who care to improve themselves: job training, high-school equivalency courses, etc. But that doesn't mean world-class law libraries, gymnasiums, cuisine, and the like. Inmates have no right to expect better living conditions than do military men, who somehow manage to survive chow lines, forced marches in heavy gear, double bunks, and collective living arrangements. Is it too much to require a convicted felon to share a cell with another inmate, or to keep it clean and neat? Is it too much to demand that he work at a prison job, helping offset the costs he's imposed on taxpayers?

Rehabilitation

A lot of money can be saved, and mischief averted, by sending the legions of prison psychiatrists, counselors, and social workers packing.

An alternative is available. For many years, clinical psychologist Stanton Samenow has been working to "habilitate" hardened criminals. His methods, which don't require advanced psychological training, are based on holding the criminal utterly accountable for his thinking and actions, and teaching him to change irresponsible mental and behavioral habits. It's a long process, requiring the criminal's sincere desire to change and willingness to work hard. Because of that, it's far from universally successful, though those who stick it out do improve.[50] But this approach couldn't be more different from the group therapies and psychological fads of the Excuse-Makers, whose premise is that the criminal is *not* responsible.

Reintegration

Excuse-Makers argue that prisons should be saved only for the hard-core offender. That, in fact, is exactly who the typical prisoner is. Releasing him back into society is a dereliction of responsibility that is itself almost criminal.

Community-based corrections is just rehabilitation on the streets—the same failed approaches, but with the added opportunity of countless innocent victims. Furloughs, work release, education release, halfway houses, pre-release centers—all should be ended on grounds of simple justice and public safety. If the primary purpose of prison is to incapacitate offenders, there's no reason for "community reintegration" programs.

Crime and Consequences

The United States was founded on the premise that each individual is an end in himself, and that he is morally and legally self-responsible. Self-responsibility means being accountable for the full consequences of one's actions, for good or ill. Thus the rewards and profits of life, in justice, should go to those responsible for making the world better; the penalties and losses should accrue to those who make it worse. Perhaps the best model of this idea is the free market economic system itself, where rewards and penalties are distributed with impartial fairness, based on one standard: the individual's capacity to generate valuable goods and services.

Under the symbol of Justitia, our criminal justice system began with the purpose of impartially meting out justice. Each person was held morally self-responsible, hence accountable for the consequences of his actions. But determinism and the Excuse-Making Industry have undermined all that.

Today, the Excuse-Makers look at the crime wave they have created, and simply shrug. The American Bar Association recently spoke for them all, saying, " . . . the public mistakenly looks to the criminal justice system to eliminate the crime problem. . . . The public's expectation that the system should control crime cannot be reconciled with the sense of criminal justice professionals . . . that the system itself has a limited role in crime control and crime prevention."[51]

That's simply more excuse-making. Citizens have a right to expect that the system is more than a procedural game to provide employment and high incomes for legal professionals. They have a right to expect not "due process" as an end in itself, which actually becomes *undue process;* they have a right to expect *substantive justice.*

Crime can never be eliminated, not if we have the power to choose evil. But it *can* be controlled, if criminals are regarded as volitional entities, fully responsible for the consequences of their actions. The answer is to reform the entire criminal justice system, from its basic premises to its routine procedures, with a single goal in mind: to reassert the responsibility of the individual.

---

1. For good discussions of these purposes see: Robert D. Pursley, *Introduction to Criminal Justice,* second edition (New York: MacMillan, 1980), pp. 352–356; James Q. Wilson and Richard J. Herrnstein, *Crime and Human Nature* (New York: Simon & Schus-

ter, 1985), chapter 19; and "What are Prisons For?" *Time*, September 13, 1952, pp. 38–41.

2. Wilson and Herrnstein. See chapter 7 for results of numerous studies.

3. Stanton E. Samenow, *Inside the Criminal Mind* (New York: Times Books, 1984), generally, and on pp. 20, 181. (See also this volume, Part I, "Basic Myths About Criminals.")

4. Wilson and Herrnstein, p. 198; David Kelley, "Stalking the Criminal Mind," *Harper's*, August 1985, pp. 57, 59; reprinted in Part I of this volume.

5. Wilson and Herrnstein, p. 196.

6. Robert R. Hazelwood and John E. Douglas, "The Lust Murderer," *FBI Law Enforcement Bulletin*, April 1980.

7. Elliott Leyton, *Hunting Humans* (New York: Pocket Book edition, 1988), pp. 311–13.

8. Ramsey Clark, *Crime in America* (New York: Simon & Schuster, 1970), chapter 13.

9. Massachusetts Parole Board, *A Guide to Parole in Massachusetts*, May 1987, pp. 13–16. [Note: citizens have led successful campaigns recently to toughen the commonwealth's parole provisions and sentencing laws.]

10. Representative Denny Smith, address before the West Salem, Oregon, Rotary, January 18, 1988.

11. "Can This Be Life?," *Corrections Compendium*, February 1987, p. 8. All data in this paragraph were current as of 1987–88.

12. Unpublished survey of states by author, summer 1988.

13. Data supplied by Contact Center, Inc., Lincoln, Nebraska; current as of 1987.

14. The failure of psychological rehabilitation was detailed in Part I, Chapter 1. On general rehabilitation failures, see also: Wilson and Herrnstein, pp. 377–78, 382–84; Samenow, chapter 12, esp. p. 193 on a 1974 National Academy of Sciences study; *Time*, September 13, 1982, pp. 38–41, and February 2, 1987, p. 61; and *Insight*, February 13, 1989, pp. 8–19.

15. Massachusetts Dept. of Correction, *Community Reintegration Program*, March 1988, pp. 1–2.

16. *Ibid.*

17. Samenow, pp. 21, 203–4.

18. See Samenow generally. Also see Samenow, *Before It's Too Late* (New York: Times Books, 1989); and Samenow's profile-interview in *People*, May 14, 1984, pp. 79–81.

19. Quoted in Norval Morris and Gordon Hawkins, *The Honest Politician's Guide to Crime Control* (Chicago: University of Chicago Press, 1970), p. 115.

20. Vernon B. Fox, *Community-Based Corrections* (Englewood Cliffs, N.J.: 1977), pp. 2, 270.

21. Morris and Hawkins, pp. 123, 141–42.

22. Fox, p. 272.

23. *Ibid.*, pp. xiii–xiv.

24. 1988 survey conducted by Contact Center, Inc.; released September 30, 1988.

25. Lester Velie, "The State That Freed Its Young from Jail," *Reader's Digest*, May 1984, p. 215.

26. *Community Reintegration Program*, p. 11.

27. Massachusetts Dept. of Correction, *Fact Sheet on Furloughs*, 1988.

28. For examples see Robert James Bidinotto, "Getting Away with Murder," *Reader's Digest*, July 1988; *Boston Herald*, December 20, 1987; and Lawrence, Mass.,

Eagle-Tribune, December 24, 1987 and January 10, 1988. For examples from other states, see Ann Rule, "A Rapist's Revenge," *Redbook,* April 1988; and Ralph Adam Fine, *Escape of the Guilty* (New York: Dodd, Mead & Co., 1986), p. 189.

29. Hearings, "Massachusetts Furlough System," Massachusetts House Post-Audit Committee, October 21, 1987; uncorrected transcripts, pp. 78–9.

30. Lawrence *Eagle-Tribune,* June 11, 1988.

31. *Fact Sheet on Furloughs.*

32. Boston *Herald,* August 29 and December 27, 1987; Warren Brookes' column, *Washington Times,* March 2, 1988; Limone's recorded commutation hearing before the Massachusetts Parole Board.

33. *Community Reintegration* Program, p. 14.

34. Massachusetts Dept. of Correction, Apprehension and Operations Research Unit, 1985 report on DOC escapes.

35. "Punishment Outside Prisons," *Newsweek,* June 9, 1986, p. 83.

36. Wilson and Herrnstein, pp. 276–77, 322–23, 388.

37. Samenow, *Inside the Criminal Mind,* chapter 6.

38. Massachusetts Dept. of Correction 1985 report on escapes, pp. 4, 6.

39. Hearings, "Massachusetts Furlough Program," Massachusetts House Post-Audit Committee, October 15, 1987, pp. 101–2, 263; October 21, 1987, pp. 95, 206–9.

40. Wilson and Herrnstein, pp. 390–91, 394–95.

41. Edwin Zedlewski, "Making Confinement Decisions," *Research In Brief,* National Institute of Justice, July 1987; released July 1988.

42. Letter to *The Wall Street Journal,* May 25, 1988, by John Larivee, executive director, Crime and Justice Foundation, Boston.

43. Hearings, "Massachusetts Furlough Program," Massachusetts House Post-Audit Committee, October 14, 1987; uncorrected transcript, p. 25.

44. "Killers At Large," *Maclean's,* July 18, 1988, p. 44.

45. *Ibid.*

46. Hearings, "Massachusetts Furlough Program," November 5, 1987, uncorrected transcript, pp. 43–44.

47. William Tucker, "Crime Victims Strike Back," *Reader's Digest,* June 1985, p. 52.

48. Estimate provided to author by Edwin Zedlewski of the National Institute of Justice.

49. See Robert James Bidinotto, "Morality Laws = Majority License," *The Freeman,* April 1987.

50. Samenow, esp. chapters 13 and 14.

51. American Bar Association, *Criminal Justice In Crisis,* November 1988, pp. 7, 51.

Index

Adler, Alfred, 56
AIDS, 266
Alaska, 76, 84, 85, 91, 93, 94, 95
Alaskan Supreme Court, 96
Alcoholism, link to crime, 38
Allen, George, 236
Alschuler, Albert W., 91, 96
American Heritage Dictionary, 156
American Bar Association (ABA), 7, 66, 76, 88
American Law Institute (ALI), 145, 281; ALI test, 145
American Psychiatric Association (APA), 144, 150, 151
Amphetamines, 36
Anchorage (Alaska), 94
Andenaes, Johannes, 86
Aristotle, 276
Armstrong, Robert, 119
Aubin, Gerald, 133
Austin, James, 195

Baby Boom, 37
Bacon, Francis, 120
Bail, 289
Bail Reform Act of 1984, 253
Barger, Melvin, 26–33
Barnes, Clifford, 288
Barr, William, 235, 250, 256
Bazelon, David, 93, 144
Behaviorism, 11, 19, 20, 21
Bell, Larry Gene, 81
Bennett, William J., 252
Benson, Bruce, 158
Berkowitz, David, 79
Bianchi, Ken, 78
Bidinotto, Robert James, 1–2, 5–25, 65–83, 181–200, 276–296

Biological explanations for crime, 20–24, 38, 54–55
Black inmates; *see* minorities, disproportionate incarceration of, 12
Black, Hugo, 71, 115
Blumberg, Abraham S., 91
Blumstein, Alfred, 246
Boalt School of Law (University of California), 140
Boone, John O., 281
Bordenkircher v. Hayes, 89, 90, 93
BOTEC Analysis Corporation, 226, 239
Bowers, Marguerite, 148
Brady v. United States, 93
Break Down the Walls (Martin), 281
Brennan, William, 133, 135
Brethren, The (Armstrong and Woodward), 119
Bronx, South, 49
Brookings Institution, The, 169
Brookings Review, The, 169
Brooklyn (New York), 120
Brooks, Alexander, 144
Brown, Ed, 117, 118
Bureau of Alcohol, Tobacco, and Firearms, 217
Bureau of the Census, 257
Bureau of Justice Statistics (BJS), 70, 80, 159, 162, 163, 211, 212, 214, 215, 217, 218, 221, 222, 223, 224, 252, 254, 260, 261
Burger, Warren E., 75, 104, 129
Bush, George, 107, 170, 235
Bush Administration, 235, 250
Butler, Willie, 132, 133
Butner (North Carolina), 184
Byrn, Robert M., 14

Cagney, James, 181
California Law Review, 133
California Supreme Court, 121
California Youth Authority, 77
Caligula, 14
Canada, 172, 222
Capital punishment, 197, 257
Capitalism, 206, 207
Cardozo, Benjamin, 71, 105, 112
Carnegie-Mellon University, 246
Cary, Mary Kate, 250–269
Casper, Norman, 108
Castle Bank, 108
Causality, 22, 23, 39, 191, 192, 276
Cavanagh, David, 226, 239
Chapman, Jim, 236, 247
Chinese-Americans, crime rate
 among, 12
Christianity, 69
Claremont Institute, 238
Clark, Ramsey, 12, 14, 26, 278, 281
Cleckley, Hervey, 42, 43, 45
Clinton, William, 250
Cohen, Mark, 224, 239
Cohen, Mickey, 27
Coleman, Lee, 79, 138–155
Collectivism, 189, 206, 207
"Community-based corrections,"
 281–286
Community service, 258
Community supervision, 270–275
Compulsion to Confess (Reik), 114
Concord Reformatory, 74
Cook County Circuit Court, 149
Cook County Psychiatric Institute,
 149
Craig v. Maryland, 265
Creedmoor Psychiatric Center, 149
Cressey, D.R., 38, 39
"Crime and Consequences" (Bidi-
 notto), 1
Crime and Human Nature (Herrnstein
 and Wilson), 20–21
Crime Bill, 1994 Federal, 183
Crime in America (Clark), 12, 26, 278
Crime rate (defined), 6

Criminal justice system, 5, 7, 9, 10,
 57, 92, 165, 171–174, 181, 183,
 187, 188, 189, 191, 193; 196, 201,
 204, 208, 217, 219, 243, 246, 257;
 disenchantment with, 1; subver-
 sion of, 65–83
Criminal Law Advisory Committee
 of the American Law Institute,
 143–144
Criminal mind, criminal nature, 27–
 46, 47–58
Criminal Personality, The (Samenow
 and Yochelson), 43
Criminal responsibility, 5–25; *see also*
 self-responsibility
Criminal Violence, Criminal Justice (Silberman), 44
Criminality, root causes of, 1
Criminals, teenage, 7–8
Criminology (Cressey and Sutherland) , 38
Criminology, 41

Davenport (Iowa), 126, 127, 128
Davis, Richard Allen, 233
Day, Roland B., 88
Delinquency, link to abuse, 38
Demery, Larry Martin, 233
Des Moines (Iowa), 126, 127
Determinism, 15, 22, 23, 34, 35, 37,
 40, 41, 45–46, 66; (defined), 21
Deterrence, 31–32
Detroit (Michigan), 241
Diagnostic and Statistical Manual, 41
Diamond, Bernard, 140, 141
DiCarlo, Philip J., 72
DiIulio, John J., Jr., 156–178
Dillinger, John, 27, 30
Doing Justice (von Hirsch), 175
Drugs, 291–292
Durham rule, 144, 145

Education release, 9
Egalitarianism, 72
Ehrlich, Isaac, 243
Eisenhower Foundation, 34

Ellington, Yank, 117, 118
Elliott, Frank A., 44
Environment versus heredity, 40
Erwin, Robert C., 96
Escape of the Guilty (Fine), 84, 86, 92
Europe, 115
Evans, Randolph, 149
Evidence, rules of, 112, 262–263, 265
Exclusionary rule, 70–72, 74, 102–111, 119
Excuse-Making Industry, 9, 10, 11, 16, 21, 23, 66, 67, 68, 69, 70, 71, 72, 73, 76, 80, 81, 199, 277, 278, 280, 281, 282, 286, 287, 288, 291, 293, 294
Ex-convicts, *see* offender release and supervision
Eysenck, Hans J., 16

Fair, Michael, 283
Fairbanks (Alaska), 95
Fatal Vision (McGinniss), 35, 36
Federal Aviation Administration, 237
Federal Bureau of Investigation (FBI), 7, 121, 122, 132, 133, 212, 216, 227, 241, 261, 277
Federal Bureau of Prisons, 162, 167, 258
Federal Prisoner Rehabilitation Act, 282
Fifth Amendment (U.S. Constitution), 123
Fine, Ralph Adam, 18, 74, 84–101, 112–137
Fisher, John, 119
Food and Drug Administration, 237
Foundation for Economic Education (FEE), 1, 2
Founding Fathers, 191, 194
Fourth Amendment (U.S. Constitution), 102, 103, 105, 107, 108, 109, 110
Franciscan Sisters of Baltimore Motherhouse, 233
Frankfurter, Felix, 120
Free will, 22, 23, 34, 45–46, 139

Freeman, The, 1, 2
Freud, Sigmund, 15, 144; Freudian ethic (defined), 16; Freudianism, 11, 15, 17, 19
Fuller, Lon, 171

Gaylin, Willard, 186, 189
General Accounting Office, 104, 172
Georgetown, 56
Glazer, Nathan, 171
Gleckman, Joseph, 134, 135, 136
Glinka, MaryAnn, 233, 234
Glueck, Eleanor, 13
Glueck, Sheldon, 13
Golden Rule, 116
Goldsboro, North Carolina, 132
Gordon, Clara, 149, 150
Great Britain, 115, 116, 142, 172, 222; English penal system, 205
Great Society, 158, 183
"Great American Lockup, The" (Zimring), 159
Greece, Ancient, 115
Green Bay Packers, 87
Green, Daniel Andre, 233
Green, Jerold, 72
Gross, Avrum, 93–94, 95

Habeas corpus, 128, 245, 263
Haley, Hugh, 288
Harlan, John Marshall, 68, 123, 124, 126
Harrison, Suzanne, 255
Harvard Law School, 87
Hayek, Friedrich, 201
Hayes, Paul, 89, 91, 92
Head Start, 183
Hecht, Ben, 27
Heffernan, Nathan S., 84
Heritage Foundation, 245, 250, 252, 256, 258
Herrnstein, Richard J., 20–21, 65, 286
Hickey, Dan, 85
Hillside Strangler, 78
Hinckley, John, 34, 79, 138, 139, 150, 151

Hitchcock, Alfred, 77
HIV testing of defendants, 266
Home furloughs, 9
Horton, Willie, 5, 9, 288
Hyperactivity, 37

Illinois v. Krull, 107
Incarceration, 209–232, 254–255, 287
India, 115
Individualism, 192, 194, 199
Innis, Thomas J., 133, 134, 135, 136
Insanity defense, 34, 47–48, 77–80,
    138–154
Insanity Plea, The (Winslade), 142, 146
Inside the Criminal Mind (Samenow),
    43
Intelligence Quotient (I.Q.), 13, 55
Internal Revenue Service (IRS), 108
International Journal of Psychiatry, 16
Iowa Supreme Court, 128
Irresponsibility, 13
Irwin, John, 195

Jackson, Robert H., 130
Jeffrey, Douglas, 238
Jews, 141
John Howard Society, 288
Johnson Administration, 26
Jones, Melvin L., 234
Jordan, James, 233, 245
Jordan, Michael, 233
Judges, legacy of activist, 170–171
Judy, Steven, 73
Juneau (Alaska), 95
Justice, 5, 22, 24, 33, 72, 87, 89, 116,
    181, 182, 186, 187, 189, 191, 192,
    193, 196, 199, 207, 208, 288, 294
Justice, distributive, 65–66
Juvenile justice system, 7, 259–261

Kamisar, Yale, 133
Kansas City, 121
Kant, Immanuel, 37, 175
Karpis, Alvin, 27, 28, 30
Keller, Edward, 149
Kelley, David, 34–46

Kemper, Edward, 77
Kennedy, Robert F., 140, 141
Kennedy, Sybol, 108
Kennedy Administration, 26
Killing of Bonnie Garland, 186
Klaas, Polly, 233, 245
Kleiman, Mark, 226, 239
Konner, Melvin, 39, 40

Langan, Patrick A., 159, 211, 214, 246
LaPiere, Richard, 16
Leaming, Cletus, 127, 129, 130
Leddy, Edward F., 270–275
Legislation, 159–160
Lewis, Dorothy Otnow, 39, 44
Limone, Peter J., 283
Lipton, Douglas, 17
Logan, Charles H., 156–178
Los Angeles (California), 95, 121, 122

M'Naughten, Daniel, 142, 150, 151;
    M'Naughten rule, 144;
    M'Naughten test, 150, 151
MacDonald, Colette, 35
MacDonald, Jeffrey, 35, 36, 44
Mapp v. Ohio, 70, 102, 103, 104, 110
Marshall, Thurgood, 69, 135, 136
Martin, John Barlow, 281
Martinson, Robert, 17
Marxism, 11, 12
Mask of Sanity (Cleckley), 42
Massachusetts Department of Cor-
    rection report on "prisoniza-
    tion," 280; prison furloughs,
    282–283
McCann, Michael, 87
McFadden, Jerry Walter, 255
McGinniss, Joe, 35, 36
Menninger, Karl, 144, 281
Mercer Regional Correctional
    Facility, 181, 182, 195, 198
Miami (Florida), 108
Milliken, William G., 241
Milwaukee, 87, 90, 92
Milwaukee County (Wisconsin), 95
Milwaukee House of Correction, 74

Mind-body dichotomy, 41
Minimum sentences, 256
Minnesota Multiphasic Personality Inventory, 43
Minorities, disproportionate incarceration rate, 12, 49
Miranda, Ernesto, 121, 122, 124; Miranda rules, 130; *Miranda v. Arizona*, 67, 68, 69, 70, 71, 72, 114, 119, 120, 122, 125, 126, 127, 131, 132, 133, 134, 135, 137
Mississippi Supreme Court, 117, 118, 119
Mitchellville (Iowa), 127, 128
Mitford, Jessica, 281
Monroe, Marilyn, 112
Moral relativism, 277
Morality, 1
Morris, Norval, 173
Murray, Charles, 10, 14

National Academy of Sciences, 216
National Advisory Commission of Criminal Justice, 88
National Campaign Against Prisons, 281
National Center for Policy Analysis, 243
National Council on Crime and Delinquency (NCCD), 160–162, 171, 195, 281
National Criminal Victims Survey, 212, 242
National Drug Control Policy, 252
National Institute of Justice, 70, 76, 91, 94, 103, 157, 168, 240, 286–287, 291
National Institute of Mental Health, 88
National Law Journal, 93
Nelson, Caleb, 102–111
Nero, 14
Neurological disorders, link to crime, 40
New Philadelphia (Ohio), 84

New Orleans (Louisiana), 76, 77, 84, 95
New York Times, The, 160
Nietzsche, Friedrich, 205
Nigeria, 16
Nix v. Williams, 106
Nixon, Richard, 34
North Carolina Supreme Court, 132
North Carolina v. Alford, 88
Nuremburg, 130

O'Brien, Darcy, 78
O'Farrell, Edward Emmett, 95
Oakland County (Michigan), 84, 95
Oaks, Dallin, 103, 104
Offender release and supervision, 270–275
Office of Juvenile Justice and Delinquency Prevention, 242
Orlando (Florida) *Sentinel*, 216
Oxnard (California), 243

Parade, 235
Parole, 5, 80–82, 270–275
Patuxent (Maryland), 184
Payner, Jack, 108
Peel, Robert, 142
People v. Love, 257
Philadelphia (Pennsylvania), 242, 253
Phoenix (Arizona), 71, 124
Plea bargaining, 8, 73–76, 84–97, 289
Pollack, Seymour, 140
Pontiac (Michigan), 76, 84, 95
Post Release Employment Project (PREP), 258
Pound, Dean Roscoe, 87
Poverty, link to crime, 37
Powers, Pamela, 126, 130
"Practice of Law as Confidence Game, The" (Blumberg), 91
President's Commission on Law Enforcement, 88
Pretrial detention, 252–253
Prince, Raymond, 16

Prisons, 160–165, 181–182, 292; expense of, 166–169; "prisonization," 280, 281; *see also* incarceration
Prison furloughs, 282–284
Probation, 80–82, 270–275, 289
Property rights, 61
Psychoanalysis, 15
Psychological explanations and excuses for crime, 15–20, 53–54, 289
Psychopathy, 41–46
Punishment, morality of, 174–176

Quarles decision (1984), 70
Queens (New York), 149

Racial discrimination, 165–166, 246
RAND Corporation, 80, 165, 168, 217, 238, 240, 247, 285
Raspberry, William, 171
Rawls, John, 65
Ray, Isaac, 142
Reader's Digest, 5
Reagan, Ronald, 138, 170
Recidivism, 9, 17, 217–219, 236, 284
Rector, Robert, 256, 258
Reed Mental Health Center, 149–150
Regnery, Alfred, 242
Rehabilitation, 280–282, 286, 293; versus retribution, 66; reintegration, 280–281, 286, 293
Reid, Sharon, 149
Reik, Theodor, 114, 136
Release-status notification, 266
Reno, Janet, 183
Responsibility, *see* self-responsibility
Restitution, 183, 290
Retributivism, 175, 187, 189, 190, 191, 194, 196, 197, 198, 199
Reynolds, Morgan O., 184, 201–208, 243
Rhode Island Supreme Court, 134
Rorschach inkblot test, 78, 148
Rousseau, Jean Jacques, 65, 205

Royal Commission on Capital Punishment, 143
Rules of evidence, *see* evidence
Rules of exclusion, 113

Salient Factor Score (SFS), 237
Samenow, Stanton, 29, 30, 32, 43, 44, 45, 47–58, 78, 79, 276, 277, 281
San Francisco (California), 12, 79
Schwartz, Bernard, 120
Science, 159, 211, 214
Selective incapacitation, 185–186
Self-responsibility, 29–30, 66, 276–296
Sentencing, sentencing laws, 279, 290–291
Sentencing Project, The, 171, 172
Serial killers, 277–278
Shields, Henry, 117, 118
Sirhan, Sirhan, 140, 141
Skinner, B.F., 19, 37, 39
Socialism, 202, 207
Socio-economic status, link to crime, 157–159
Sociological excuses and explanations for crime, 11–15, 49
Son of Sam, 79
Sondheim, Stephen, 47
South Africa, 171
Soviet Union, 171
Speck, Richard, 205
Sperry, Roger, 41
St. Elizabeths Hospital, 45
Stanford University, 16, 18
Star Chamber, 116
Steinmetz, Donald A., 88
Stevens, John Paul, 130, 135, 136
Stewart, James K., 157
Stewart, Potter, 129, 135
Stewart, Raymond, 117
Stewart, Roy Allen, 121, 122
Stratton, Hal, 218
Sutherland, E.H., 38, 39

Tangled Wing (Konner), 39, 40
Texas A&M, 243

Texas Penitentiary, 255
Third World, 12
Tonry, Michael, 173
Tucker, William, 289–290
Treasury Department, 217
Treatise on the Medical Jurisprudence of Insanity (Ray), 142
Truth in sentencing, 234–249, 255
Truth in Sentencing Act of 1993 (H.R. 3584), 236, 247
"Twinkie" Defense, 79
Two of a Kind (O'Brien), 78

Uniform Crime Reports, 7, 160, 211
U.S. Constitution, 1, 69, 102, 103, 104, 106, 111, 125, 128, 130, 131; Fourth Amendment, 70, 71; Fifth Amendment, 67; Preamble, 191
U.S. Court of Appeals, 93
U.S. Department of Justice, 34, 73, 172, 209–232, 242
U.S. National Advisory Commission on Criminal Justice Standards and Goals, 75, 87
U.S. Parole Board, 237
U.S. Sentencing Commission, 239
U.S. Supreme Court, 66, 67, 68, 69, 70, 71, 75, 84, 89, 91, 92, 102, 103, 105, 107, 108, 109, 111, 112, 114, 115, 118, 119, 121, 122, 123, 124, 125, 126, 128, 130, 131, 132, 135, 145, 202, 265, 266
U.S. v. Calandra, 104, 105
U.S. v. Ceccolini, 104, 105, 106
U.S. v. Leon, 107
U.S. v. Payner, 108
University of California, Berkeley, 159
University of California Medical School, 140
University of Chicago, 103, 243
UCLA Neuropsychiatric Institute, 18
University of Oklahoma, 18
University of Pennsylvania, 242

Utilitarianism, 175, 183–187, 188, 190, 194, 198

Vanda, Thomas, 78, 148, 149
Ventura County (California), 84, 95
Victims, rights of, 263–266, 289, 290
Vienna Psychoanalytic Association, 114
Vignera, Michael, 120, 121, 122
von Hirsch, Andrew, 175
Vulnerabilities to Delinquency (Lewis), 39

Walden Two (Skinner), 37
Wall Street Journal, The, 31
Walter, David, 59–62
War on Drugs, 159
War on Poverty, 158
Warren, Earl, 68, 119, 120, 121, 131
Warren Court, 203
Washington, D.C., 56, 93, 118, 145, 171, 234, 254
Washington, D.C., Circuit Court, 111
Washington Post, 159
Watts district of Los Angeles, 49
Webster, Daniel, 114
Welfare, welfare state, link to crime, 14, 59–62, 206–208
Welfare "Rights" Organization, 61
Wendt, Kenneth, 149
West Side Story, 11, 47
Westover, Carl Alvin, 121, 122, 124
White, Byron, 68, 69, 125, 130
White, Dan, 79
Whitman, Christine, 236
Wicker, Tom, 160, 171
Wilkey, Malcolm, 111
Wilks, Judith, 17
Williams, Robert, 126, 127, 128, 129, 130, 131
Wilson, Donald Powell, 281
Wilson, James Q., 20–21, 32, 33, 65, 86, 185, 237, 286
Wilson, John G., 281

Wilson, William Julius, 158
Winslade, William, 142, 146
Wisconsin Supreme Court, 84, 87, 88
Wolfgang, Marvin, 242
Woodward, Bob, 119
Wootton, James, 233–249
Work release, 9, 284–285

YMCA, 126
Yochelson, Samuel, 29, 30, 32, 43, 45
Young, Don, 236, 247

Zedlewski, Edwin W., 168, 240
Zimring, Franklin E., 159

About the Publisher

The Foundation for Economic Education, Inc., was established in 1946 by Leonard E. Read to study and advance the moral and intellectual rationale for a free society.

The Foundation publishes *The Freeman,* an award-winning monthly journal of ideas in the fields of economics, history, and moral philosophy. FEE also publishes books, conducts seminars, and sponsors a network of discussion clubs to improve understanding of the principles of a free and prosperous society.

FEE is a non-political, non-profit 501(c)(3) tax-exempt organization, supported solely by private contributions and sales of its literature.

For further information, please contact: The Foundation for Economic Education, Inc., 30 South Broadway, Irvington-on-Hudson, New York 10533. Telephone (914) 591-7230; fax (914) 591-8910.